Fashion under the Occupation

Fashion under the Occupation

Dominique Veillon

Translated by
Miriam Kochan

Oxford • New York

English edition
First published in 2002 by
Berg
Editorial offices:
150 Cowley Road, Oxford, OX4 1JJ, UK
838 Broadway, Third Floor, New York, NY 10003-4812, USA

© Berg Publishers 2002

Originally published in French as
La mode sous l'Occupation
© 1990, Editions Payot, Paris
© 2001, Editions Payot & Rivages

Published with the assistance of the French Ministry of Culture –
Centre National du Livre.

Library of Congress Cataloging-in-Publication Data
Veillon, Dominique.
    [Mode sous l'Occupation. English]
    Fashion under the Occupation / Dominique Veillon ; translated by Miriam
Kochan.
      p. cm.
Includes bibliographical references and index.
"Originally published in French as La mode sous l'Occupation, (c)1990, Editions
Payot" – Verso t.p.
    ISBN 1-85973-543-6 (cloth) – ISBN 1-85973-548-7 (pbk.)
    1. Costume–France–History–20th century. 2. Fashion–France–History–20th
century. 3. France–History–German occupation, 1940–1945. I. Title.
    GT880 .V4513 2002
    391'.00944'0904–dc21

                                              2002007694

British Library Cataloguing-in-Publication Data
A catalogue record for this book is available from the British Library.

ISBN 1 85973 543 6 (Cloth)
1 85973 548 7 (Paper)

Typeset by JS Typesetting Ltd, Wellingborough, Northants
Printed in the United Kingdom by Biddles Ltd, Guildford and King's Lynn

Contents

Preface

Is fashion anything more than a frivolous activity, changing with each new collection? Apart from the continual changes that, until World War Two, primarily affected the wardrobes of the elite, and are mainly remembered as a female phenomenon, is fashion not also significant for being rooted in the social context? To what extent does it offer the historian a field of study? These questions deserve to be considered seriously. Fashion is an expression of every aspect of life; it is a way of existing and behaving, and is, in fact, an observation point from which to view the political, economic and cultural environment of an historical period. The dark years from 1940 to 1944 offer ideal terrain for carrying out this sort of research because they cover a short, eventful period: they provide the best opportunity to discern the correlation between 'the phenomenon of fashion' and political upheavals, between ways of dressing and the adoption of attitudes induced by the extraordinary events affecting the country.

The arrival of the Germans in the summer of 1940 radically changed the overall picture. The end of the Third Republic, its replacement by the Vichy government, and the appearance of new economic and political structures had unprecedented effects even in the field of fashion. One of the first consequences of the defeat and occupation was to move the country from a situation of plenty to one of organized scarcity. In the space of a few months it became difficult to obtain items such as woollen cloth and leather shoes except at high black-market prices. Moreover, French life was subjected to a system of ration cards and coupons, and ruled by red tape. The Vichy government regulated every aspect of life, trying to place its imprint on everything. Regional and folk costumes were brought back into fashion, some *couturiers* making them the focal point of their collections. Several women's magazines held up as an example the image of the traditional homemaker, as opposed to the model of an over-Americanized French woman.

Did the population follow similar directives? Dress as an indication of identity can be a sign of approval as well as of resistance. In that case, fashion goes beyond frivolity and cannot be dismissed as a transient phenomenon: it is much more than a matter of changing dress-styles. It is a way of living in the climate of the time – suffered here, accepted there, rejected elsewhere. Sometimes synonymous with courage, it is also the reaction of an offended dignity that refuses to give up. Sometimes provocative, fashion can become a means of revolt against the occupier. In some cases, a well groomed and inventive attire, stylishness, even seduction, became psychological weapons against external aggression. Several examples of this are given here.

The wartime fashion that was born as the months went by reflected two trends, mirroring the dual nature of society. Whereas the majority of the population, subject to endless aggravation, just about managed to get along, and created its own style of dress, the way of life of the rich minority was almost unchanged. High society, actors and comedians continued to go out and to entertain. Restaurants and theatres, patronized by well-dressed men and elegant ladies, who were dressed by the *grands couturiers*, barely suffered. Photographers like the Seeberger brothers captured well-known profiles such as Geneviève Fath and the Countess d'Oncieu de Chaffardon on film, while actresses like Ginette Leclerc, Edwige Feuillère, Renée Saint-Cyr and so many others were the stuff of dreams for female newsreel audiences. The 'stars' in women's magazines set many a female heart fluttering.

The defeat did not interrupt the *couturiers'* creative activity; they adapted to circumstances and continued to produce. However, things did change. The number of models, the quantity of fabrics, the type of material, even the line of the gowns, were all revised to take account of restrictions imposed by the Germans. More than a change in ways of dressing, fashion here appears to be an important economic and cultural factor. It was an economic factor because the Germans were greatly in need of raw materials and imposed strict rationing, which affected creative *couture*. It was a cultural factor because at the outbreak of war the prestige of *haute couture* was at its height. Paris was the capital of elegance, and the reputation of certain *couturiers* went far beyond national frontiers. Every collection was an opportunity for the creators to dictate a style that spread throughout the world. Both the United States and Latin America were accustomed to follow French fashion; France was the depository of a cultural heritage that it was determined to defend. The envious conqueror aimed to break this hegemony. In addition to the highly skilled workforce, the Germans wanted to take over the great Paris fashion houses and transfer the biggest names to Berlin. In the face of attack, *haute couture* defended itself. Lucien Lelong, leader of French *couture*, attempted to oppose the occupier. This involved a certain degree of compromise, which he had to justify after Liberation. The *grands couturiers*, like other trade associations, displayed the whole gamut of attitudes towards the Germans, ranging from minimal cooperation to complete collaboration. The first edition of this book, in 1990, exposed for the first time certain hitherto neglected compromising attitudes on the part of the fashion houses. The present edition goes much further by integrating the results of recent work. This is also true of the fate of the Jews – particularly numerous in small dressmaking ateliers and in the leather and fur sectors – who were the target of practices aimed at eliminating them from the manufacturing processes and from drapers' shops.

Studying fashion under the occupation means first of all reconstructing the past, the images of women in wooden soles, short skirts and extravagant hats, the elegant ladies in custom-made model gowns, rubbing shoulders with the occupier on race courses and at receptions. It also means attempting to understand something that may seem trivial in comparison with the Resistance and the deportations but that is actually very significant – that is, how a society reacted in its ways of living and dressing, and how the men and women who created its clothes behaved in an unusual situation. Lastly, it means trying to assess within the framework of a general history of fashion whether those four years represented a parenthesis, a turning point or a complete break.

Acknowledgements

At the outset of this new edition I would like to thank the Institut d'Histoire du Temps Présent, its director Henry Rousso, as well as my colleagues and friends there. I hope they will regard this as the expression of my gratitude for the exchange of ideas we have had, particularly in the internal seminar. I want to express particular gratitude to Anne Boigeol, Anne-Marie Pathé, Michèle Ruffat and Jacqueline Sainclivier for their support and advice; to Danièle Voldman, who helped me in the difficult periods of proofreading, combining efficiency and friendship; to Jean Anstruc and Maryvonne Le Puloch for their help with documentation and their professional competence.

Thanks too to the researchers and friends in the study group on fashion that I have led at the Institut d'Histoire du Temps Présent since 1999: Farid Chenoune, Françoise Denoyelle, Valérie Guillaume, Martine Lemaître, Michèle Ruffat; also Eléonore Testa who did her utmost to make my task easier. Warm wishes to Lou Taylor, professor at Brighton University and Valerie Steele, of the Museum at the Fashion Institute of Technology, New York, who joined the group.

My thanks also go to the Archives Nationales where I was able to round off my research when new deposits were opened up in the Musée Galliera, where the librarians Annie Barbéra and Sylvie Roy helped me in my search for documentation. Thanks to them I was able to finish off examining specific reviews. The same is true of the Bibliothèque Forney and the Bibliothèque Historique de la Ville de Paris. Lastly I do not want to forget the Bibliothèque Municipale de Versailles, where I was able to borrow the basic works on fashion and consult a number of articles and reviews on the spot.

I would like to thank my American friends, Sarah Fishman, Miranda Pollard and Paula Schwartz for their encouragement; Dominique Missika for her friendship throughout this work; Claire Marchand and Philippe Verheyde who facilitated my research; Christophe Guias who edited the text with insight and intelligence; Françoise Narti and Jacqueline Eichart who guided my choice of iconographic documents.

Sincere thanks to Céline Assegond who helped me to gather documents. I would also like to thank Michèle Ruffat and Steven Zdatny for their help with the translation.

Lastly, I have not forgotten the incalculable support of Bruno, Emmanuel and Véronique, Antoine and Marine (including Marie and Grégoire). Each in their own way has helped me.

–1–

The Last Good Days

At the end of August 1939 it seemed that summer would last for ever. There were storms but the weather was still hot, the sky barely tinged with grey. Men still wore light suits and women their flowery summer dresses. They wore tiny hats on their heads, trimmed with foliage or ribbons, unless they were lucky enough to own one of those delightful hats decorated with feathers. For most town dwellers the holidays were drawing to an end.

At Deauville, the smart seaside resort frequented by Parisians, there were fewer summer visitors. The brightly-coloured cotton beach pyjamas and pareos, previously so widespread, had almost disappeared from the promenades, where large white sun-hats worn with light-coloured outfits had also become less common. One did meet jockeys leading their horses along the racecourses to train, but there were few signs of life in the racing clubs, which were shunned by high society. A few players were hitting balls to and fro on the tennis courts. The fashionable restaurants were open – 'Women come there in glittering dresses and men in dinner jackets or suits. The service is always impeccable, the food exquisite . . . At the Casino in the evening, the croupiers repeat the traditional "rien ne va plus" ("this is your last chance"), without batting an eyelid.'[1] But the luxury hotels were emptying because the diplomatic tensions convinced their international clientele to leave France. With a little bit of luck it might have been possible to catch a glimpse of an actress or two on the *Normandy*, particularly Corinne Luchaire, surrounded by a crowd of admirers, including Prince Ali Khan. However, the time for festivities seemed to be over and few people attended the Deauville Grand Prix, which customarily marked the end of the social calendar. The Begum Aga Khan caused a sensation in the enclosure, draped in crepe printed with navy-blue leaves on a white ground, and the princess of Faucigny-Lucinge, known as 'the lady of 365 toilettes', was wearing an ensemble from Lanvin and was much admired.

In Paris a few wealthy couples prepared to desert the capital out of a pressing need to take the cure at Vichy. The autumn season there promised to be enjoyable. There would undoubtedly be plenty of fun and dancing at the Casino, where evening dress was *de rigueur*. More than one lady of fashion spent a long time in front of her looking glass debating the composition of her wardrobe. Should she take the tight-fitting beige gown with the transparent lace bodice with which Coco Chanel had caused such a stir that season, or one of those magnificent gypsy

– 1 –

dresses blossoming out like the corolla of a flower? Or should she instead take the black and red tartan velvet ensemble from Marcel Rochas, worn with a black satin jacket? One item was essential: she would not forget to slip a knitted costume, so cosy for the fresh autumn evenings, into her luggage.

There were crowds at the entrances to the Paris stations that last Sunday in August. Alongside reservists called up to rejoin their units in this period of calm, were throngs of young men and women bent on experiencing the joys of camping. These open-air enthusiasts surged on to the trains. Like their idol Marlene Dietrich, who made slacks fashionable on the beaches of the Côte d'Azur where she had stayed that summer, many of the young women sported outfits that they found practical – to hell with the frowns of the critics! Some even risked wearing shorts. At the gates of the capital, couples of bare-headed 'tandem-ists' wearing matching shirts and cycling culottes took to the road after a preliminary glance at the sky.

The atmosphere varied from one district to the next. On the Champs Elysées the pavement cafés were doing good business, periodically invaded by hordes of foreigners, particularly the English and some Americans. At Fouquet's, when high society met to sip port, a striking collection of hats by Rose Valois was on show, absolutely the last word in fashion. They included 'several suede or antelope fezes, decorated with ostrich or egret feathers held in place by a jewel, and one large black felt wide-brimmed hat tilted over the left eye and laden with satin ribbons'.[2] The displays of jewellers and of shoeshops were riveting. Toutmain, the new fashionable boutique (26 Champs-Elysées), created in 1932, advertised unbeatable prices for its winter collection. To judge by the publicity, it seemed that a woollen costume with a fur collar for added warmth was an essential that season. Elsewhere, more than one woman was dreaming her way along the fronts of the great fashion houses, almost all located between the Champs Elysées, Place Vendôme and Faubourg Saint-Honoré, in what was customarily referred to as the temple of elegance. How many secrets and how much genius those facades concealed!

The most aristocratic of the *couturières* held court at 136 Champs-Elysées: Maggy Rouff, daughter of Besançon de Wagner, who was head of the house of Drecoll, was born and bred in the seraglio. Every season, the most select clientele as well as the high aristocracy from all over Europe rushed to her premises (Princess Marina of Kent was a regular customer). Every new season, Maggy Rouff went to the Dutch court, accompanied by a head saleswoman from her atelier and a mannequin, to show her collection to the royal family. By her own account, however, her favourite clients remained 'Baroness J. de Rothschild, who has a magnificent body, ideas and charm, then Gabrielle Dorziat, and the irrepressible actress Alice Cocéa who enhances whatever she wears'.[3]

At number 22 Rue du Faubourg Saint-Honoré was the house of Lanvin, whose reputation in the world of fashion and perfume was second to none. Looking at the famous Lanvin label, window shoppers might have wondered why it displayed the image of 'a young woman with a little girl'. Very few were able to solve this mystery. In fact, no one seeing Jeanne Lanvin, doyenne of fashion and at the height of perfection in her art, could imagine that she had risen from very modest beginnings. Yet when she was thirteen she was an apprentice milliner, running to and fro from morning to night delivering hats and was not able to set up on her own account until she was twenty-three. She came to *haute couture* later, thanks to her daughter. She made Marie-Blanche's clothes herself and they were so delightful that it was not long before her friends asked her to make dresses for their little girls (hence the mother-daughter logo). From being a children's dressmaker, she became a dressmaker for young girls and then for young women and was soon on the way up. She had a varied clientele: a lot of big names, many actresses (Arletty, Madeleine Ozeray) were loyal customers. Everyone knew that Yvonne Printemps 'was dressed both for town and for the theatre by Jeanne Lanvin'. Only a short time before, everyone had had the chance to admire the gowns that the star wore in the film *Les Trois Valses*, which were produced in the Lanvin ateliers. Rumour had it that when the actress left for a tour of the United States, she demanded to take eighty gowns from Lanvin with her. It was also whispered that Sacha Guitry, that eternal and incorrigible lover, swore by nobody but Lanvin, entrusting her with exclusive responsibility for dressing his four successive wives, the most recent being Geneviève de Séréville. In Rue Cambon, a crowd gathered in front of Chanel's window to admire the display of perfumes and the very bold, very imaginative jewellery: 'one piece is made up of baroque pearls, separated by red stones with a 'crackle' effect, and looks like an ancient necklet of a maharajah . . . Also very original is that harlequin trapeze artist, fully jointed, and with a face formed from a ruby. He hangs by both hands from a trapeze, the trapeze itself being connected to a chain which encircles the neck'.[4] The famous Mademoiselle was certainly as fascinating as ever. What happened to her was the stuff of dreams for young dressmakers! Orphaned when she was six, Gabrielle Chanel was put into a convent at Moulins; twelve years later, when she was eighteen, she left to become a salesgirl in a ready-to-wear dress shop. This was the start of an incredible story.[5] Spotted at the age of twenty by an officer, Etienne Balsan, who became her protector, Gabrielle left Moulins to discover the amazing fashionable world of the racetrack. Shortly afterwards (1911) she met an Englishman, Boy Capel, and they fell madly in love. Thanks to him, Coco Chanel managed to gain relative autonomy. She began to make and sell hats, then she opened a couture house in Deauville (1912) and, after the war, set up in Paris at rue Cambon. Then began an ascent that turned Chanel into one of the most famous personalities in fashionable Paris. Friend of the Grand Duke Dimitri and mistress of the richest man in England, the Duke of Westminster, she was surrounded and inspired by a court of artists and writers: Cocteau, Dali, Picasso, Iribe, Reverdy . . . 'all crowd round her like drunken moths'.[6] Many women were grateful to Chanel for supplying the means with which to express their new desire for emancipation. Many unhesitatingly adopted the style she created, marked above all else by the 'luxury in simplicity' that her tweed and jersey ensembles symbolized. Nevertheless, some critics did not hesitate to accuse her of borrowing from men's clothing (berets, trousers, sweaters and so forth). No-one, however, remained unaware of her style.

A little further on in place Vendôme, a crowd of both informed and curious bystanders gathered in front of a beautiful eighteenth-century *hôtel*, one of the shrines of fashion. Elsa Schiaparelli, the most original of the *couturiers*, established her kingdom there in 1935; today it stretches over four floors, with a boutique at ground level selling perfumes, jewellery and accessories. She too had an amazing rise to fame which fascinated her admirers. At first nothing predisposed this great lady to plunge into *couture* other than innate good taste and a great deal of imagination. An Italian born into a well-to-do and cultured milieu in Rome, she enjoyed a gilded youth. After her marriage she lived in the United States for a few years until her divorce in 1930. She then decided to settle in Paris, where she earned her living making luxury knitwear – pullovers, sweaters, jackets – enlivened by surrealist or cubist decorations. Her success was soon assured. American buyers fought for the increasingly varied range of her creations. Her inventions, which entranced and shocked to an equal degree, were soon known throughout the world, in particular her lucky colour, a slightly bluish pink, christened 'shocking pink', which spread like wildfire. Her collections were the object of perpetual astonishment, if only for the themes employed: the circus, with performing elephants and horses embroidered on boleros; the *Commedia dell'Arte*, with Harlequin's coat, launched by Arletty. The window, displaying the suede and copper telephone bag, especially designed for the *couturière* by Salvador Dali, aroused much comment, as did the jewellery devised by artists as famous as Giacometti and Cocteau. Also on view was a bottle of *Shocking* perfume, its shape inspired by the bust of the American actress Mae West! Many women would have given their eye teeth to own one of these treasures, even if some of them had mainly comedy value, such as the bags that lit up or played a tune when opened, or the 'escarpin' or 'cotelette' hats! From the Comtesse Crespi to the Duchess of Windsor, not to mention Arletty, Marlene Dietrich, Cécile Sorel, and Joan Crawford, the most elegant women in the world voted for 'Schiap'. Only that summer, at the Eiffel Tower gala, the *couturière* had launched 'the jubilee hat', original both in its shape and its arrangement of black feathers. A photograph of it that appeared in the weekly *Match* on 9 June 1939, was subsequently reproduced on several occasions during the war in a number of magazines, in particular in *La Semaine, l'hebdomadaire de l'actualité mondiale*.[7]

Along the boulevards the queues outside theatres and cinemas stretched further and further. Abel Gance's latest film, *Louise*, was a sell out because of its cast: Ginette Leclerc and Robert Le Vigan. In the auditorium, the dresses were predominantly lightweight for early autumn, their dotted or checked fabrics marking the transition from the medley of summer prints to the dark plain cloth of winter.

Whether they had a premonition or whether it was their natural reaction, people wanted to make the most of these last fine days. Hardly any attention was paid to the alarmist rumours of tensions in Poland in the newspapers or on the wireless. After all, many people remembered the Munich Agreements, which had defused the crisis in September 1938, and it was hoped that the storm would once again be dispersed.

In the world of elegance, one event dominated conversation: the unveiling of the winter collections. For several weeks, *couturiers* had been held in the grip of creative fever as, in the greatest secrecy, they prepared the new collections for winter 1939. The creators had scoured the world to find the 200 designs that made up their presentations. They gathered round them the most unusual and valuable objects.

> The sheep-farmer from Australia, the goatherd from Tibet, the diver from the Persian Gulf, the trapper from Kamchatka, the prospector from the Klondyke [sic] who washes gold from the rivers or the miner from the Transvaal who digs for diamonds, and the dyer, tanner and weaver from Flanders and Picardy, the silk merchant from Lyons, the florist from the rue du Sentier, have all sent the products of their husbandry or their cultivation, their hunting or their labour.[8]

Now, alone in their workroom, with scissors, safety pins and a battalion of large wooden dolls, the *couturiers* drew, cut and prepared the fabrics, which they fitted on their mannequins. A whole team bustled about in their wake, everyone from the most important to the lowliest, from the manager to the errand girl, playing a part in the success of the collection. Little by little, fairyland took more definite shape and came to life: live mannequins replaced the wooden dolls. 'For the last time, the inspired designer places the rough scratchy cloth on these beautiful, thin and supple girls, adds a pin here, a charcoal line there.'[9] Then it was the turn of thousands of apprentices to take hold of the chosen fabric, and to pin, sew and embroider. Thanks to their skill, combined with the genius of the creators, the miracle was achieved: under their nimble fingers, a Paris gown was born.

Now it was fever pitch. Everything was ready for the grand parade. Reporters and buyers had arrived from New York, Chicago, Montreal, Buenos Aires and London, ready to choose, buy and peddle Parisian fashion all over the world. Installed in luxurious salons, the hand-picked spectators waited for the show to begin, vibrant with anticipation. The decor surrounding them was luxuriant hangings and panelling in pastel shades, chairs upholstered in green silk with gilded backs, precious objets d'art, all coming together to create an atmosphere of refinement (the prize goes to Robert Piguet, who transformed his salons in the style of Italian palaces, with heavy drapery and ceilings covered with cloudy skies). In the front row of this private view sat the American Janet Flanner, the correspondent of the *New Yorker*, who never missed a fashion show. Her cabin on the great transatlantic liners was booked from season to season. Thousands of her compatriots hung on to her every word, and her articles, illustrated with sketches thanks to telephotography, were among the first to be published. Not far from her, Edna Woolman Chase, editor in chief of American *Vogue*,[10] was seated beside Michel de Brunhoff, who had been responsible for the French edition of the magazine since 1929. Both of them, pencil in hand, were examining the papers handed to them when they came in. Among the journalists, André de Fouquières, arbiter of elegance who attended every reception, exchanged a few words with his neighbour, the columnist Lucien François, editor of *Votre Beauté*. The new trends in the collection were not their sole subject of conversation, however. They were tormented by the same question: 'Do you think that Hitler will dare to go to war?' Lucien Lelong, leader of the French *couturiers*, would not let the gloomy diplomatic situation cloud the atmosphere. People were only too happy to repeat the optimistic remarks of the man at the head of *haute couture*: 'Our role is to give France an appearance of serenity; the problems must not hamper the creators. It is their duty to hold aloof from them. The more elegant French women are . . . the more our country will show people abroad that it does not fear the future.'[11]

Indiscreet remarks, which had filtered through to the press, hinted that the collections would be influenced by the fashions of 1880. The *couturiers* had once again kept their promise: thanks to them, a new type of woman was born. 'The Paris peasant woman', naïve and fresh, chic and attractive, of the previous summer, was replaced by the more sophisticated lady from *Maxim's*. The following advice, which appeared in August 1939, seems very trivial and far removed from the reality of the day:

> From now on if you want to be up-to-date, make an effort to act naturally in your new role – this winter's very extravagant fashion calls for a certain dignity and an enormous amount of style and not a simpering manner. Learn to moderate your long athletic strides, at least when you are wearing an evening dress. Have a relaxed and not a provocative deportment . . . Learn to handle a fan gracefully and to wrap your stole round you. Goodness knows, it is rather a big jump from the little girl model to the lady from *Maxim's* but with your feminine skill you will manage it.[12]

> In the salons, where the temperature has reached hot-house levels, conversation has ceased. The windows are shut, beams of light from large reflectors converge on a door at stage level, masked by drapery. The drape is raised, the model appears, takes a few steps, spins round then crosses the room. A name or a number circulates and is repeated in the major European languages.[13]

The collections had to follow an established sequence: first, casual costumes; then town or afternoon outfits in wool, crepe and satin; then the grand finale with evening gowns and wedding dresses. At last, buyers and critics were witnessing the much-discussed new line. The waist was small and was emphasized, often held in a light drape. Skirts had fallen again and were three centimetres longer than in the previous season.

The creators anxiously awaited the verdict of the spectators. As was her wont, Mademoiselle Chanel was seated on a step right at the top of the staircase and cast a final glance over her models, who nodded to her before moving off. 'Why,' the audience wondered, 'is there so much decoration, trimming, frogging, shoulder braid and tassels on the boleros and jackets . . . By bringing the very old military uniforms back into fashion aren't the creators – at least some of them – allowing themselves to be influenced by these troubled times?'[14] Surprise, even irritation, reached its peak when the millinery models appeared. Shakos, chéchias, busbys and even the French guards' tricornes – this winter's woman would certainly take on a military appearance, which some found attractive but others deeply displeasing. Luckily, the parade of evening gowns was greeted with cries of admiration. Brocade and brocaded fabric made for gowns that enhanced the figure. Reports noted many tight-skirted gowns with the fullness at the base or draped in a panier on the hips. Madeleine Vionnet, who had brought drapery back into fashion several years before, received loud applause for a two-coloured evening gown, 'emphasizing the hips with a ruche of black lace like the skirt'. Also found worthy of note were a blue-and-gold lamé siren gown worn with pearls and coloured stones at the house of Worth – which traditionally dressed royal families – and a long gown in Albène lace from Calais, re-embroidered in silver, shown by Lucien Lelong.

To judge by the applause, orders were bound to pour in at the end of the show. The rooms emptied; some foreign correspondents immediately telephoned their impressions to their papers. It was certainly still true: French fashion took first place on the international scene and Paris remained the capital of elegance. But for how much longer?

On 3 September 1939 it was 'farewell' to the good days. No one wanted to believe it but the evidence was unavoidable: war had come: Britain and France had officially declared war on Germany following the German invasion of Poland. General mobilization was ordered. From one day to the next, life was turned completely upside down. Women made up parcels for their soldiers, slipping in a woolly here, a photograph from the good times there. As the moment of parting drew near, a procession of bright dresses, like so many floral wreaths, accompanied the conscript to the station or to his call-up centre. Although not all were in uniform, it was easy to spot those leaving laden with luggage or armed with a haversack. Despite the tears they held back and the distress that gripped them, young and not-so-young women found the courage to make themselves beautiful in order to create a pleasant, lasting impression. But behind the rather tight smiles, one burning question was on everybody's lips: 'When will we meet again?'

After a few days of confusion, when trains were stormed by tearful civilians and lines of cars dashed towards what they thought to be more clement climes, the country settled down. France, trying to give the impression of normality, put on its customary airs. The press unanimously emphasized the courage of the population and, if the skilfully orchestrated propaganda is to be believed, life everywhere resumed its normal course.

In Paris, as elsewhere, whole families had fled in overladen cars, equipped with blankets, thermos flasks and sandwiches. Pure mohair overcoats from Creed were glimpsed inside limousines driven by uniformed chauffeurs, as were elegant tartan coats carrying the Lanvin label, and hair tied tidily back by jersey turbans from Agnès. Then the city adjusted to the new situation. Despite closed boutiques, Paris, in the daytime at least, regained its animation. Only its external appearance had changed: some luxury shops had protected their frontage with wooden panels and had stuck strips of paper over their plate glass windows in the hope of reducing the damage from bombing; in preparation for the worst-case scenario and obeying the air raid precautions,the principal monuments were covered in sandbags, while windows were painted blue to prevent the slightest ray of light escaping.

Most cellars had become shelters, and hastily posted notices indicated where to seek refuge in case of alerts. A striking feature of the streets, where one or two officers were to be seen in uniforms impeccably cut by the best establishments, was the absence of children, often evacuated to the countryside, and of young men, almost all mobilized.[15] Furthermore, a new object had appeared, supplied to every civilian: the compulsory gas mask. The fear of a gas war was such that, for a few months, the population barely moved without this piece of equipment. In the market, at school, in the cinema, at the theatre, in a restaurant, in the metro, the mask was always present, everywhere. It became the symbol of war time. Some women displayed enormous ingenuity in camouflaging it or matching it to their outfit. Consequently, it was common to see masks concealed in bags made from fancy fabrics or, in chic districts, in leather or satin holders. Advertising and the luxury trade took advantage of the opportunity. A miniature model gas mask became a perfume flask or 'the newest and most practical lipstick case' of the year. Across the Atlantic, cylindrical hat boxes launched by Jeanne Lanvin were a great success. The same was true of the cylindrical bags that every Argentinian and Brazilian woman fought for because they were the very incarnation of Paris fashion.

New days, new ways. The war and the first measures that accompanied it (such as air-raid warnings, and power-cuts) dictated a change in behaviour, particularly for the female population. Some eccentrics walked about in khaki shirts, with gilt buttons, epaulettes on their jackets or proudly sported shakos, chéchias, busbys and other garments worn by operetta soldiers. Many a young woman, her face still tanned from the holidays, had no hesitation in going about with her hair flying loose and her hood folded back on her shoulders, until she needed it to protect her from the cold.

Some women even sacrificed their carefully arranged curls in favour of a simpler upswept hairstyle. Hairdressers explained that the current situation called for adaptability, and that never, absolutely never, would curls have stood up to gas-mask straps or electricity cuts. Consequently, the only solution lay in the scissors.

Air-raid warnings also called for a revision of the female wardrobe. Under the title 'Tout ce qu'il Faut pour Descendre à l'Abri' ('Everything you Need for your Shelter'),[16] a Paris department store offered its customers a faithful reconstruction of a cellar. It had everything: a table, benches composed of a plank supported by sandbags in place of legs, a lamp, sleeping bags and, on the benches, casually spread out, a whole range of warm clothes: padded waistcoats, fleecy hoods, siren (boiler) suits in leather or waterproof material, sheepskin jackets. If she did not take some elementary precautions, a shelter could be very uncomfortable for a woman who felt the cold and who had been dragged out of bed. Ski clothing, being both practical and warm, was particularly popular, and large woollen fur-lined coats with hoods were soon all the rage. Some women made themselves one-piece outfits with zip fasteners, which were easy to pull on, as was the wool jersey siren suit which *Mode du Jour* recommended to its readers in autumn 1939. It was gathered at the yoke and fastened with a buttoned strap, while the legs were extended by socks; a pair of rubber boots could easily complete the outfit.

Elsewhere, elegance lost none of its privileges: the shelter in the Ritz, for example, strongly resembled the most recent fashion salon. The cellars were pleasantly furnished with fur rugs and sleeping bags from Hermès. The newest war-time outfits were paraded here, worn by women well known for their refinement. The three-piece ensemble from Schiaparelli – trousers, blouson and hood in transparent blue-green waterproof material, lined with violet flannel – did not go unnoticed. Next to it was the already classic siren suit in iron-grey wool, worn with a cape by Robert Piguet, in pink, white and grey squares and a hooded cloak lined throughout with grogram brought murmurs of approval. A common feature of these outfits was the number of pockets of various shapes and sizes. Large and deep with gussets, or very small and flat, they were indispensable for protecting papers, jewellery and money. Heavy footwear, fur lined for warmth, and knitted gloves completed the air-raid outfit.

There were times when the love of finery and desire to show off overcame fear for some fashionable ladies. Witness this scene, which took place in Deauville in the grand hotel 'Normandy' right at the beginning of the war: strident wailing rent the night, general panic followed, and people in often sumptuous night attire barged into each other, shouting, and accosting one another in the corridors. Suddenly, there was complete silence. All eyes turned towards Cécile Sorel who was coming down the staircase as majestically as if she was at the theatre. 'She was wrapped in a sort of large blue cape which covered her whole body down to her ankles, her head was crowned with an admiral's hat to the most striking effect. Her face was made-up as for the grandest of first-nights, her hair curled as if she had emerged from the greatest Paris hairdresser.'[17] She passed slowly by and disappeared into the night.

During the first few weeks the winds of moralism and virtue shook the land, and this was reflected in its dress. Paris, both the heart and mirror of France, set an example of respectability. The city of lights was dark at night, semi-deserted, as if numbed. There were few entertainments. Horse-racing was considered unsuitable and was cancelled until further notice. Initially closed down, cinemas and theatres re-opened but were subject to draconian regulations.

A sign of the times was the proliferation of women in uniform; they were visible everywhere in the Paris streets. 'Wearing a black costume, with a white shirt and black tie, they took over the job of emptying the post boxes in various districts of the capital.'[18] There were also a lot of Red Cross nurses. Most of them wore the usual outfit – 'strictly tailored costume, classic coat, a dark blue felt hat with a brim turned down in front'[19] – which the newspapers reproduced on innumerable occasions, some dailies even providing patterns of these outfits for sale by mail order. Society ladies, whose day principally revolved around a cup of tea or a charity sale, and who had been idle only twenty-four hours earlier, became conscious of their responsibilities and enrolled in the medical or social services. Florence Gould, the wife of the American railway king and a Parisian by adoption, was a good example of this, as was Gogo Schiaparelli (Elsa's daughter), who became an ambulance driver in the mobile medical sector. Some *couture* houses seized their chance. 'Dressing according to the instructions of the Red Cross and the directives of the *grands couturiers*' was the purpose of this new crusade. The exceedingly chic uniforms from Schiaparelli and Lanvin were objects of envy.

In the bars at lunch time a swarm of seamstresses and employees drank their coffee and ate their sandwiches standing up. The atmosphere was less gay than before as they discussed the latest news. Clothes also became more sober. Gone were the gaudy gowns, the eccentric hats, the showy jewellery and the too-red nails. The fashion was for strict tailoring, relieved only by a crepe blouse. A small dark felt hat decorated with a ribbon and a large handbag completed the ensemble.

For homemakers, 'the war became a sort of war of movement'.[20] The new life they led, divided between the children in the country, parents in the provinces, and husband at the front, forced them to make incessant journeys and called for practical and comfortable clothing. It was with them in mind that those costumes made from thick fabric – tweed, jersey or wool – were created, as well as full coats, roomy enough to be worn over the costume and equipped with large pockets and often with hoods so that they could dispense with bag and hat. The days of affectation were gone. Solid laced-up shoes and thick stockings, which only a few weeks before no woman would ever have wanted, had become the common garb.

There was also a fashion prescribed for the army:

Our soldiers at the front, exposed to wind, rain and all sorts of bad weather, appreciate to the highest degree the comfort of fur clothing. The large chasuble-shaped sheepskin jackets worn on top are providential for our look-outs, the infantry, the pilots and for our gallant soldiers. Patrols and trench life have brought into general use those waterproof jackets called Canadiennes [lumber-jackets] that are lined with sheepskin, lambskin or some other fur. A belt with a buckle draws them in at the waist. A wide fur band at the neck frames the face and protects the chest against damp and cold.[21]

The repercussions of the war also spread to high fashion, where the key words were discretion and elegant comfort. Once everyday life had resumed, the small world of fashion also continued on its way, while at the same time taking into account the new situation. However, some of its best elements had been lost along the way. Some fashion houses had closed. The American *couturier* Mainbocher had fled to the United States. In December 1940, Madeleine Vionnet, who, at the time war was declared was the master of the art of draping, chose to close her fashion house. Marcelle Chaumont was her self-appointed successor. The 'Grande Mademoiselle' did a moonlight flit. As soon as she heard the news, Chanel decided to leave the capital. Driven by her chauffeur and bodyguard, she left by car to take refuge in the south. And then, despite appeals from her colleagues and friends, she obstinately refused to re-open her salon. She who had previously been so tenacious, and who had struggled to make her style rule supreme, withdrew from the business world and put her life on hold, spending her time making up parcels for soldiers. Jean Marais's war-time pen pal, she ended up adopting his whole squadron, sending pullovers and mittens to the lonely.

The young designers Christian Dior and Pierre Balmain were called up. Other *couturiers*, like Marcelle Dormoy,[22] until recently still grouped around Jean Patou in Biarritz, decided to return to Paris. With Lucien Lelong, they worked tirelessly, determined to offer their clientèle new designs that were better adapted to the circumstances. The 1939–40 winter collection was presented to the public late, but the delay was used to good effect to bring the creations up to date. Speaking to a journalist who had come to interview her about the state of Parisian *haute couture*, Maggy Rouff intimated that it was unthinkable in view of the needs of the time to adopt, unaltered, the collection shown to journalists and buyers in August-September. 'Born in peacetime, created for carefree days, our gowns have retired for a deep and unexpected sleep within the protection of their wardrobes,' she explained.[23] In their place, another fashion was born, and a new word, 'utilitarian', appeared. Knitwear, pullovers, dark-coloured woollen dresses, heavy overcoats, classic costumes, a lot of furs; every *couturier* was set on preparing a 'real' collection, even if the customary ritual was somewhat upset.

And then in rue Royale, place Vendôme and in the Champs Elysées, the liveried commissioner of happier days resumed his guard in front of every door surmounted by a well-known name. His face bore more wrinkles, his back was rather more bent, he had taken the place of a friend who had left for the front, but he was there. The fashion houses were open again and that was the main thing. The atmosphere may have buzzed as much as ever but it was less frivolous than usual and the public was not exactly the same. Of course, the fashion designers and a few foreign journalists were there, loyal to their jobs, as were, first of all, the permanent correspondents of the major magazines. Carmel Snow who had resigned as editor in chief of *Vogue* and moved to *Harper's Bazaar* in 1932, came to see for herself the state of Parisian fashion. She was accompanied by Marie-Louise Bousquet, who helped her with the Paris edition. Both carefully noted the changes that had occurred. The management of the Paris office was left in the hands of Daisy Fellowes, whose contacts in society and the arts were major assets. Thanks to the 'clipper' planes, American buyers, who were able to reach Paris from New York in only two days, prepared to carry back their booty, particularly the evening gowns made specially for them.

The front rows at the shows were occupied by a tightly-packed battalion of spectators who were attentive but, judging by what else they were doing, had no intention of remaining idle. They included the wife of General Gamelin, wearing a hat, dressed all in black, and setting a serious tone by enthusiastically knitting up a ball of khaki wool. Alongside her, others skilfully knitted away, ensuring that the army lacked neither mufflers nor gloves, nor even balaclavas. When something approaching silence was obtained, the parade finally began and the compère announced the designs, whose names, lines and colours had all been affected by events of the day. The gown 'Un soir près de toi' ('An evening near you') was now baptized 'Permission' ('Leave'), while pyjamas were called 'Alerte' or 'Au coin de feu' ('By the fireside'). Lanvin won applause for 'Spahi', a costume in soft, sand-coloured wool, with wide pockets on the jacket and a dark belt. Robert Piguet had a great success with 'Service Secret', an ensemble with a large number of buttoned pockets. Schiaparelli embellished her collection with numerous strokes of genius, including the enormous pocket bags that replaced handbags. There was even a pocket closed by a zip fastener on the inside of the hem of a dark skirt. Also from Schiaparelli, the new 'laveuse' dress in 'camouflage' green shot silk, caused a sensation. Short and draped for daytime wear, it could, with a flick of the wrist, become long for the evening.[24] Colours were also discreetly influenced by the events of the day. New colours had appeared: 'Royal Air Force blue' was the great event of the season, followed by 'Maginot Line blue' or 'tempered-steel blue', 'aeroplane grey', or even 'French soil beige'. 'The president of the Chambre syndicale indicated his preference for a colour verging on bronze, a bright, deep bronze evoking, not the broken muzzle of a cannon, but a sturdy bell singing of hope'.[25] Hats were not to be outdone. The astrakhan chéchias, so disparaged the previous month, came back with a vengeance, while the tartan beret, imported from Britain, inspired many a casual hairstyle. Some pretty designs slipped into this military collection – for example, a little two-tone felt hat in sweet pea mauve and pink, reminiscent of the English forage cap, was the work of Rose Descat.

When the applause had finally died down and the lights of the ramp had been switched off, the *couturiers* wondered how this collection would be received by both the French and, especially, their foreign clientèle. Would they succeed in keeping the flag of Parisian *haute couture* flying high as they had in the past? Or would they have to give way to competitors who were eager to seize their opportunity? Rumours were already rife that some *couturiers* in the United States were claiming they were ready to supplant Paris. People were asking, 'Where have the good old days gone when orders flowed in from the four corners of the globe and when the sale of a luxury gown enabled the state to buy ten tons of coal, and the sale of a litre of perfume two tons of petrol?'[26] What would become of a work force that had attained a high level of skill by dint of unspeakable sacrifice and effort? Was it generally known that it took at least seven years to become a 'sleever' or a 'skirter'', and that only a tiny minority reached the envied grade of 'head' of an atelier? Would the 25,000 women working in the fashion industry have to be made redundant?

This context makes it easier for us to understand the significance of Lucien Lelong's approach to the authorities to obtain an assurance that they would support the *couturiers'* efforts. It was vital, he explained, for French *couture* to defend its share of foreign markets at any cost: 'luxury and quality are national industries. They bring millions of foreign currency into the state coffers, which we need now more than ever . . . What Germany earns with chemical products, fertilizers and machinery, we earn with diaphanous muslins, perfumes, flowers and ribbons.'[27] By continuing to produce beautiful evening gowns for Americans, Argentinians, Brazilians, and so on, who were not at war, one section of the ateliers would not be made redundant.

By defending *haute couture*, France was defending a part of her industry that was also part of her culture, because the majority of rich or well-off women throughout the world dressed, made up, styled their hair and decked themselves out not only according to Paris fashion, but also with the intention of imitating Parisian women. According to Lucien François, Parisian women had a duty to continue to be elegant. Addressing those who set the tone in the type of lyrical flight of fancy of which he was a past master, he had no hesitation in writing, 'The day when you cease to be coquettes [and like pretty clothes], half Paris will be unemployed, because foreigners will no longer want what has not been created to answer the needs of the women of our country . . . Every woman in Paris is a living propaganda poster . . . the universal function of the Parisian woman is to remain a coquette.'[28] Coquetry became an indispensable weapon in the economic war. Not only fashion writers enrolled in its service, but also the *couturiers*, the designers and everyone who helped to create fashion. Time and again, they mounted the battlements to criticize women for indifference to their external appearance. Each had their own refrain according to their speciality but all tried to get people to spend patriotically. 'Jeanne Lanvin confirms the need to maintain the radiance with which Paris illuminates the world . . . do not women have a duty in these tragic times to keep a small scented corner in the very heart of France for dreams, luxury and beauty?'[29] To let hair fly loose, styled heaven knows how, did not befit the situation, growled Madame Agnès, one of the most prominent milliners in Paris, using the powerful argument of soldiers' leave. 'Do not forget, ladies, that the soldier on leave wants to find you as beautiful and as elegant as you were when he left you; be more sober in your dress but do not renounce elegance altogether.'[30] And she ended by recommending to those concerned 'a little toque in woollen lace; the transparent effect is becoming and it is at the same time practical since it conceals slightly disordered curls.'

The same tone of reproach was sounded by Maggy Rouff, Robert Piguet and Molyneux[31] who fulminated against the carelessness of some and the casualness of others. With emotions running high in the first days of September women had been overcome by an attack of virtue and took refuge in wartime fashions. Without succumbing to excess, the time had come to resume the traditions of good taste. Some women's magazines, including the weeklies, published articles that contained banal clichés, notably the deeply rooted image of a woman for whom frivolity was a necessary weapon. 'The existence of an army of carefree women whose beauty brings a little gaiety to our somber days is a necessity. Nursemaid to her man,[32] the attractive woman knows she has a role to play: to please. Because nothing is more cheering for soldiers on leave than to find a smiling, carefully made-up face and a pleasing figure. When they go back, they carry with them an image of optimism, courage, hope and beauty.' As if to echo their thoughts, Paris came back to life.

Cautiously, cinemas and theatres opened their doors wider, adopting a recipe of pre-dinner performances. The Comédie-Française was packed despite its wartime appearance. The busts of Molière and Corneille that had once greeted audiences had been taken away for safe-keeping and only Houdon's large Voltaire remained at the top of the staircase because it could not be transported. In the auditorium, there were many lounge suits and a few sports jackets among the men, and few women wore long dresses, Most had adopted simple but refined clothes. Many of them wore little black woollen dresses, others evening costumes in black or navy faille, brightened up with sequins at the yoke and on the skirt. A few turbans and a large number of heavily trimmed hairnets replaced evening headwear, some with blue or black sequins and others embroidered in gold. The Théâtre de la Madeleine did not witness the excitement of the great evenings until the beginning of November. In fact, the first 'first-night' of the war took place from the 5th to the 7th: this was a charity gala organized by Sacha Guitry, which included three of his plays. The money it raised was earmarked for the purchase of an ambulance for the Red Cross. Fashionable Paris had taken seats in the boxes – the Duchess of Windsor in a blue gown from Molyneux, next to her husband, the Duke; the extravagant and exquisite elderly Lady Mendl, known for her fêtes; Madame Paul Reynaud, soberly and classically dressed by Jeanne Lanvin. Elsa Schiaparelli and her daughter Gogo were the centre of attention, one wearing a black-and-pale-pink ensemble, a short jacket over a pink blouse enriched by embroidered beading, while the other wore a 'sleeping' blue faille gown, with black stripes. On that particular evening the prize for elegance went to Geneviève Guitry who was wearing 'a tailored coat of Persian blue Duvetyn, with a flared skirt'. Paul Valéry and Jean Cocteau in evening dress were not far behind.

At the ABC and Bobino's, where variety performances had resumed, the atmosphere was different. They were crowded with soldiers on leave, avidly seeking distraction and trying to forget. As before the war, their companions were painted and made up and, under the compassionate eyes of some and the merry gaze of others, they took out and plied their powder puffs and lipsticks. Side by side with some pretty hats that were a credit to the good taste of their wearers and to the Paris milliners, some jovial characters did not hold back in their loud criticism of a 'titfer' that looked like a 'pancake for Little Red Riding Hood' or another resembling 'a fruit basket'. Laughter spread around a felt stove-pipe from which a few permed curls escaped. 'What will women think of next?' some people sighed.

As time went by, the gloom of war tended to fade among those at home, and the soldiers at the front settled down to a 'phony war' where nothing happened. The year 1939 slipped quietly away, a night of snow in the midst of uneasy voracity. People wanted to forget; those seeing in the New Year made an attempt at gaiety. Not for ages had restaurants in the capital, from the humblest to the most luxurious, seen such crowds. After dining with friends, couples, who could not go dancing because dances were still forbidden, went on to the Casino de Paris to applaud Maurice Chevalier and Mistinguett. Despite the cold, the new year gave many young girls the opportunity to wear a shift for the first time, with its straight lines and soft cut, and fastened at the neck with one of the gilt brooches that were so popular that winter. Amazing feats of imagination, they came in a variety of designs, but none went unnoticed: a key for hope; Anglo-French flags; a weather-cock with the inscription, 'Until the end'; and so forth. One young engaged woman had even hooked a framed photograph of her beloved on to her bodice, plus the insignia of his regiment, thereby earning enthusiastic applause from the assembled company.

Further on, gourmets and connoisseurs competed for entry to the chic establishments, looking for a carefully prepared menu and a happy atmosphere. Three-quarter length mink coats, astrakhan capes and toques, nearly all of them from Révillon, the fashionable furrier, crowded the doorways.

British and Polish Allied airmen found themselves squashed among the evening gowns and dinner jackets in the Boeuf sur le Toit, where everybody was enjoying themselves. If you failed to catch a glimpse of Jean Cocteau, a regular habitué, you could at least, and with a certain degree of malice, spot several Marlene Dietrich look-alikes, platinum blonds in lamé dresses and red nails, with cigarette holders dangling from their lips.

Thus Paris, like much of France, drowned its sorrows and tried to forget the war by putting down the enemy. A report in *Match* on 11 May 1939 had already stated, 'Germany is held together by its ersatz' products, and used photographs of mannequins to illustrate their 'new discoveries' in the realm of fabrics and footwear, describing them as unsatisfactory. The general feeling was optimistic and people had a good laugh on discovering that the poor Germans were reduced to a system of ration books and clothing coupons to dress themselves. Every time they wanted to buy an item of clothing they had to tear off coupons giving them the right to such and such an article! Thank heavens there was no risk of such a misfortune coming to France, where everything of that sort existed in abundance. One only had to look in the windows of Samaritaine or Bon Marché to see the bargains they offered during the sales! It was not government measures that risked hampering the smooth running of the luxury trade. Paul Reynaud, Minister of Finance at the time, had said repeatedly to a delegation from the Fédération des commerces et industries d'art de qualité who had come to plead their cause: it is essential that luxury crafts and *haute couture* continue to sell, in France of course, but above all overseas, to ensure that the state coffers were well lined. However, the fur trade was witnessing the beginnings of a serious crisis. According to experts, 'this crisis is partly due to contracts based on business carried out in previous years, contracts which have become impossible to fulfil because of the war, the restrictions resulting from it, and the disappearance of the biggest fur markets: the North and the East [of France].'[33] Furriers in the Lower Rhine had been obliged to leave their businesses and take refuge in the Dordogne, where they were dispersed.

As if they had learned their lesson, the *couturiers* created gayer and also more colourful styles in their spring collections. (If 'RAF blue'[34] was still the most popular colour, the shade of red christened 'scarlett' and bright green could also be found, as well as raw silk and every shade on the colour chart between caramel and

– 16 –

maize.) The creators had achieved the dual distinction of satisfying the slightly controlled elegance of French women in wartime, and the more sparkling, more imaginative elegance of foreigners who were enjoying the benefits of peace. In France, elegant ladies no longer had the time to change their dresses several times a day, as pre-war fashion required. As a result, suits that could be worn from morning till night, became the most popular costumes, or else a simple dress worn with a long jacket and often a belt in a contrasting colour. Everything lay in the choice of fabric, which had to be of irreproachable quality and cut, which could come only from a *grand couturier* (even if prices had climbed dangerously that season). The more sophisticated designs, in which silk and organdi were prominent, were intended for overseas. There was an endless variety of prints: Bayadère bands with little stylized flowers, paisley patterns, sweet peas, eglantine, enormous sunflowers, and marguerites on blue, yellow and black backgrounds offered an infinite choice. Patriotism was not entirely absent, with a model by Jean Patou, 'Cocorico', featuring a seed-plot of red and white cockerels on a blue background. Sensibly, the prime concern of everyday fashion was to encourage clothes that could be worn in both town and countryside. The cheap women's magazines were full of co-ordinated designs: a plain fabric worn with another with narrow stripes, or a small check matched with a large one, and so forth. At the summer 1940 preview, some designers presented smart, fresh outfits in the style of pinafore dresses, which were described as ideal for gardening and the sea. Flowers were scattered over the summer hats and everyone wanted a little boater trimmed with bunches of primulas, myosotis, cornflowers or roses.

A few weeks before the blow fell, spring, already anticipated by fashion, really arrived, enchanting Parisians with its incredible beauty and sweetness. The chestnut trees on the Champs Elysées were in flower. For days on end the sky remained a cloudless unchanging blue. More than ever, the war seemed far away and the singer René Dorin's refrain: 'Will it be tonight, will it be tomorrow?', which was on the wireless and then on every tongue, was a fair reflection of the sentiments of a population that no longer believed that danger was imminent. The Parisian woman whose photograph appeared on a cover of *Vogue* remained the symbol of elegance: a smiling blonde, tastefully dressed and coiffed, followed by two Allied officers, visibly charmed by her grace.[35]

Paris meant more than elegance and beauty at the end of April 1940. It also remained the city of entertainment, as the Swiss journalist Edmond Dubois noted, counting 105 cinemas, twenty-five theatres, fourteen music halls and twenty-one cabarets still open. On the occasion of a gala charity show to take place at the Opéra in the presence of the President of the Republic, Albert Lebrun, one lady journalist devoted an entire article to the ideal outfit for such an event: 'The difficulty of a gala in wartime does not lie in its success . . . The most important thing is to know how to dress appropriately for the occasion.'[36] There should be no showiness, but also no carelessness. A dress that was too gaudy or too modest would be out of place. If gentlemen thought tails excessive, did not sports jackets risk appearing like 'a sort of vestimentary defeatism'? There were always dinner jackets . . .

With the help of the weather, morale was therefore set fair. The lilacs had faded but the roses were in bloom and the merry month of May saw the return of the Paris season, the return of elegance! When, in the early hours of 10 May, the French, including the Parisians, learned that the frontiers of Holland and Belgium had been violated, the awakening was painful. Anguish and stupor were written on every face. The false calm had come to an end. A week later the great surge of people from the north began. They came from another world: harassed families seeking refuge, shaken old men, exhausted little girls, women, hatless and in smocks, grey with fatigue, dragging perambulators or bent under the weight of baggage; they were a pitiful sight and they reminded everyone that the war was for real.

L'Oeuvre recommended that the women who welcomed the Belgian refugees in the hall of the Gare du Nord should apply only a light make-up; to do otherwise would be 'outrageously out of place amidst these exiles, worn out by fatigue and restrained grief'.[37] *Paris-Midi*[38] announced a new style, intended for those women who spent their days in the reception centres for refugees: 'a leather bag attached to the waist by a belt', which left the hands completely free.

Panic soon hit the capital, where a retreat began according to social status. It started in the smart districts (Etoile, Passy . . .), where those who had learned to take the time to put on suitable outfits, as if they were going on holiday, drove off in their beautiful cars for their seaside villa or country house. At the same time, the sleeping-cars – where there was no shortage of elegant travelling clothes and leather luggage – were besieged by people wanting to travel to the Riviera and the Basque coast, and a notice was posted up saying that they were fully booked. Then, without undue haste, the middle classes joined the movement, adopting the advice that appeared in *L'Action Française*[39] on 4 June:

> If you are going away to some provincial refuge, as so many others have already done, take with you things that can not easily be replaced. Ladies, abandon your sun dress rather than your plain clothes. Do not forget to equip yourself with a pair of sensible shoes in case of storms, leave a hat rather than a book or a cherished photograph . . . think of the future and make sure you take blankets and woollen clothes . . .

Paris-Soir addressed middle-class women more prosaically. 'Here is some useful advice for those of you who have been evacuated: wear flat shoes, since you will have to walk around a lot on foot, lisle rather than silk stockings or even bare feet in sandals, and take a hairnet or kerchief to tie back your hair'.[40]

At the beginning of June, it was the turn of the working-classes to take to the road by any means they could: old jalopies into which whole families piled with assorted goods, lorries or bicycles. There were record crowds at stations; trains were packed. Many of these people were wearing their Sunday best and were too warmly dressed for the time of year, the women with hats and sometimes even gloves. One thing seemed to be uppermost in the minds of all the travellers: to get away without leaving anything behind. It was common, on those scorching hot days, to see a single person wearing a jacket and a coat, a mackintosh and a suit. Their shoes were often too flimsy, the heels too high. Soon northern France, panic-stricken under the German planes and bombs, fled towards the south. The exodus speeded up – what else could they do when the enemy was at their gates? Very early on 14 June the first Germans entered a Paris that was half empty and from which all life had fled. From behind their shutters those Parisians who remained looked with amazement at their conquerors. They were so different from what they had been led to believe: young, athletic boys whose uniforms were cut from substantial cloth and some of whom even wore superb leather boots. There was certainly no sign of the ill-clad, badly-dressed horde they had been led to expect. When they risked going out they saw flags with the swastika flying on the principal monuments and did not understand how they got there. The waves of refugees had settled in central and southern France, but were still suffering from the shock of their ordeal. The government had taken refuge in Bordeaux; the town was over-crowded, the atmosphere heavy. Even though people were counting on Maréchal Pétain to steady the ship, they knew that he had decided to ask the Germans for the conditions of an armistice. A very large majority of the French approved of the Maréchal's decision, which they thought would end the suffering of the people on the roads. In a few weeks many would discover the real meaning of the armistice: occupation. Summer had suddenly ended, bringing the good days to a close.

–2–

New Formulas for New Times

The shock of the defeat left the French numbed, incapable of understanding what had befallen them. This reaction was strengthened as yesterday's enemy, anxious to appear in a good light, curbed its appetite for conquest; for a time, the wolf donned lamb's clothing. In Paris where they were expecting the worst, a sort of status quo was established between occupier and occupied. Everyday life resumed. On 18 June the shops raised their iron shutters. The department stores Louvre, Trois Quartiers, Galeries Lafayette and La Grande Maison du Blanc re-opened:

> The window displays are not impeccable, the counters are a bit untidy, there are fewer personnel, but the clientèle pays no heed to this. At the perfume, textile and clothing counters women are buying, fingering the fabrics, chatting. A few weeks ago, house-wives were making sometimes ill-considered purchases of sugar, preserves, pasta. Today Parisians are buying woollens and footwear for the winter.[1]

The cafés on the Champs Elysées set out their terraces as before. The only change was that German officers had replaced the Allied soldiers of the past. A few days later, Maxim's again became the place to be seen. Groups of 'tourists' in uniform and armbands with swastikas, photographic equipment across their shoulders, invaded the Louvre, Notre-Dame, the Eiffel Tower and the Arc de Triomphe. If the majority of the population remained on their guard, a few by-standers applauded the occupation troops as they passed. In Rue Lafayette an old crone with a shawl on her head, arms akimbo, shouted out 'Aren't they beautiful!' when she saw 'them' pass, which earned her a serious reprimand from her comp-anions. Young high-school girls in skirts, blouses and bobby socks, ribbons in their hair, sometimes plucked up courage to smile at the conquerors. 'They are well-behaved' and 'How polite they are' were the comments most commonly heard. Operation seduction was in full swing; in the metro, 'they' gave up their seats to the elderly or to people with children.

Behind this correct behaviour, however, the realities of the occupation had to be faced. Substantially provided with money, which was greatly to their advantage because the exchange rate of the mark was fixed by decree at 20 francs whereas it was worth 12 at the most, the Germans rushed to the shops to buy everything that was in short supply back home. They could be seen standing immobile in front of the fine lingerie and perfumes, symbols of Parisian luxury. From silk stockings by the dozen to shoes to beauty products, they bought everything. Within seconds, luxury products were swept up (Hermès at Rue du Faubourg-Saint-Honoré had a few days of excellent business), while the women's ready-made clothing department was stripped bare. To avoid mistakes, some produced photographs of their wives as a way of specifying the size they required. There was no limit to their needs; their compulsive hunger was so great that the salesgirls derisively nicknamed them the 'Colorado beetles'. At first, some shopowners were naïvely delighted, unanimously exulting, 'they pay cash'. But the moment they understood they had been cheated by the German rate of exchange, the grumbling started. A few shops took advantage of the exchange rate to raise their prices sky high – at Lancel, Avenue de l'Opéra, for example, the price of a suede bag rose from 950 to 1,700 francs in the space of ten days – and were severely penalized by the officials of the Prefecture of Police when inspections were carried out. As for the Parisians, they saw themselves as being supplanted by these insatiable shoppers with whom they could not compete, and looked upon this frenzy of expenditure with sadness.

During the summer the first 'refugees' returned, having lost their linen, clothing and personal possessions during their trials and tribulations. Their only hope was to resume a normal life – like the teacher who returned to her little flat in Montmartre on 15 July after endless wanderings. The first German who crossed her path in Place du Tertre brought tears to her eyes, then she was filled with anger at the sight of the Moulin de la Galette, which was surrounded by the enemy, accompanied by 'French women flashily dressed and outrageously made up'.[2] The day after her arrival she went into her usual shop to look for shoes and something warm to wear. To her surprise, the shelves were almost empty and the only shoes left were old fashioned or their soles too thin. To find a comfortable pair, she writes, she had to scour 'eight shops and almost as many for a cardigan'.[3] As misfortunes never come singly, Paris had assumed an occupation look. On the conqueror's orders, the sandbags had been taken off the monuments, but the Nazi emblem was present everywhere. Traffic signs in German had appeared on every street corner, but there was less traffic on the roads. Hence the strange impression which Jacques-Henri Lartigue recorded:

> Paris is fading away. One can scarcely hear her breathe. She has fainted in her party dress . . . without cars, the avenues, boulevards and roads have become enormous and look like parts of an aerodrome . . . The Germans talk about Paris as if it were a toy they had just been presented with. A large toy full of subtleties which they do not suspect.[4]

However, activity in *haute couture* resumed. The creators had pulled themselves together. This was the conclusion of an article by Violette Leduc, who questioned *couturiers* on the survival of their art for the new woman's magazine, *Pour Elle*, at the end of August 1940.[5] Barbas, the manager at Jean Patou, who had only recently returned, emphasized two points which in his opinion were essential: on one hand, it was necessary 'to leave the past behind, convince oneself that one was not building the new with the debris of the old, and rejuvenate fashion'; on the other hand, Parisian *haute couture* had to recover 'the sense of moderation and simplicity and cut out the foreign influences that had ruined its international reputation for good taste'. If it wanted to survive, it had to change. In Jeanne Lanvin's white boutique the atmosphere was bustling. 'A young girl is choosing cheerful silk scarfs . . . soldiers are buying perfumes . . . a lady is having a suit copied.' The fashion house had not closed its doors since war was declared and as one or two 'good' customers were now frequenting it, it had gone back to work. And Jeanne Lanvin explained: 'It is necessary to adapt to present circumstances by creating simple things, which will be very beautiful. If on resuming we succeed in exporting to Germany and Italy, then the 700 employees of the House will not be unemployed this winter.' Nina Ricci, who re-opened on 1 July, appeared resolutely optimistic about the future of fashion: 'My clients, who had lost everything during the exodus, come to see me and replenish their wardrobes. Others are completing interrupted fittings . . . I must tell you that all this is very encouraging and that my workers have lost none of their agility and ingenuity during their enforced inactivity.'

As for the top rank milliners and hairdressers, it was clear that they would reopen. Madame Suzy swore that she never lacked work thanks to orders from people who had never left Paris. Rose Descat was delighted to find her clients again when she returned from Biarritz. As for René Rambaud, his sales of beauty products increased and he was able to replenish his stocks. In his hairdressing salon, he re-employed two manicurists and two hairdressers.

Haute couture and luxury were not dead. Parisian elegance resumed its traditional features. At the end of October 1940 Lucien Lelong presented his collection, followed soon afterwards by other big names. 'Thus, that autumn, the first autumn of a Paris recovering after its tragic hour, they anticipated women's desire only to dress wisely and with dignity. They have also adapted utilitarian designs to the circumstances of their new life, without ever robbing them of anything that might give a new tone to their elegance, however discreet.'[6]

Nevertheless, it was impossible to forget the context. The armistice, signed on 22 June, set the seal on France's defeat and formed a framework for Franco-German relations. France was cut in two by a demarcation line defining an occupied zone and a free zone where French sovereignty theoretically prevailed. The atmosphere was perceptibly different from one town to the next, depending on circumstances, even if those who found themselves on the good side of the demarcation line were generally filled with a slightly cowardly relief.

Until 7 July, Lyons was occupied by the Germans at the very same time that it was having to deal with an influx of refugees. Like the Parisians, the Lyonnais were dismayed to see the enemy ransacking shops stocking women's and children's clothing and clearing the shelves of jewellery.

In addition, people who had lost everything during the exodus tried to build up a basic wardrobe once more, sometimes buying what they could find at exorbitant prices, with the result that the population as a whole began to experience material difficulties even before the end of the summer. When the armistice came into force, the Germans left the city. Yet even though Lyons had become 'free' again it would soon take a veritable *tour de force* to obtain wool or cotton and, disaster of disasters, in the capital city of silk, prestigious fabrics disappeared from the counter, waiting for better days when they would not be sent to Germany. Silk was highly valued by Field-Marshal Goering for its finish and natural elegance and he had no hesit-ation in buying vast quantities to be sent on to him. In response to a request by Lyons industrialists, and because he had dealings with a number of silk merchants, the *couturier* Marcel Rochas decided to present his collection at Lyons on 9 to 12 December 1940. In fact, what he showed were basically dress 'materials' suggest-ively displayed and not finished designs. A presentation of hats – the shortage of raw materials meant that only two or three copies could be made – accompanied the 'gowns'. 'Silk brocade, shot silk, old ribbons originating in Lyons and made up in Paris'[7] gave each one a touch of personality. Although reserved for a few privil-eged people, the presentation was appreciated because it brought a breath of air from the capital.

The Côte d'Azur, with its rather flashy elegance, hitherto the refuge of wealth, changed its style. A few rich foreigners, who had only very recently enjoyed the coast, had left. Luxury faded away. Bicycles and cabs were seen on the streets instead of the fine automobiles of yesteryear. Well-off families, who had spent time on the Riviera not so long ago, made it their safe haven. They settled there with all their belongings and appeared mindful of their dignity, far removed from the eccentricities in which they had indulged only a little while before. To remain plain, and not to make a show, was the order of the day. Many young women, in keeping with government instructions, gave up sophisticated makeup and dressed more soberly. The fashion, as the president of the Chambre Syndicale de la Couture de Nice emphasized, was for simplicity. A journalist who came to investigate expressed the same opinion: 'Everyone is very respectable in this large village, which runs from Nice to Marseilles . . . people are no longer dressing like savages and they are no longer carefully stripping to get tanned'[8] – and this was not only because Ambre Solaire was unobtainable! Other factors had to be taken into account: an immediate consequence of the defeat was a wave of moralism that washed over the region, some municipal decrees going as far as to forbid the wearing of shorts or bathing costumes outside authorized zones.

However, a few palaces survived, like islets, and the Riviera, because of its specific clientèle kept the flavour of forbidden fruit. Artists lived side by side there with the millionaires of international high society, both torn between 'ostentatious luxury' and 'inimitable discretion'. The Tout-Cinéma had taken refuge there: Danièle Darrieux and Micheline Presle. In Nice, the *thé dansant* at Maxim's was always an attraction, and the women there competed in coquetry and pretty dresses. According to Jacques-Henri Lartigue, 'the Grand Hôtel at Cannes is like a sort of liner standing still in the midst of war.'[9] All the great fortunes, precious stones and showy jewellery had gone there to seek refuge, 'to pass the time while the war lasted', in company with theatre and cinema people and in a pre-war atmosphere punctuated by gala evenings where it was good to show one's face. Edith Piaf's soirée and the gala of the inevitable Maurice Chevalier were a sell-out.

Alongside these privileged people, refugees who came later had trouble finding somewhere to live. Between August 1940 and October 1941 there were several thousands in Nice. They included tailors, embroiderers, furriers, almost all of them Jewish. Threatened by the race laws, the first of which was promulgated in Autumn 1940,[10] they hurriedly left the occupied zone for Nice, Marseilles or Cannes. For them fashion had a very precise meaning: far from being its beneficiaries, they were its servants. Bruno du Roselle, in his *Histoire de la Mode*, rightly stresses that the arrival of these families largely contributed to the development of the clothing industry in these regions. Their decision to settle brought with it the establishment of ateliers. The example of the Corot family was repeated more than once, though without their notoriety. After closing their Paris shop, Raymond Corot and his brother took refuge in Cannes where they opened a clothing business that flourished because they were lucky enough to have a supply of fabrics from their pre-war stocks.[11]

At the top of the rag-trade hierarchy were some of the great Parisian names who had settled in Cannes, where they had branches before the war. Discretion and a casual note marked their collections. In fashion at Hermès were a classic grey flannel costume edged with braid and, in particular, a two-coloured woollen dress (pink bodice, blue skirt) with piped pleats. Jacques Heim, the *couturier* so highly regarded by the young, launched into chic casual clothes. Like his colleagues he had trouble obtaining wool, and as a result he took advantage of the region's craft resources. His costumes were cut from hand-woven tweed. The range of checks was so varied that it became one of the season's most popular fabrics. Noteworthy, too, at Kostio de War were very fine denier lisle stockings in place of the unobtainable silk stockings. Despite some problems of variety the fashion industry was maintaining its momentum here.

The arrival in the provinces of *couture* craftsmen did not go unnoticed. Thus, 'the president of the Chambre de Commerce de Roanne complained to the "sous-préfet" about the influx of Jewish refugees, wholesale cloth merchants, from the eastern territories. He stated that there was no Jewish household in his town in 1939 and that there were seven of them in January 1941.' 'Roanne cannot take all the Israelite cloth merchants whom the Germans do not want in the occupied zone.'[12]

The other centre of attraction was Vichy, where the Maréchal and his government had been established since July. A watering town and the seat of the French state, it was also, at least at first, one of the centres of elegance. It was a rendez-vous for fashionable Paris, for everyone of some social standing: stately dowagers, high officials, members of high society, actresses and writers. All this fashionable society had invaded Vichy, forming a peculiar upper crust. Lucien Rebatet painted a realistic picture of it in the early days of the French state: 'Vichy was humming like Deauville in its happiest days. A sea of smart dresses flowed from the station up to the River Allier, interspersed with cleverly contrived bathing costumes, and jackets from the great tailors: Hollywood, Juan-les-Pins, the Champs-Elysées, all Auteuil, all Passy, all the great Bernstein and Jean Cocteau "first nights", *haute couture*, banking, the Comédie-Française, the cinema.'[13] The casino gave way to the Hôtel du Parc, which became government headquarters (and incidentally a place of pilgrimage for the French!). Almost every evening its great hall was transformed into a gaming room or into a salon, where you pretty much had to be if you were one of the insiders. 'Off-duty officials played poker. Admirals took a turn at the billiard tables.'

These gatherings sparkled with fashionable outfits, furs and sumptuous jewellery. Dress was always formal, the men happy to wear 'civilian suits of military chic'.[14] A few actresses were present at these soirées, including Mary Marquet, the brains behind André Tardieu, obviously very comfortable in this milieu, Elvire Popesco and Françoise Rosay. Corinne Luchaire, who accompanied her father to Vichy at the end of August 1940, remembers a very chic and very gay dinner when she entertained a whole galaxy of show business people at her table, including Jean-Pierre Aumont, Claude Dauphin, Jaboune (alias Jean Nohain) and Mireille.

The top people also made up the audience at concerts, where, in particular, Alfred Cortot and Jacques Thibaud performed,[15] and attended charity galas, organized under the patronage of the wives of the most prominent political personalities. At the beginning of September 1940, for example, the Petits Chanteurs à la Croix de Bois gave a concert. Seen at that function were the wives of Maréchal Pétain and Admiral Darlan, and Mesdames Alibert and Baudoin, all dressed in dark-coloured, strictly tailored costumes, with only the hat lending the ensemble a bit of colour. The first theatrical gathering, devoted to poetry and organized by Jean Nohain and Dario Moréno, was a sell-out, attracting a varied but uniformly elegant public. In 1942 the majority of entertainments were always regularly attended. 'Red Cross nurses sold the programmes and, though correct dress is essential, this does not mean that one must wear a tuxedo or an evening dress.'[16] Given the problems with supplies, the restaurants had become the fashionable places to be – the 'Chantecler', for example, where diners not only ate well but were certain to meet fashionable Vichy and see a striking concentration of jewellery and mink coats. It was also chic to patronize a vegetarian restaurant near the Hôtel du Parc or to meet on the golf course. From 1941 to 1943 race courses attracted a much-photographed fashionable public.

The rest of the time one had to reckon with people taking the cure who, despite the defeat, had not deserted the town, and who still swallowed their fifty grams of mineral water, be it Chômel or Grande Grille. They included 'wealthy stockbrokers with their ribbons and their paunches', and above all elderly ladies with frizzy hair who carefully hid their faces under a veil and 'fluttered about in the supreme refinement of their white costumes and sunshades'. When the time came for the daily promenade, this loyal clientèle invaded the cool alleyways and pastry shops to peck at what their stomachs and, soon, their supply of ration tickets permitted. But as soon as the Maréchal appeared, they abandoned these occupations to form a guard of honour and shout 'Vive le Maréchal!'

Despite the creation of the new French state,[17] the lives of these people had not really changed. These women still had the means to visit the beauty parlours, which were particularly numerous in Vichy, to ferret out the best milliners able to fashion a more Parisian hat than Paris ever saw, and to frequent the fashionable shoemakers. As the demarcation line between the occupied and the unoccupied zones prevented some elegant people from buying their clothes in Paris, local *couturières* were overloaded with work, busy satisfying the demands of their clientèle. This was all the more praiseworthy in that needles and thread were hard to come by because the defeat brought material consequences there as elsewhere. The town had its share of refugees, including some who, in order to make a living, reverted to the small crafts of yesteryear, such as hairdressing in their homes, embroidering, repairing sewing machines, all of which either directly or indirectly contributed to women's apparel. On 25 September 1942, Danièle Darrieux married Porfirio Rubirosa, *chargé d'affaires* of the Dominican Republic in France. The bride was 'blonde under a heart-shaped tartan hat', which the Vichy craftsmen did not fail to copy.[18] This watering place, promoted to the rank of capital, housed a large ministerial staff. Prices had increased so much, raising ordinary goods to the rank of luxury items, that typists and secretaries sometimes found it hard to make ends meet. Despite this, they held their own, smartly and prettily made-up, living up to what was expected of them. To meet the ever-growing demand for lipstick, the Société d'Exploitation Thermale considered manufacturing an authentic French brand in the region, 'Le rouge baiser', hitherto produced in the Paris suburbs. On Sundays these young girls in their flimsy dresses met on the banks of the Allier to go boating. However, in contrast to pre-war practice, few dared to appear in shorts, which had become the object of general disapproval. A page had certainly been turned. Was the age of liberty at an end?

Before summer 1940 was over the majority of the French had discovered to their surprise, and sometimes indignation, the hardships of defeat, and had grudgingly buckled down to a new way of life. No region or area was protected from this tidal wave. Petrol, which the Germans desperately needed to feed their war machine, was the first product to be rationed. Suddenly, the population had to manage with the means at its disposal and adapt to the situation. Without cars, bicycles became the most widespread means of transport throughout France. Through necessity they took pride of place. Every day, people brought out machines that had long lain disused, or they paid exorbitant prices in the shops to grab the latest models (from 8 million machines in 1940, the figure rose to 10 million in 1942 and 11 million in 1944). From one day to the next in Paris, Vichy, Lyons and Marseilles, every age-group, every social class got on their bikes.

Léon-Paul Fargue, an old Parisian, was surprised to see that the bicycle was the indispensable companion of 'the girl student, the young sports-loving girl or the future star, legs bare, hair flying in the wind', but also 'of serious, grey-bearded gentlemen with pince-nez.' [19] According to Edmond Dubois, in Paris 'the whole town is on wheels and pedalling . . . Housewives do the rounds of their suppliers, baskets and saddlebags on their luggage-carriers . . . Mothers transport their progeny on special seats; a crowd, a large crowd of women follow the throng as best they can. Lastly, there are elegant ladies who ride their bicycles because it is good for them.'[20] In Nice, Mistinguett did not move without her brand-new machine, drawing admirers in her wake. In short, necessity imposed a fashion: the fashion for the bicycle. For four years, this was a thorny problem for women: what was the most suitable outfit to wear? In July and August 1940, a number of cyclists adopted the little spotted or striped print dress normally reserved for seaside or country holidays, which had become a classic in this post-exodus period, even for town wear. If young girls deliberately left their hats in the wardrobe, some women who were careful about their appearance remained loyal to this accessory. They considered it indispensable, notwithstanding the problems posed by gusts of wind, which gave them the choice of the lesser evil when their skirts blew up or their hats blew off . . . Sometimes, the outfits that these amateur sportswomen wore were a little odd. 'The women who pass silently by on their bikes with their flowery hats look as if they are on the way to the Carnival',[21] remarked Jacques-Henri Lartigue.

With the autumn and the onset of the bad weather, the cyclists obviously had to rethink their outfits. Although some women, particularly in the rural areas, fell back on practical garments of the slacks and anorak type, divided skirts, hitherto reserved for sport, won the day. Made from tweed or thick woollen cloth, they 'were worn next to the knickers, which matched the colour of the dress above'. If one can believe a writer who was sympathetic to the Maréchal and the occupation, Alfred Fabre-Luce did not find this fashion so unpleasant. According to him, the elegance of Paris was very real, even in these difficult times when there were numerous cyclists.

When they pedal, our elegant ladies do not have their grandmothers' terrifying gravity. They laugh when they meet one another. It is like a farce to them, a Carnival convention . . . Boycotted by America, they even issue a challenge: they would wager that their divided skirts and hoods, born of the scarcity of transport in Paris, would soon be chosen abroad for their aesthetic appearance.[22]

Woollen, or better still, fur hoods covered the ears of the chilly, who also donned warm mittens as well as fur boots to protect them from cold. A sling bag and a saddlebag on the luggage rack were essential pieces of equipment. Winter 1940–1 was so harsh that despite these precautions cyclists had freezing hands. To remedy this they were strongly recommended to have, fixed on their handlebars, 'wind-breaks for hands', which were very common in Holland and Belgium. 'These consist of cups, preferably made of leather, that are fixed in front of each fist.' As recent restrictions on leather severely limited its use, people were advised to replace it with felt from an old hat or by a piece of oil-cloth! An unexpected result of the use of bicycles at every hour of the day and in all circumstances was that 'smart short dresses which a mackintosh can cover are now acceptable evening wear'.

In 1941, during the Russo-German war, the occupation became more of a burden and repression intensified and spread over the whole country. However, some elegant ladies were solely concerned with finding the best possible dress or skirt to suit the bicycle they had adopted. Instigated by the journal *Paris-Midi* and assisted by the *grands couturiers*, Wednesday 23 July, chosen as the day of the bike, a contest for the most beautiful cycling outfits was organized. Against the verdant backcloth of the Armenonville pavillion and before an admiring crowd, the models perched on their two flower-decorated wheels and presented designs which demonstrated that it was possible to remain attractive while making sacrifices to the demands of the time. Several awards were bestowed. The first prize, that of 'Practical Elegance', was awarded to Bruyère for a two-piece outfit worn by the model Moussia. It was composed of a divided skirt in black and white crepe-de-chine with a matching shirt, worn with a finely made black felt hat and a hooped-shaped bag in black velvet. Jeanne Lanvin took the prize for 'Casual Elegance' with a very chic black linen costume matched with a shirt, tie and turban in kingfisher blue. Lastly, the prize for 'Parisian Elegance' went to Lucien Lelong for a red divided skirt worn with a blue and white pleated tartan skirt and a white blouse, although the use of the three colours seemed to leave the audience cold on this occasion. Its organizers wanted the day of bicycle elegance to replace the traditional day of automobile elegance, which had had a resounding success in pre-war days. The bicycle had won its royal warrant!

Later, some young girls and sometimes women used bicycles for other purposes. As liaison agents with the Resistance, they were charged with carrying urgent letters, their over-riding concern being to avoid being noticed. Consequently, when these messengers, who were risking their lives, dressed for cycling, their main aim was not to be conspicuous but to melt into the crowd.

Nothing stayed the advance of the *couturiers*. From season to season they vied with each other in ingenious ways to make the divided skirt invisible. 'M. de Rauch conceals the crutch by means of tight pleats; Jeanne Regny hides the culottes under a skirt buttoned from top to bottom; whereas Worth contrives an invisible zip down the centre of the front.'[23] The aim of all these solutions was to allow the woman to leave her two wheels at the door of the smartest establishments and go in without making herself unacceptably conspicuous.

Thus, up to the end of hostilities, the bicycle was a force to be reckoned with. Alongside the designs that *couture* created especially for the two wheeler, it also had a fashion of its own: a light dress or shorts in the summer, a sheepskin jacket and divided skirt[24] or slacks in winter, an oilskin mackintosh for rainy days, cap, gloves and gaiters. In the Riviera, some prefects, including one in the Alpes Maritimes, who were particularly fussy and jealous of their prerogatives, at first forbade women to wear male clothing. In spring 1941 they agreed to lift the prohibition, provided that 'trousers be accompanied by a bicycle', proof if ever there was that function creates dress. However, in its ten commandments for the Parisian lady the magazine *Marie-Claire* included 'Only on a bicycle shalt thou wear culottes.'[25]

For women who did not want to have anything to do with bicycles because they considered them incompatible with their rank and their wish to make a show, there were two other solutions: taking a horse-drawn fiacre as in the past; or hiring a 'velotaxi'. This latter form of transport was very popular, at least in summer. This new form of taxi was made up of a bicycle harnessed to a wicker cabin or basket suspended on two rubberized wheels. Athletic men in bathing costumes propelled the vehicles at various speeds. Inside the taxis was a wooden bench covered with cushions. The whole velotaxi was painted in bright colours and had a name fixed to the rear or perhaps a slogan: 'Cleave the breeze' was much used. Artists who were too well dressed to risk damaging their gowns on a bicycle, or unused to tiring themselves out when they travelled, as well as women in the public eye, greatly appreciated this rapid and efficient system of locomotion. It had an additional bonus – the height of refinement: it allowed them to match their outfit to the velotaxi they hired. When they ordered it, they would say, 'Send me the blue cabin – the one that goes so well with my dress.' In the evening, in front of the night clubs or certain restaurants, the velotaxis wisely waited for their passengers and when the well-dressed figures followed one another out of the door it was almost like attending a fashion parade.

At Longchamp or Auteuil, when the horse racing season came round, 'bicycles, velotaxis, wagons drawn by heavy draught horses . . . all formed a sort of "strange"

– 30 –

Noah's ark'.[26] Alice Cocéa chose to go to the races at Tilbury on a horse belonging to her friend Nicole Gallimard. Tandems harnessed to multicoloured carriages transported gentlemen in stiff collars or elegant ladies with parasols. Voices were sometimes raised and disputes broke out when everyone wanted to use the most chic vehicle, which consisted of 'a long negro shining like ebony and a young very white, very blond girl, the pair dressed "like sisters" in the same 1900 football-style sweaters . . .'[27]

There was a means of transport available to the well-dressed Parisian that had long been shunned by high society: the metro. 'That brave, faithful metro which is found to be much quicker and more practical than was ever thought possible and which becomes the focus of many an encounter'.[28] Its usual clientèle was joined by people who had previously only travelled in their own cars or by taxi. 'After giving a final touch to their makeup, without which a Parisian women would no longer be a Parisian woman',[29] lower middle-class women, secretaries and dress-makers' assistants rubbed shoulders with society ladies, en route recognizing an outfit or a hat that bore the signature of the best makers. 'Entering the metro, clad in woollen stockings, they continue to wear the furs that suit their complexion, and the hat that makes them look a little immoral, and their bearing is still that of a creator of fashion.'[30] The metro was now part of the war-time background of Paris, to such an extent that one *couturière*, Madeleine de Rauch, built her collection around a journey on the underground. She christened her designs with the names of stations: 'Here is 'Mabillon' in a pink gown; 'Auteuil' in a severe costume with a supple line; 'Solferino' in a tailored red coat ; 'Austerlitz' shows a yellow jacket; 'Madeleine' in a black costume presents a beautiful white blouse, with sleeves formed of pleated frills'.[31]

Catching the last metro became an obsession for people who went out in the evening to dine in town or go to the theatre; because of the curfew imposed by the occupier everyone had to keep half an eye on their watch. Worse still, some sources also blamed the curfew for the disappearance of the long dresses in which it was so difficult to run. Now, to make the walk or rather the procession to the station easier, fashion suggested dresses that did not touch the ground, because it was important to catch the 23.00 train; missing it meant spending the night in the police station. All the same, this last metro resembled nothing so much as a fashionable salon or the wings of a theatre, so striking was the number of well-cut costumes and gowns from the *grands couturiers*. In fact it was common to meet the stars of current shows there, also reduced to using this means of transport. Ginette Leclerc hid behind dark glasses to remain incognito. In winter 1940–1, Edwige Feuillère,[32] who was acting in *La Dame aux Camélias*, was one of the metro's most faithful passengers. The same was true of Edith Piaf – recognizable by her large eyes – who almost always wore thick white woollen socks, a short skirt and flat shoes. At the Pigalle station the young ladies from the music-hall got on, often out of breath from running. They obviously had not had time to remove their makeup: their hair was too yellow, their cheeks too red, their eyes too blue. There they were, exactly as one would expect them to be – laughing, chattering, mocking. All were warmly dressed, muffled up in woollies.

Bicycles and the metro were not alone in dictating clothing laws. The cold weather also caused the adoption of new practices that women tried to turn to the best account. Habits had to conform to winter hardships. In October 1940, the combination of a bad winter and inadequate heating meant that dresses were not only required to be smart and pretty but also, and above all, warm. For the common run of humanity a bulkier figure was no longer a crime but a necessity in the battle against the cold. In the absence of warmth from the radiators the writer Colette advised people to line their underwear with sheets of newspaper, which was marvellous insulating material if not exactly elegant. 'Placing two light materials on top of each other, separated by a layer of feathers, kapok or even paper vermicelli',[33] was better protection against bad weather than heavy clothing; consequently this method was commonly applied in the manufacture of plastrons that were slipped on under a coat or dressing gown. Outfits appeared that owed more to miracle formulas than to creative imagination, and these were the ones that triumphed on the street.

Everyday winter fashion was for extra heavy clothing and contrasts; when *Marie-Claire* suggested that its readers wore the 'thousand-pieces', a series of different-coloured garments worn on top of each other, it was doing no more than popularizing an already widespread idea to bring it into line with the spirit of the times. Strange sights met the eyes of passers-by, who ended up not being surprised by anything. January and February 1941 were marked by heavy snowfalls: straight away skiers proliferated, and heavy shoes, woollen stockings and trousers were very popular. Except when she was going to the high school where she taught, Simone de Beauvoir[34] swapped her skirt for slacks, which kept her warmer. On 5 January 1941 a schoolgirl noted in her war diary: 'Today I tried to put on papa's big hob-nailed boots and I went for a walk . . . my shoes feel heavier than roller-skates. I have blisters. All the women are wearing shoes like that in Paris.'[35] 'On the university benches under the gaze of the professors who are the only ones to wear a gown, sit the students huddled into ski jackets and trousers. But after the lecture they have no hesitation in donning a town coat with an inordinately high collar which meets a tiny hat at eye-level.'[36]

Keeping one's feet warm soon became an obsession, everyone resorting to their own remedy. Certain women suggested inserting a cork sole into the existing sole, which, it seemed, made it possible to splash through snow and mud with impunity. Others advised putting mustard in stockings or socks, an infallible recipe employed by the Russians. The fact was that the formidable ordeal of queuing, which forced the population to go out in the morning in the dark and in temperatures of $-10^{\circ}C$, was transformed into a competition in how best to avoid the traps of winter. Chilblains and Siberian cold overcame the last remnants of reserve and everyone strove to improve their equipment without worrying what the neighbours thought. Typical of this attitude was a Parisian lady who explained as she surveyed her attire:

> Double, triple woollies, an appropriate shawl hidden under my caped 'gunner's' coat, my head muffled in a woollen hood, heavy knitted stockings, so thick that they stand up on their own like the waders of a sewer worker, 'elegant' fur-lined shoes . . . Most beautiful is my peplum: a large grey shawl with pink stripes, discovered in London a good twenty years ago, which I drape round me; this does not prevent me hiding my hands in a bald muff. Oh, I am such a pretty sight, I positively look as if I were in fancy-dress but people are so preoccupied that they do not notice me.[37]

Thus, as the months went by, the attempt to make the contents of one's wardrobe yield the maximum warmth was a major occupation that left no one untouched. The young Christian Dior, at the time starting out as a dress designer in the Riviera, contributed to the women's page of *Le Figaro*. He suggested a series of ideas that were easy to put into practice and illustrated them with sketches.[38] One of these, for example, described how to make a coat cosier: adding a detachable cape and a camelhair plastron doubled its efficacity. There were other, equally radical, methods: cut a band of tartan or coloured woollen cloth 40 cm wide, put it on your head, then catch it at the neck with a metal loop and lastly secure the two ends of the scarf with a belt. Neither needle nor thread was necessary for the latter design: all you had to do was drape two straight pieces of jersey or other warm fabric 50 cm wide from front to back into a belt. Schiaparelli recalls the hard times in her own way: 'Because of the lack of buttons and safety pins, there were dog chains to close suits and to hold skirts. Maurice Chevalier's latest song was printed on one scarf, the restrictions that Parisians endured on another. Thus: Monday – no meat. Tuesday – no alcohol. Wednesday – no butter. Thursday – no fish. Friday – no meat. Saturday – no alcohol . . . but Sunday – toujours l'amour.'[39]

Although the countryside faced the same problems, the solutions were often different. There, people could obtain local wool at a certain price or by spinning and carding it themselves. It was then possible to knit stockings, socks or even, for the more daring, pullovers, although it is true that they were all in rather rough material.

In Paris, a certain Raymond Duncan, 'an advocate of anti-mechanism', taught women how to spin and weave their own clothes. 'In eight days he has taught more than 100 women how they can weave wool taken from their mattress on a simple loom to make themselves a peplum (which they will be able to use as a spring coat).' Faced with the problems of costume changes posed by her profession, even the actress Hélène Perdrière, Sacha Guitry's partner at the time, learned to weave her own outfits.[40]

Many town dwellers did not hesitate to play at being farmers' wives and bought wooden clogs. Stuffed with straw they were very warm. Above all, tanned rabbit skins gave rise to a profitable trade. They were very popular for making coat linings, foot warmers, muffs, mittens and for trimming hoods and even ankle boots.

In autumn 1940, there was extreme excitement in the world of Parisian *haute couture* because, despite the problems of the day, the *couturiers* had succeeded in setting up a winter collection, both a symbol of hope for better times and, more prosaically, a concrete means of fighting the unemployment that threatened them. Designers and creators were largely governed by economic conditions in practising their art. They had been forced to take into account the shortage of raw materials, but also new living conditions that were emerging: the absence of means of transport, and the inadequate heating that did not always spare the rich, their principal clientèle! It was even said that 'Countess Greffulhe has had a heated cabin installed in her salon; she only quits it clad in a fur coat to warm herself up under its wainscotting as in the open-air'.[41]

How then could they reconcile elegance, cold and shortages, while at the same time offering a 'real' collection, one capable of being an effective weapon against the rigours of the temperatures both inside and outside the house? What to suggest to women who did not always have the opportunity to change their dresses before going out to dine at a night club? These were some of the problems confronting the masters of *couture* and that they aimed to solve, hoping also that they would be well received. Bruyère was not afraid to spell out the rules of the game loud and clear when she presented her creations: 'The collection has been entirely conceived with regard to the Parisian woman's new way of life: her comfort, walking, the terrible cold, all are provided for, but elegance is maintained.'[42]

Renewing links with the past, coquettes and society ladies flocked to the traditional fashion shows that 'bore the hallmark of a sober and purified chic', and were the last word in simplicity. In the salons, where the graceful movements had begun in front of a loyal clientèle interspersed with a few German uniforms, 'the chatter was less exuberant, there was a certain gravity but no sadness'.[43] At Robert Piguet's, the privileged who had obtained authorization to attend the parade of the collections always pretended to be knitting for the most unfortunate, a good way of being useful and acquiring a good conscience. However, the evocative names of the designs were linked to the reality of the present: 'Bicycle', 'Coal', 'Black coffee'. Many of the little gold chairs were no longer occupied by transatlantic buyers as in the past. On the other hand, the number of fashion writers who had come to glean information or steal ideas had risen. They included a young beginner, Violette Leduc, who stood out from the crowd because of her modest dress, shabby raincoat, worn shoes and by the letter of recommendation she handed with a determined air to the official in charge of seating her. Armed with a pencil, she took endless notes during the fashion parade presented by Lucien Lelong. Her article waxed so enthusiastic that, to thank the young girl, he offered her a costume and hat bearing his label.

The critics greeted this first collection of the occupation as was fitting. 'In the heart of a Paris which no longer looks the same but which still preserves a calm smile, the seasonal fashions are born. We were feverishly awaiting the fashions for 1940–1. It does not surprise us, since it expresses that faith in the future which gives everyone courage.'[44] This was the opinion of a writer in *La Femme Chic*; it was shared by her colleagues, who also stressed the tact that the new collections showed: 'Everyone trying hard to be simple, but what elegance! What concern for the comfort and present possibilities of women!'[45] They admired, congratulated and applauded the suggested innovations. One such innovation was greeted by women with slight surprise, even incredulity, but they quickly became accustomed to it and soon would not be able to do without it: fashions for indoor clothes.

No collection left out this new category. In the parades, 'indoor pyjamas' and 'housecoats' made a breakthrough, replacing lace and muslin negligées and other flimsy robes. There were comfortable outfits with evocative names. Nina Ricci offered 'Veillée' ('Vigil'), black jersey trousers worn with a warm jacket in old rose velvet, its pockets enhanced by embroidery; or two housecoats 'Tiédeur' ('Warmth') and 'Douillette' ('Quilted housecoat'), whose elegance and refinement lay in the fabric employed and the high quality of the workmanship. For dinner with friends or a tête-à-tête there was 'Dîner improvisé' ('Improvised dinner'), an ensemble composed of trousers worn with a large quilted housecoat. 'Tibétaine' ('Tibetan woman'), from J. Lanvin, a black cape worn around the shoulders with a soft astrakhan collar draped around the neck, could give additional warmth when worn with the other ensembles.

A stream of regular customers passed through the doors of Madame Leroy's – at the head of Fourrures Max – every day. Here the cold was overcome by elegant garments and the heating problem resolved in ingenious ways. The customers had the choice of a range of warm outfits, each bearing the name of a method of heating and each intended to replace the failing stoves. There was 'Salamandre' ('Salamander' stove, a slow-burning stove), a long indoor garment lined with squirrel or mink, 'Mirus' or 'Chauffage central' ('Mirus' or 'Central heating'), short fitted jackets in delicate green, convolvulus mauve, and praline pink, lined with red guanaco 'which enables even the most demanding woman to keep warm and good humoured'. Paquin was thinking of the comfort of the long winter evenings when he conceived 'On lit mieux quand on a chaud' ('One reads better when one is warm'), a thick red woollen cardigan, easy to slip under a skirt and enhanced with amusing slashes in trompe l'oeil.

Every winter, freezing apartments and the problems of daily life returned like a leitmotif running through many presentations. In winter 1941, Bruyère enjoyed an undisputed success when she showed red dresses in soft jersey, angora or woollen cloth, which she baptized 'Robes thermiques' ('Thermal dresses') because they were warm both to the eye and to the touch. In December 1942, Jeanne Lanvin based her whole collection on a day in the life of a Parisian lady, from 'Je fais la queue' ('I join the queue'), a comfortable coat, up to 'Je sors ce soir' ('I am going out this evening'), a short formal dress. There were some indoor outfits in between: 'Je me réchauffe' ('I warm up'), 'Je remplace le chauffage central' ('I replace the central heating') . . . Outside it was cold; snow, rain and ice increasingly poisoned everyone's life. The *couturiers* therefore used furs and animal hides, which remained the best defence against the cold. People with means could plump for astrakhan, beaver and broadtail, or even chinchilla and sable, which were like collectors' items – they were so expensive and incredibly rare. 'The same is true of skunk, which was once used to dress coachmen from good establishments and which now fetches crazy prices.' Maggy Rouff offered two designs: one was a long, classically cut beaver coat called 'Marchons' ('Let's walk'); the other 'Bourrasques' ('Squalls'), was in the same fur but fuller, its softness and the freedom of move-ment it gave making it suitable for sporty women.

Alongside these heavyweight creations, the *couturiers* also suggested 'practical and attractive fantasies in sealskin, guanaco and also cat. Thanks to the regular pattern of their markings the skins of these animals fit together well and produce pleasing effects. Black cats, ginger cats and ash gray cats are mainly used.'[46] High quality furriers also tackled rabbit, which they had hitherto scorned. 'Shaved, plucked, polished, rabbit becomes a fur of utmost chic "at a very modest price"; moleskin-style, civet-style, otter-style, castor-style – bunny rabbit is unrecog-nizable.'[47] Necessity rules and everyone goes mad over it. Likewise, the goat, mole and sheepskin that Germaine Lecomte worked with produced relatively accessible furs, used to make not only coats but also trimmings.

Times were hard for everyone. 'The big stores closed down one department after another. The luxury trade, magnified by an impressive presentation [shows] its last merchandise. Hermès, deprived of leather, is lending its shop window to the antique dealer, Jansen. There are still a few decorative displays to be seen but then a small card makes it clear that nothing is for sale.'[48] Each *couturier* strove to attract as many people as possible by showing how adaptable or imaginative they were. Maggy Rouff allowed clients to bring her their furs or fabrics to be made up into models from her collection. Marcel Rochas did the same. As for Nina Ricci, she proved both practical and inventive: to help people who had to walk in the icy blast of the cold north wind she had the idea of creating leggings which could be adapted to any outfit. This, madam, did the trick; now you can laugh at your thermometer and no longer suffer. All you had to do was cover your legs in leggings – 'amazing in their cut and their comfort', according to the publicity material. Made in fine woollen jersey, one could choose from beige, grey or brown to match the colour of one's dress and coat. Customers who had come to the show, some on foot, some by bicycle, some on the metro, chilled to the bone, their legs spattered with mud, left wearing a pair of leggings, their equanimity restored, disarmed by such an appropriate means of relieving their discomfort. The wish to help elegant ladies by taking their requirements into account, caused Lucile Manguin to produce

a dress which is as unexpected as it is ingenious: it has a short skirt which can be lengthened instantly by using press-studs. When Madame goes out at dawn to do her shopping, Madame can therefore carry in her handbag the woollen or moire "accessory" that will at an opportune moment transform her afternoon outfit into an evening gown.[49]

Its creator hoped that this cunning device would answer her regular customers' expectations.

'Le cyclo-pédestre', de Bruyère design, from *Les Nouveaux Temps*, 5 April 1941.

Dictated by circumstances, a new way of life appeared that tended to modify customary ways of dressing and impose a style suited to the times. Although *haute couture* survived with its own rhythm of collections, it could not cut itself off completely from its environment and adapt in its own way. The cold and the lack of transport had to be taken into account. The thermal gown and the leggings were direct attempts to deal with the frost while at the same time maintaining elegance. Scarcely had the bicycle or the metro acquired a following in privileged circles than one or other of the *couturiers* took advantage of the situation. There was the short dress that could be lengthened as circumstances demanded, or the metro gloves containing a small pocket on top to hold the ticket.

Fear, hunger, cold and lack of transport were the common evils, whereas the crowded metro and in particular the bicycle provided additional constraints. Practical outfits appeared: divided skirts, sheepskin jackets and hoods in the winter, bare heads and short dresses in summer, which ended up as the dominant fashion, because in life it is numbers that count. The traditional image of woman subjected to the whims of fashion and to strict rules was shaken. A new style was about to be born.

–3–

Hard Times

In the space of a single season daily life took a serious turn for the worse for the majority of the French. Bread, sugar, milk, meat and many other products which were already rationed became scarcer, and consumers were divided into categories and assigned coupons giving them the right to a specific quantity of food products determined by their age and, theoretically, their needs.[1] Day after day, before their outraged eyes, the scale of the restrictions and shortages became clear, affecting an area to which they remained traditionally attached and which, only shortly before, was renowned for its choice and quality: clothing.

Finding new footwear or a warm garment soon became something of an achievement, unless one was able to resort to the parallel market, better known as the black market. The crisis affected everything connected with clothing fashions. For the general population, this took concrete form through a series of measures, the most spectacular being the introduction of 'footwear coupons' (January 1941) and the issue of a clothing card on 1 July 1941. This latter innovation was resented all the more because many Frenchmen had had a good laugh when it was adopted by the Germans in 1939, never for a single moment imagining that their own country would one day be reduced to the same position. 'How and why have we fallen so low?' groaned some individuals, lamenting their fate.

There were various reasons for this clothing shortage, closely linked to the defeat. The demarcation line, a veritable frontier cutting through the country, and the division of France into several zones, resulted in real difficulties in moving supplies between regions. Paris no longer received cloth originating from the north, from the Pas-de-Calais, and the Vosges, on which it largely depended. The shoe factories situated in the occupied zone could not meet the needs of the free zone, and so on.[2] Added to this was the manpower shortage, because one-and-a-half million prisoners of war were held in Germany and they included tens of thousands employed in the textile and clothing industry who could not be replaced.

Nevertheless, one of the basic causes, and the one that weighed most heavily in the eyes of the population, was German requisitions. 'They are taking everything away from us,' was a complaint that recurred like a *leitmotif* in the litany of grievances that everyone recited daily, grumbling about the absence of footwear or woollies from the shops, whereas the conquerors had a right to everything. Without

– 39 –

knowing the exact amount of the requisitions, many people soon understood that France, bound hand and foot, had surrendered to the enemy. In addition, there was the black market, the establishment of parallel networks, which diverted some of the raw materials away from their intended destination. Some industrialists, despite the regulations, dealt directly with the occupiers.

Under the conditions of the armistice, the Germans had the right to demand a certain quantity of raw materials, preferably the scarcest and most expensive available. 'Plans' were brought in for wool and leather, providing for strict delivery dates (the Kehrl plan for textiles, the Grunberg plan for leather).[3] The consequences of this were soon felt. Severe retrenchment ensued, while a cumbersome and complicated administrative and legislative apparatus was established to handle the clothing shortage.

On 1 September 1940, a decree signed by Maréchal Pétain was published in the *Journal Officiel*. It controlled and limited the quantities of textiles manufactured to 30 per cent of sales in 1938. These had to be fairly 'distributed' between wholesalers, department stores and retailers. It was the first step in the intrusive legislation that lasted throughout the occupation.

By virtue of the law of August 1940,[4] which reorganized French production and placed each branch of industry under the direction of a 'Comité d'Organisation', the 'Comité Général d'Organisation de l'Industrie Textile' made its appearance in October 1940. At its head, Robert Carmichaël 'represents the industry in its relations with French and foreign, public and private agencies'. It was up to him to take every measure he considered useful 'in technical, economic or social matters'. He was helped in this task by the directors responsible for each of the ten branches comprising the main textile body (cotton, wool, silk fabrics, artificial fibres, linen and flax, jute, rags, dyeing, hosiery, clothing).[5]

Within the Comité général d'organisation de l'industrie textile, the clothing branch, because of its importance, became a separate agency in its own right with the creation of a Comité d'Organisation du Vêtement, itself divided into seven distinct groups:

Group 1: *Couture*, decorations, fashion, made to measure clothing, lace, tulle and embroidery. Director: L. Lelong.

Group 2: Men's clothing. Director: H. Darnat.

Group 3: Women's clothing. Director: J. Guenin.

Group 4: Manufacture of men's shirts, underwear and ties, lingerie. Director: J. Berthelot.

Group 5: Furs, skins. Director: R. Binet.

Group 6: Related industries (hats, cravats, scarves). Director: J. Deligny.

Group 7: Cloth trade. Director: D. Moreau.

A textile section of the Office central de Répartition des Produits Industriels (Central Office for the Distribution of Industrial Products)[6] had also existed since 24 September 1940, headed by the same Robert Carmichaël who distributed all the materials. The least one can say is that textile fibres and the clothing industries, fashion and couture monopolized the attention of a considerable number of people, and the same names appear again and again in lists of those in positions of high responsibility. Frequently, the director of a Comité d'Organisation was also head of the section for the distribution of products, thus combining considerable power. A Lyons industrialist, Jean Barioz, at the head of a Comité d'Organisation for silk, was a good example of this.

A Comité Général d'Organisation de l'Industrie du Cuir (leather) was created according to the same pattern at the end of October and entrusted to Roger Ribes. A separate committee for footwear was formed within this body, grouping together all the industries and craftsmen engaged in the manufacture of these goods. The fame of André shoes, 'The shoemaker who knows how to make shoes', was no longer a factor among footwear manufacturers. Before the outbreak of war it was one of the largest French firms. Its factories produced some four million pairs a year and employed more than five thousand people. But the owners of the group, the cousins Roger and George Levy, were Jewish and therefore victims of aryanization. Hereafter, clothing and footwear manufacturers were subjected to a regime of supervision and red tape. It should be mentioned that 'more than 80 per cent of businesses declared "Jewish" and affected by the process of aryanization proved to be, for the main part, constituted of small, even very small, units, primarily in Paris and two-thirds engaged in textiles and leather'.[7]

In the summer, leather was strictly regulated, for it remained the raw material for the manufacture of footwear and accessories. In July 1940, as a first step towards governmental control, administrative memoranda reminded craftsmen, shoemakers, leather workers, and so forth, that they had to declare the state of their stocks. Despite censorship, a newspaper report on a footwear factory in Romans in September 1940 let it be understood that the situation was difficult. 'Because of the lack of available materials, tanning products and above all thread, they are reduced to using silk thread in place of linen and cotton thread!'[8] Nevertheless, propaganda asserted that French children would be supplied with 'clogs' (a sort of ankle boot mounted on a wooden sole) and male customers would be offered national footwear (in box-calf or calfskin). Three models – laced boots, the Derby and the Oxford – would be launched on the market at between 120 and 150 francs a pair! These promises were a long way from being fulfilled. People had to rely on what they already owned and depend on a craftsman to do his best to preserve one's possessions.

A survey of 7,000 of these cobblers in the Paris areas carried out in November 1940, revealed the difficulties they were encountering in properly resoling the shoes brought to them, at precisely the time when the number of repairs required was growing ceaselessly because of the new living conditions. An old craftsman explained that under the prevailing terms of distribution, he received five kilos of leather[9] for the month of December, which, he said, would barely enable him to work for a week; the rest of the time he would be out of work unless he found alternative solutions.

These began to appear in January 1941. In addition to rubber, old tyres and plaited straw were used for resoling. Many women, forced by the demands of style to wear high heels, adopted an ingenious method of preserving their footwear: steel pads. 'Since the restrictions on footwear, I, like all my friends, have had little steel pads screwed under the tips of my soles and under my heels in order to spare the rare leather', one of them explained. The result proved visually satisfactory, but the noise shocked her. 'This "click-clack" echoes so loudly that you can hear it everywhere, it punctuates girls entering and leaving their offices!'[10] In Passy, a very elegant Parisian lady attracted a lot of attention: her feet were clad in golf sports shoes, the colour of box calf, raised on a thick cork sole concealed under a double ridge.[11] Soon palliatives were no longer enough; the day was not far off when wooden soles, used experimentally in 1940, would become the last resort for almost everyone, including the most chic society ladies.

The figures speak for themselves. Before 1939, according to the trade journals, '60 million pairs of shoes were manufactured. Of this quantity, the fair sex alone was allocated nearly 40 million pairs of fancy shoes, sports shoes, etc.'[12] Now, barely 8 to 10 million pairs were produced with leather soles. But, under the agreement between Jean Bichelonne[13] and Dr Grunberg signed on 4 November 1940, France had to deliver 6 million pairs of shoes to the Reich in 1941, a very high figure in view of the numbers available.[14] This was the problem faced by those in positions of responsibility. 'Another agreement, that of 25 May 1941, relating to the plan for the production and delivery of leather is revised downwards, it stipulates the delivery of 1,100,000 pairs of shoes to Germany, comprising 575,000 pairs of men's town shoes and 525,000 pairs of town shoes, with delivery spread out from July to November 1941.'[15] In response to German demand, and faced with the increasing scarcity of leather, the state intervened in authoritarian fashion. Supplying the population with shoes became the object of a law establishing a system of vouchers issued by the local authority, which, as from January 1941,[16] represented the right to an allocation of one pair of shoes per person for a given period. Jean Luchaire's paper, *Les Nouveaux Temps*,[17] triumphantly announced that the Maréchal had put in a request for a shoe voucher and reproduced the docket:

Name:	Pétain
Date of birth:	24 04 1856
Residence:	Hôtel du Parc
Profession:	Maréchal of France, head of state
Business address:	Vichy
Order number:	1672

At the same time, the legislators established various categories of shoes (such as work shoes, town shoes, indoor shoes, sports shoes) and pored over the doubtful cases. The public was informed through the press that the measures had been taken in order to enable little girls to obtain the white shoes they needed for their first communion. Families were simply asked to be good enough to attach a certificate signed by the parish priest![18]

In order to encourage economies in leather, the thickness of soles and the shapes of shoes were closely examined and regulated, which inevitably affected style. A regulation published in the *Journal Officiel* on 28 December 1940 prohibited shoes with double or triple leather soles as well as high boots and ordinary boots made of leather. The sole must not in any case 'project'. Despite these requirements, which forced them to pay close attention to their manufacturing processes, footwear specialists and shoemakers strove to offer their female clientèle a range of articles that they hoped were attractive and accessible. Leather boots were forbidden. Never mind, henceforth they would be made from tartan cloth or some thick material. They followed the example of the Italian shoemaker Ferragamo, who had launched the wedge heel – a thick sole made of cork or some other substance – in similar conditions of scarcity before the war.

Wooden 'soling' began to spread in 1941. 'They come from the forest, the shoes of the armistice', *Marie-Claire* informed its readers. 'And women as a whole will be taller by wearing them because the wooden soles – the only ones that can be sold without coupons – are 2 to 3 cm thick.'[19] Henceforth, instead of choosing a leather at the shoemakers one was offered 'clogs' made of bark, 'bakou' or sisal. Bertrand Heyraud, who was one of the very first to use this process, presented his creations in March 1941, emphasizing their innovative aspect dictated by the needs of the day: light shoes mounted on a small wooden base. He recommended, among other things, the 'Gitane' sandal in lacquered wood, furnished with anti-noise, shock-proof and non-skid features, or, better still, the 'Sablaise' with a thick, light sole.

Fairly soon, in order to improve the quality of the product, a French group secured the use of a German patent, the Zierold sole (soon known by its French name, Smelflex). It was made of plywood, cut to standard measurements. According to the manufacturers, zig-zag cuts with the saw made it very supple and thus ensured that walking was relatively easy. 'Are we really going to wear those heavy wooden clogs like "farmers' wives at the operetta"?, we asked ourselves when these "monuments" appeared, with their uppers made of such strange and varied materials.' But that remained the only question.

At first, users resorted to this expedient with a heavy heart, complaining of the stiffness of the material, to which they found it hard to become accustomed, not to mention the absolute impossibility of running when wearing clogs of that type. How many women in illegal situations, with faked papers, secretly cursed these shoes, which prevented them from fleeing when, for example, they saw a police checkpoint appear on the horizon. 'I would have made a run for it', explained Michèle, whose heart was in her mouth when she presented a false Ausweis to a German officer, 'but wearing shoes with wooden soles this was not easy and I would soon have been caught.'[20] Fortunately, on this occasion she escaped with no more than a dreadful fright, because she managed to get through the barrier.

Remote from such concerns, the creators confided to the press that five minutes were 'normally' enough for a woman to learn to walk properly, while admitting that men needed three times as long! However that may be, the process made headway and the wooden sole became an integral part of the perched-up wartime female image. Maurice Chevalier even made it the theme of one of his songs, 'La Symphonie des Semelles de Bois' ('The Symphony of the Wooden Soles'), while some writers nostalgically recalled the famous click-clack. 'To the clicking of wooden heels,' noted Colette,

> I can dream that I am again at Belle-Isle-sur-Mer, at the time when the tide bringing in the boats calls to the sardine fishers on the quay. But it is nothing more than a flight of young girls whose shoes are clattering under the galleries, leaving the Comédie Française.[21]

As far as the *grands couturiers* were concerned, Maggy Rouff acknowledged that she had solved the problem of leatherless footwear by showing shoes with wooden soles with her spring dresses in 1941. Alix[22] complemented her peasant-type summer dresses with wooden sabots, a fashion she was happy to launch. Moreover, because it was impossible to obtain the smallest pair of shoes without a voucher, craftsmen adopted the habit of using diverse materials. Loyal to his vocation as a creator, the famous shoemaker Perugia, by dint of his innovations continued to make shoes for elegant ladies: 'My soles are not made of wood but of artificial or vegetable fibre. I use a compound which looks like leather, which wears well and which above all eliminates that exhausting and not always pleasing noise of sabots.'[23] For the uppers, he used bark, raffia, matting or synthetic hemp that looked like silk. Grésy showed clogs for townswomen, with very thick soles cut from pieces of wood topped by sandal-type uppers, open-toed to varying degrees.

'Nothing could give our descendants an idea of the orgy of creativity in our shoes during 1941,' commented the fashion editor of a Parisian political weekly.[24] Our journalist saw a good number of designs pass by as she sat on the terrace of a café on the Champs-Elysées, and indulged in a few sketches, which she matched with disagreeable comments. She had an *embarras du choix*.

> The woman who is passing by, unfortunately without any flexibility [in her step], has chosen sabots, the genuine article, which clack on the asphalt. To decorate them, she has fixed a small pink knot on top, but nothing gives any impression of comfort. Now comes an austere lady who has taken no trouble with her dress and who is putting down a matronly foot bound with white bands on a black base.

What else does our observer see? 'An improbably thin insect-woman . . . she is walking on blue buskins raised on soles which are so high that they look like two platforms.' And then there comes 'the image of youth and elegance, a beauty dressed to kill, but peculiarly shod: she is wearing worn out shoes which are soon going to part company with her. The nail of her big toe is sticking out at the end while the sides and stiffening are slashed, cut . . . This shoe is the last word in elegance!' There was such a wide variety on offer that the list of what was fashionable would be endless. Pedestal heels made of the new 'compounds' – wood or lacquer, not to mention rubber or straw – with many arched or curved shapes, were meant to attract both the most sensible and the most whimsical woman.

By 1941 'wood takes over from leather' had become a regular slogan. Now it was quite usual to see an advertisement praising the virtues of wooden soles prominently displayed in shoe shop windows – even in the free zone. In Lyons in June and July 1941 queues formed in front of a reputable shop which was offering a very successful range of summer footwear, advertised using a persuasive argument: 'Wearing shoes with wooden soles in summer saves your leather or rubber shoes for the bad weather.' In any case, walkers hardly had a choice. Scarcity, advertising and propaganda all drove them to adopt this fashion.

In order to spread the news about advancements in this field professionals were invited to participate in a competition. They were asked to offer 'unrationed' shoes, that is to say shoes containing no rationed materials (skins, leathers). All they could use were types of artificial leather, any sort of textiles, felts, oil cloth, lino, rubber, compounds of cork, wood, raffia, straw and rattan, to the exclusion of any other material. The results were shown at an exhibition held in Paris at 75 Champs

Elysées from 3 to 14 July 1941. The exhibition was opened by Roger Ribes in the presence of Dr Grunberg, head of the leather office in Berlin. Replying to the address welcoming the professionals, Dr Grunberg praised the good taste of the French creators 'who were not content to copy the German and Italian models but have invented new designs'.[25] He ended by stressing how much the exhibition reflected the collaboration between France and Germany! Amidst the flowers and skilful lighting, in a symphony of mauve and pink, the latest strokes of genius (or 500 designs) were offered to the public, who were given all the time in the world to admire the skill and know-how of the creators. The curious throng crowded around number 417, remarkable for its plastic sole, number 401 with a metal jointed sole, or even a strange shoe with a rounded wooden sole and straw uppers. The models filed by, shod in the latest fashions, and people went into raptures over the reds, blues, blacks, pale gold and natural straw colours that characterized these new-formula shoes. The exhibition also included a range of designs for men and children. At the end of their visit, each participant was asked to state his or her preference so that the ten most frequently named creations could be rewarded. A jury composed of experts (Hellestern, Pilmis, Kezler) and personalities from the world of arts and fashion (Lucien Lelong, André de Fouquières) picked the winners. The prize was . . . a pair of 'unrationed' leather shoes . . .

In summer, it was relatively easy to solve the shoe problem. In the south of France raffia espadrilles or beach sandals won the day, whereas sabots or beach sandals with wooden wedge soles (unrationed) were popular wear with summer outfits in the town. Perugia designed a light sandal in 'paper' net (this was a sort of strong but light lace thread), which could be painted to match hats and handbags. It was difficult to solve the problem in winter, however, and smartness, which had already been put to some hard tests, suffered a serious blow. In fact, the only solution for many women in the countryside was to fall back on wooden sabots that were put on over a pair of socks. In the town exhorbitant prices were paid for ankle boots lined with felt, fabric or, for the lucky ones, fur.

From month to month, the footwear question caused increasing anxiety to all ages and all income groups. Despite promises, schoolchildren were the most affected, since it became difficult even to exchange vouchers for clogs. In view of the impossibility of meeting German deadlines, a new regulation in May 1941, annulled all preceding ones: '4 million slippers will be handed over to Germany and 650,000 pairs of fashion shoes will be made available to German buyers in French retail shops on presentation of special vouchers.'[26] 'In total, the French are no longer allowed more than one re-soling a year and one pair of new shoes every four years at the most.'[27]

A massive increase in purchases of shoes by the occupier was registered almost immediately. The prefect of the Doubs noted in July 1941 that more than 700 pairs had been sold to the Germans in the town of Besançon alone, whereas in the same period there were only 400 available for the locals. Likewise, at the end of August 1941 the mayor of Versailles informed the prefect of Seine-et-Oise that for fourteen days German soldiers, abundantly supplied with vouchers, were 'buying men's, women's and children's shoes, which they pay for with brand new bank notes'.[28] So substantial were these purchases that there was a serious danger that the basic needs of the French could not be met. In August 1941 administrative reports stressed widespread complaints from the population. In Rennes, 9,000 vouchers were distributed, 3,600 for ordinary shoes and 5,400 for fashion shoes, to meet the needs of a department of nearly 600,000 inhabitants. In Saint-Quentin, 400 vouchers were put into circulation for 45,000 inhabitants, and so on.[29]

For children a system was introduced whereby used shoes could be exchanged for new shoes. The old shoes were repaired and put back into circulation for use by others. Soon, in 1942, there was nothing to be found even with vouchers, to the despair of mothers of families who had difficulty dressing their children, and who laid siege to craftsmen. 'At my request', explained Edmée Renaudin, mother of six, 'a sympathetic cobbler agrees to lengthen the toes of shoes which were too small for F. with a piece of leather that he had. My son wore them for three days and it is to his credit. They look like long pointed shoes on him, with turned up toes.'[30]

For adults the problem was even harder to solve (of the 18 million pairs planned, production in 1941 barely reached 6 million). According to *Le Journal de la Chaussure*: 'In 1942 the scarcity of leather only makes it possible to produce one pair of leather shoes at the most for every 4 or five inhabitants, or 9 million pairs of leather shoes. The difference is made good by wood. Twenty million pairs of shoes with wooden soles will be produced plus 5 million pairs of clogs and wooden pattens for resoling' (June 1942).

The good old shoes that had held out till then were beginning to wear out and people no longer recounted the incidents – comical to varying degrees – which occurred from time to time. Often, when the event took place under the eye of the occupier, shame, even hatred, were close to the surface. When she was out walking with a friend a young girl suddenly saw 'her sole leave her shoe and circle through the air: she got home as best she could . . .' A fifteen-year-old high-school girl decided to make her own shoes as everyone around her was doing. She bought 'a cork sole with a heel some 10 centimetres high and used some blue leather salvaged from a bag to make the uppers'. The result proved very encouraging.

In August 1944, a Paris daily, *Le Matin*, published the method for making one's own moccasins, like the Indians. All you needed was a discarded satchel or an old felt hat strengthened with synthetic leather. Absurd ideas bubbled out of the brains of coquettes, like the lady from Nantes who cut up her father's billiard cloth to make her own shoes, or the Lyons woman who made indoor mules from tapestry. The misfortune of some was the good fortune of others. Flea markets had never had it so good. 'People jostled each other in front of a pair of wrinkled leather shoes, sold for 120 francs.'[31] Second-hand shoes that looked new were snatched up: they might not have been fashionable but they still looked good. The black market was also very active, as the shoemaker Maurice Arnoult explained, summarising the way it worked.[32] The high school girl, Michèle Bood, on holiday in Verneuil, took advantage of her stay there to ferret out a pair of winter shoes. She finally succeeded in obtaining a pair (at a price) via a pregnant woman's voucher. This was the only category that had a right to 'vouchers for town use', that is to say to shoes 'soled' in rubber.

Faced with the scarcity, a few serious gentlemen, concerned about the well-being of their fellow men, suggested the adoption of new 'soling' processes. M. Lebossé of Sainte-Adresse, near Le Havre, thought seriously about doing research into shoes with metal soles: steel, duraluminium or light alloys, and offered his services to the Minister of Industrial Production. An investigation was launched and reached the following conclusions: 'From a technical point of view the duraluminium sole offers even worse sanitary guarantees than the wooden sole. The alloy may be too cold in winter and too hot in summer.'[33] Developing it proved much too expensive and the idea was abandoned. The wooden sole survived and gained customers from month to month, its increasing popularity demonstrated by a gala November 1943 called the 'Gala of the Wooden Sole', when Marie-Josée Carlatti, Michèle Darlan and Suzy Solidor showed the most beautiful designs.

The restrictions forced craftsmen to obey new, often strict, rules if they wanted to carry on working. From January 1941, leather belts for women could not be more than 4 cm wide. For men they could never exceed 2.5 cm, 'whatever the physical requirements or wishes of the purchaser'.[34] As a result, very narrow belts, for small waists, became fashionable – quite appropriate, 'restrictions' being what they were. In some shop windows in Rue du Faubourg-Saint-Honoré or Rue de la Paix, some creators exhibited extravagant designs which in their own way mocked the times. One example was a black suede belt on which was engraved in gold the name of the vegetable that the French abhorred because it was the symbol of scarcity: the swede. Another one was fastened by a model of a tiny stove containing the 90 g meat ration.[35] A craftsman offered a belt for sale for a slender waist on which was inscribed: 'Just another notch.'

At Cannes, Kostio de War, who specialized in knitwear and crochet, catered for sporty types by offering them a knitted belt with a zipped pocket. In the 1941 spring collection all sorts of imaginative designs were offered. Two of them were particularly appreciated because they were easy to make up even by beginners: one was composed of two wide bands of lamé (unrationed), cut on the bias, which ended in a buckle; the other was a sort of braid consisting of three plaited strands, in royal blue, light blue and orchid pink, with a muslin scarf in the same colours. For a belt, the clever customer of modest means could buy furnishing straps and selvedges on which she embroidered simple logos or designs, with a cord threaded through a ring serving to fasten it. Lastly, to restore a rather jaded leather belt to its former glory, some fashion columnists advised embroidering it with woollen or silk motifs in varied colours, or better still encrusting it with gilt spangles. The prize for ingenuity in this field undoubtedly went to Josèphe Cardin, a young high-school girl at the collège Sévigné. When the Germans published a decree at the end of May 1942 ordering Jews aged six and over to wear a yellow star, she was over-whelmed with the desire to revolt. She sought a concrete way of showing her sympathy for the outcasts and made a cardboard belt bearing the word 'Victory', each letter being composed of tiny yellow stars linked together. As a result of her daring, she was arrested and imprisoned for defying the occupier, and the notorious belt was also seized.[36]

In 1941, following a decree forbidding their manufacture, the large leather bags which were so popular because of their carrying capacity, gradually disappeared from the streets, where people had become accustomed to seeing them. Suddenly, women who were lucky enough to own one of these marvels, became all the more attached to them because they were so special. The other side of the coin was that it suddenly became easy to identify the bag or its owners – and later a few young girls learned to their cost that, in these times when the enemy was king and when denunciations were rife, they could be spotted by their bag and then given away when it was used to transport subversive newspapers for the Resistance.

A coveted object because of its rarity, this sort of bag easily lent itself to barter (classified advertisements sometimes contained notices saying: 'Would exchange fur coat for a leather bag'), or the black market. However, some women fell back on substitute products which they adapted very cleverly. The fashion was for very large shopping bags, made of patent 'leather' or, better still, snakeskin, particularly python, the ultimate refinement being to match the fabric to one's belt.

Cloth shoulder bags were all the rage and there were several versions, ranging from the most ordinary to the most sophisticated. The first category included a very popular model, called 'Restrictions'. This was a large bag, often in oilcloth, closed with a cord. A woman's day-to-day companion, it could even become elegant when it was made – as Worth made them – of thick fabric. Inside, it could contain small bags made of light material which were used to cover up boxes of 'coffee', 'tea', 'sugar', 'coupons' so that nothing would show. Thus, when invited to tea or dinner, Madam could arrive with her quota of food, or even come equipped with a shawl or warm slippers, everything buried and protected from prying eyes.[37] Equally practical were the tartan bags which all the young girls adored. When her kilt proved too short to wear, Michèle Bood, who had no intention of parting with it, looked round for an ingenious means of putting it to further use. She then had the idea of making it into a bag, with overstitching and a shoulder strap, and the result exceeded her wildest hopes, to the point of arousing the jealousy of her friends.

The basic material changed according to custom or season, with the exception of gros-grain or moleskin, which were in demand because they were strong and easy to care for. In summer, ribbons and straw were used to create fresh designs, although they were less resistant to wear and tear. Right under the eyes of the flabbergasted occupier, it was not rare to see brazen French girls proudly carrying one of these fragile tiny masterpieces, as if they wanted to prove to the world that, despite the difficulties of the day, French taste was alive and well. In winter, felt and cheap fur vied for public favour. For a privileged clientèle who were able to pay high prices, the *grands couturiers* displayed elaborate compositions in which a little leather, suede or box-calf mingled with authorized materials. Here too, 'felt in clear hard colours' was used a great deal. The first to encourage its use was Christian Bérard. Expensive but also in demand were lizard and crocodile. Dubost, at 6 Rue Royale, manufactured a travel bag in claret-coloured crocodile, which he christened 'Sleeping'. A sense of humour was maintained, and in February 1941, instead of leather bags, Lucien Lelong, showed a design cut out of raw wood with the amusing appearance of a hewn log. The example caught on, and shortly afterwards innumerable wooden bags, polished or varnished, plain or coloured, round or square, invaded the towns.

The shortages also directly affected an accessory that had even been expensive in normal times: fur. In 1940 stocks diminished perceptibly. This unprecedented situation was largely due to the clientèle, who were smart enough to anticipate the crisis in raw materials, and the occupying forces, who did not hesitate to buy up interesting rare commodities. It was compounded by the severity of the winter. Lack of warm underwear drove many women to buy the fur-hooded waistcoats that still existed on the market. To meet the heavy demand, craftsmen then resorted to rabbit skin, which was strictly controlled by the Fur and Skins Section of the Central Distribution Office. All undressed rabbit, hare and wild rabbit skins were centralized in the hands of specialized merchants, appointed 'wholesale classifiers'. It was from them that furriers and clothing manufacturers obtained their supplies in 1941, provided they were equipped with the necessary purchase licence. From 23 to 30 January 1942, in the hope of increasing production, the Committee for the Organization of Skins and Furs forced screenings of a film on rabbit breeding through the medium of International ACE Newsreels! When they could not procure the skins of the precious 'national rabbit', furriers turned to skunks, ferrets and moles with limited success!

Silk stockings took pride of place among those accessories affected by restrictions. Their almost total disappearance in 1940 was a real problem for those who wore them. At that time, stockings, like hats, were indispensable components of female dress and no lady would think of dispensing with them for fear of breaching that code of good manners called fashion. It was an established fact that no lady worthy of the name could go out without stockings. It is not hard to imagine the problem that the lack of material posed for the masters of elegance. In the cold season, thick woollen stockings appeared, followed by leggings, the latter encouraged by the *grands couturiers*, and enthusiastically adopted by many women. For style's sake, a minority remained faithful against all odds to transparent tulle stockings, stubbornly 'maintaining an expensive fashion unseasonally and unreasonably'.

In spring 1941 the problem returned all the more acutely since wear and tear had caused pair after pair of silk stockings to disappear from drawers and because, despite the occasional miracle, it was becoming hard to replace them. Pulling on their last pair, these women lived in terror of ladders or of inadvertently snagging their stockings. Of course, there were repair shops that mended laddered stockings but there was a point beyond which nothing more could be done. 'What can we do in these circumstances?' 'How can we replace the irreplaceable?' A few very young girls began to mutter fearlessly: 'It doesn't matter, summer is here. We'll go without stockings as we do at the seaside.' But for the majority of people living in the city this was not a solution and the question hung in the air.

'In order to make up for the disappearance of silk stockings, Parisian ladies are colouring their legs with iodine dye,' Maurice Arnoult reported.[38] A major perfume brand, Elisabeth Arden, offered a solution, and others soon followed: dyeing one's legs with an easily applicable lotion that browned the epidermis but was transparent enough to allow the skin to show through. The ultimate achievement was to draw a black line on the calf, giving a life-like imitation of the seam of a real stocking. Meanwhile, the press reported, 'Elisabeth Arden, who never misses a trick, is giving us the chance to cover our legs as is fitting, without fear of the frisson of laddering and without putting a strain on our finances, in preserving the correctness of our attire and our elegance – and all this in the simplest possible way.'[39] It was an enormous success. 'The artificial silk stocking is born,' stated the critic, welcoming its invaluable qualities: 'Nothing is as reliable as these stockings'; they never moved, they never fell down. They could take the worst showers without being affected. Catching them on something was no longer a drama.

All things considered, women were only too happy to grab at these miracle bottles, the price of which varied according to the renown of the perfumer: 33 francs from Elisabeth Arden (plus 2 francs for the bottle), 30 francs from René Rambaud – who boasted 'the ladderless stocking' in a range of three shades: flesh, gilded flesh, tanned flesh – and 25 francs in the department stores under evocative names. 'Filpas', which the advertising described as 'The silk on your legs without silk stockings', was very popular. It was a liquid guaranteed to be harmless, which did not stain and was water-resistant. 'It is not a dye; it covers the skin and sheaths the legs like the prettiest stockings', making ankles and calves look thinner.[40]

"Ambresoie" replaces silk stockings, does not stain dresses, does not mark in the rain.'[41] The brand was distributed by L'Oréal. A less prestigious perfumer, Dorin, had no qualms about claiming to be the 'creator of leg make-up'.[42] A Montmartre painter suggested painting multi-coloured flowers on legs, but nobody paid any attention. Despite these substitutes, some people remained nostalgic for silk stockings and lamented the good old days. The most depraved and corrupt were well aware of this and *Au Pilori*, a violently antisemitic newspaper that collaborated with the Germans, offered three pairs of stockings as first prize in a despicable competition. Entitled 'Where to stick them?' the competition was only open to women and required them to imagine ways of 'cleansing' the country and getting rid of the Jews. It found a winner: a Parisian lady who was visibly delighted with her prize, particularly valued in those hard times.[43]

Stockings were the object of a considerable black market. The legal rate for a pair of lisle or rayon stockings varied between 25 and 30 francs, for better quality rayon between 33 and 38, and for silk stockings between 65 and 85 francs. An investigation by the General Commissariat for Jewish Affairs in Troyes in January 1943 reported the following prices on the parallel market: 125 to 150 francs for a pair of ordinary rayon, 165 to 190 for better quality and 250 to 300 francs for a pair of silk stockings.

The shortages affected everyone, or almost everyone. Every man and woman rummaged among their hidden treasures for something that might be turned into an accessory to complement their outfit. A belt could be made of plaited straw or papier mâché, while nimble fingers could give new life to the smallest piece of string or lace. In her chronicles devoted to Paris in these dark years, Colette describes how an Indian cashmere shawl that came from her mother, 'threw out its last blaze of colour in the form of a handbag mounted on light-coloured tortoise-shell', which was, after all, according to the writer, a happier fate than ending up as a tablecloth!

Never had accessories been so prized. Gloves were increasingly popular. There were all types for all tastes. Plain gloves, *crêpe de chine* gloves, printed to match gown or hat. They were rarely made of leather, almost always cloth. The most dressy were made of drawn-thread material or lace, the smartest of silk piqué, the newest of jersey or crochet. The sumptuous days were over. Henceforth it was an illusion to hope to wear the appropriate clothes for every occasion, as fashion used to dictate. Women therefore counted on accessories to help them adapt their outfits to their needs.

Taken from *Mode du Jour*, 20 February 1941.

-4-

Making Do and Looking Smart

When the measure introducing clothing coupons in July 1941 was announced in the press, it dealt another blow to an already debilitated French morale. There had certainly been early signs that suggested that the situation was serious, but no one dared believe that it could actually come to exchanging coupons for clothing.

It was nevertheless a *fait accompli* at the beginning of 1941. Under the law of 11 February 1941, the temporary regulation of the sale of clothing and textile articles was replaced by a provision for

> supplying a card comprising a certain number of points to every customer holding a food ration card. The [new] card would allow the acquisition of clothing and textile articles according to a scale based on the nature of the article and a determined number of points.[1]

It took experts twenty-three sessions between 23 February and 30 April 1941 to work out the details of this card.[2] While waiting for it to come into circulation, items of clothing were subject to limitations. For women, the limit below which a request for coupons could be made was as follows: two dresses, two aprons or overalls, a raincoat, two pairs of winter gloves, a winter coat, three dresses, two slips, three pairs of knickers, six pairs of stockings, six handkerchiefs. No comment!

There were enormous crowds at the Paris department stores on 14 February, the last day of free sale. 'Amidst harassed but smiling salesgirls at the Printemps department store, two or three hundred women armed with order numbers awaited the arrival of woollen goods, while other women were queueing up to try on items in the dress and coat department.'[3]

After that date, all purchases of clothing and underwear were forbidden without coupons. Nevertheless, from April, consumers were allowed to acquire one new garment in return for providing the supplier, free of charge, with 'a double quantity of the same products, worn but capable', the decree specifies, 'of being assigned to a new vestimentary use' – provided that a tailor assessed them! From 1 July 1941 the needs of the consumer were satisfied essentially by a system of coupons torn out of a book. Considering what textile goods were available, the government acknowledged that it was impossible to satisfy all demands and consequently it decreed that only coupons numbered from one to thirty could be used immediately.

A terrible dilemma then faced the common run of mortals and particularly women who traditionally looked after the clothing of the whole family: what to do with their thirty coupons?

From the housewife to the secretary, not to mention the well-to-do working girl, student, or shopgirl, the same problem preoccupied them all: 'How to make the best possible use of the meagre quota?' Everyone tried to build up a wardrobe according to their lifestyle and the means at their disposal. It was the subject of many conversations, and the press and the women's magazines sketched out solutions to help their readers. The advice varied from paper to paper according to their readership.

Several case studies were given. Madame X, whose maternal duties tied her to the house, could at a pinch make do with a skirt made from an old pair of men's trousers and a re-knitted woollen waistcoat. To dress up to go out, a tulle or lace dress, which she could buy without coupons because they were on free sale, would suffice. With her thirty points she could, for example, buy three pairs of cotton stockings (twelve points), a short-sleeved blouse (four points), and a sleeveless waistcoat (five points). On the other hand, Nicole's work as a publicity agent brought her into constant contact with clients. She absolutely had to look smart and right from the beginning she took great pains over her everyday dress. Two skirts made of ersatz wool (twenty points), one of them black, which she would wear with a casual or an angora sweater (not subject to rationing), with matching ankle socks, gloves and turbans, would form her basic wardrobe. She could make an elegant scarf out of two silk handkerchiefs (again unrationed), which would put the finishing touch to her cycling outfit. If she was invited to a formal dinner Nicole would get her dressmaker to make her a lamé suit (without coupons). She would use the rest of her points on lisle stockings. Colette, the young student, would exchange two used costumes, which had become too short for her, for a new one. It should be in a neutral shade so that it would go with everything. Her coupons would allow her to buy a silk dress for going out (eighteen points), as well as the indispensable divided skirt her bicycle demanded.[4]

Le Figaro, whose provincial, well-to-do readership did not lead the same sort of life, emphasized the need to choose a wardrobe that would last more than one season, specially adapted to a period of restrictions. It had to meet three conditions:

1. Only a minimum length of fabric is needed;
2. Must not be too strongly identified with current fashion so that it can outlive it;
3. In the case of an ensemble, the 'pieces' should be interchangeable.

It also proposed a basic wardrobe consisting of a classic costume, of which the skirt should go with another jacket, and the jacket with another skirt, matched with several blouses, a black woollen dress, a casual ensemble with culottes and a check scarf. All these models, it assured the reader, could easily be made by a dressmaker.[5]

Soon the whole of France was trying to circumvent the restrictions by employing a variety of inventions gleaned from almost anywhere. Word of mouth, the press and the wireless all freely gave advice to the lady of the house and ended up imposing their law on everyday fashion. It mattered little that a band was missing here or a corner there in order to finish a dress. 'There is a solution that is widespread in both town and country: the use of cuts-off (which everyone or almost everyone carefully keeps in a cupboard) which can still be useful if put together.' And the fashion spread for dresses made of different fabrics – which also made it possible to transform worn out outfits cheaply. The real inspiration was called 'The dress of a million pieces' and was very widely adopted in 1942. Neither beautiful nor really elegant, it was everywhere, so much so that it became fashionable by force of circumstance.

A sort of marketplace of ideas was spontaneously established, everyone exchanging their dressmaking tips. 'My dress,' one woman explained, 'did not cost me a penny. I happened to have a short length of claret-coloured woollen cloth, which I supplemented by cutting a bodice and collar out of an old tartan skirt.' 'I do the same sort of thing,' another replied. 'The coat you are looking at is made from two cast-offs, overlooked at the back of a drawer: one brown, the other check, it was such a tight squeeze that I had nothing left to make lapels, so I made an "aiglon" collar which is attached to the yoke.'[6] Lucie Hirigoyen, fashion editor, raved about the quality of a three-quarter length casual garment worn by one of her friends, and tried in vain to understand where this marvel came from. She eventually learned that it was a renovation: it had been made out of a travelling rug, now quite useless as there were no cars.

As if by magic, what might once have seemed ridiculous suddenly became street fashion. Colette, so aware of her companions' misfortunes, was transformed into a good fairy, amiably handing out advice: 'Do you, Madame, own two tight skirts which fashion condemns and use has made shabby? Is one beige and the other brown? You put one into the other and do it so that the top of one, cut out in points, provides the width that is lacking in the other. Rather like the triangles in the game of backgammon – do you get the picture?'[7]

Thus miraculous solutions were found and people discovered ways of evading the inescapable clothing coupons. The women's press played an essential role here in the service of its readership. It would require countless pages to list the tips it passed on. Alongside their role of providing entertainment and advice on how to overcome problems, these magazines gave women the help and strength they needed to solve their everyday problems. The practical information was greatly appreciated and the magazines became increasingly popular during these four years.

Le Petit Echo de la Mode, which had 209,000 subscribers in 1941, had 253,000 in 1942, and was able to overcome the obstacles of the occupation, defending itself tooth and nail in order to obtain permission to continue to appear. The magazine 'renders the greatest service to the mass public, strengthening the courage of wives of prisoners and troubled households without ever encouraging them to complain, helping them by its practical character to endure both the clothing and food restrictions'[8] wrote the editor in 1942 when threatened with a reduced allocation of paper.

Marie-Claire was a modern magazine, influenced by the American press. Born in 1937, the magazine had a circulation of nearly a million before the war and devoted considerable space to sport, body care and fashion. Withdrawing to Lyons in the free zone in 1940, *Marie Claire* changed its formula and became more traditional. It sold very well and set out to be the champion of bright ideas. The political dailies, for their part, also understood the importance of the subject and, despite difficulties, retained a weekly page devoted to fashion. All the advice – which as the months went by tended to become rather repetitive – could be summed up in a few lines: times are hard; you do not have the right to throw anything away; we are living at a time when the smallest piece of cloth is precious; learn how to make the best use of everything. This is a national duty. Look in your cupboard: perhaps you stacked away some old worn, velvet, cretonne, chintz or taffeta curtains several years ago. Now is the time to take these old things out and to cut a jacket, a pair of trousers or a skirt out of the good bits. What would you say to getting a new jacket – without points or black market – from a jacket or dinner jacket that your husband no longer wants? 'A pair of men's trousers can become a pretty dress. All you need to do is turn them inside out after carefully unpicking them. The dress is made of four panels to which you will add a yoke of striped or knitted fabric.'[9] Your plain dress is sadly worn out and shiny, but what does it matter! You can still use it by inserting strips of different coloured cloth to form a good contrast. In order to revive your classic black dress what do you think about a wimple, cuffs and bows, or perhaps you would prefer a little bolero made from a scarf?

Among the innovations, ribbons, only recently the poor relations of dress-making, came in to their own. 'Ribbons!' enthused the editor of the women's page of *L'Œuvre*, 'what a resource for us and more so now than ever before because we can buy them without points up to a width of 20 cm. What pretty things we can make with them! Whether they be narrow or wide, in soft or cheerful colours, striped, tartan or spotted, in faille, satin or gros-grain, we'll turn them into blouses, waistcoats, boleros . . .'[10]

The same was true of the chamois leather that *Marie-Claire* suggested its readers make into a waistcoat – 'You have often coveted a leather jacket or waistcoat, but you have to do without them because of their high price. Go and buy some chamois leathers in the market or at a department store. Cut them into pieces 9 cm x 12 cm and stitch them together . . . you then have a new type of fabric, soft, warm, strong, which you can cut like a material bought by the metre . . .'[11]

To complete this picture, there was the increasing space given to patterns, lessons in cutting-out, and booklets sold by post and intended to initiate the housewife into the secrets of dressmaking. Hélène Pasquier, for example, was the popular author of *Elégante quand même. Comment Tailler et Exécuter un Tailleur, un Manteau, une Jupe-culotte, Transformations.* (Elegant Against All Odds. How to Cut Out and Make Up a Suit, Coat, Divided Skirt, Renovations).[12]

Today this very prosaic advice seems both perplexing and amusing. In 1942–3, at a time when the war had reached world-wide proportions and bloody battles raged, and when in France confrontations between occupier and occupied in the form of assassination, sabotage and executions were becoming more violent by the day, it may seem surprising to see such a large place reserved for such apparently minor subjects. In reality, these useful tips show just how much clothing, closely linked to context, is a social phenomenon. They conveyed a social fact: the precarious position that the French population had reached within the space of a few years. Fashion had assumed a new meaning; what only recently would have been unthinkable had actually happened. Renovation had to be recognized as a necessity, because there were no means of acting otherwise. These recipes formed part of the system of dressing. Unable to change clothing at will, people made it over. Belcolor announced a new dress that was cheap and did not require coupons. 'Fine dyes that hold, transform faded cloth into sparkling fabric.' It was left to the advertising material to state: 'so simple a child could do it'!

Beyond the desire not to yield in the face of adversity, the words behind the conventional language should also be read as the wish to safeguard an identity. While everything, or almost everything, was lacking, people followed the suggested solutions to camouflage the mediocrity of the present and keep up appearances.

The shortage of such indispensable raw materials as cotton and wool, the lack of cloth, and clothing coupons were not easily endured. Complaints poured into government offices from all sides. The Saint-Etienne syndicat patronal des tailleurs confectionneurs français, (employers' association of French ready-made tailors) expressed its anguish at the allocation of 100 points (thirty of which could be used immediately) from the clothing card. As this number of points was insufficient to buy any article whatsoever from tailors, the result was that consumers no longer bought anything but small items such as socks, shirts and handkerchiefs.[13]

The prefect of the Hautes-Pyrénées was hard pressed to answer a letter from Madame Pujos of Tarbes asking for an additional allocation of textile points. He opted for the truth: the small quota, which allocated half a textile point a month per

100 inhabitants. However, to buy a coat required 145 points. In these circumstances, any request, even the most justified, could not be favourably received.[14] As for the law of 17 June 1941 introducing the rationing of sewing thread, dressmakers let it be known that they could no longer practise their trade. In spring 1942, the widowed Madame Salmon from Precy-sur-Vrin in the Yonne, wrote to the director of Home Trade and asked him for an additional allocation of thread, explaining that she needed it in order to continue to work. The answer, handwritten by the director, was not slow in coming. It was a refusal in the purest bureaucratic style:

'Madame, I have the honour to inform you that the thread or silk must be supplied by your clients. They will be able to obtain it with coupons F and L from their ration book for clothing and textile articles which gives each person the right to 8 g of thread or cotton, or 3 g of silk . . .'[15]

Added to the difficulties they were experiencing obtaining skins, professionals such as furriers listed the lack of linings and quilting, and the almost insoluble problem of the shortage of needles and thread.[16]

Consequently, people salvaged. They salvaged thread that had already been used, and they 'drew' thread from pieces of cloth. In a word, once again, they managed to get by. But nothing in the escalating discontent exceeded the anger that the introduction of wool coupons aroused in summer 1941. Under French regulations, these coupons were reserved exclusively for children under three and pregnant women. However, under the terms of the directive issued by the German occupation authorities in the occupied territories, it was decided at the end of 1941 that every German soldier possessing coupons could also have an allocation of wool. Since August 1941 the French had already had to suffer the sight of Germans granted coupons for cloth amounting to 75 points. This time it was too much. Small revolts broke out in the provinces and in Paris. In March 1942 the manager of the department store Grands Magasins du Louvre refused outright to honour the coupons that came his way, pleading a lack of supplies.[17] Shortly afterwards, he was arrested by the Germans after a soldier complained about his refusal; he was sent to prison. A circular from the French government (June 1942) reminded shopkeepers that they were obliged to honour these coupons.

However, the wool question was still not totally settled. Once in possession of their coupons, mothers-to-be went to the shop of their choice where they were handed the desired items. But there was no question of being able to choose the colours they wanted for knitting their baby's layette. Expectant mums had to take what they were given – that is to say anything but the blue, pink or white, to which contemporary fashion in babywear remained very attached. Therefore, some women who hitherto accepted footwear coupons and a clothing voucher, for good or ill, revolted and refused to be allocated skeins of wool in shades of khaki. They followed the example of actress Simone Signoret: she was several months pregnant and exploded in anger: 'I thanked the draper. I took back my coupons. I again climbed the three floors of the town hall. I returned the coupons to Madame Fichini de Fleurville Rosebourg. I said to her: 'I do not know if I am going to have a boy or a girl. I want blue, pink or white wool. Whatever the case, I do not want to dress it as a soldier already.'[18] Faced with this insurrection, which became general, a government communiqué called the unruly to order:

> In the present circumstances it is not permissible for parents to refuse to buy dark coloured wools for their children: questions of fashion and personal preferences belong to a period which the defeat of France ended for the indefinite future. Children of two or three can be dressed perfectly well in dark coloured or even black knitwear. It is more important that they be dressed warmly than elegantly.[19]

In this realm where Ubu was king, the wish to rule everything took hold of officials accountable to the government. Nothing was left to chance, the urge to legislate being a characteristic feature of Vichy. Certain measures taken in April 1942 to save material were breathtaking – for example, the recommendation that trousers be made without turnups, or the prohibition on the production of jackets with inlays, and of overcoats with half-belts, and, best of all, the imposition of a maximum hem length. In July 1942 the manufacture of the following items of clothing was prohibited:

> Short, tight small boy's jacket, called an 'Eton';
> Single or double breasted small boy's jacket;
> Blouse with a sailor collar or revers, called 'Américain';
> Small boy's waistcoats.[20]

Boys below the age of fifteen did not have the right to wear long trousers without an exemption, grudgingly granted, on grounds of size.[21] Every case was carefully studied (clothing for colonials, pregnant women . . .). The majority of the population found this intrusion into its private life hard to bear and only accepted it because it had no choice.

'Salvaging' had become the prime preoccupation of serious civil servants who watched the rag-pickers' collection operations with interest: costumes, skirts, lounge suits and other articles of clothing could, after sorting and treatment, become new textile raw material capable of being used for curtains, dusters . . .

Whereas clothing was closely rationed and accessories like footwear and bags, belts and gloves were subject to regulated norms, headgear witnessed an explosion of shapes and colours and a riot of materials: tulle, veils, lace. feathers, artificial flowers, grosgrain, felt ribbon, straw . . . Never before had so many bizarre ideas and preposterous creations burst forth as between 1940 and 1944.

At the time when the Germans settled in Paris, the skill of Parisian milliners was world famous: some ten of them, perfect masters of their art, even had an international reputation. They each specialized in a specific range: 'grand style hats from Caroline Reboux; hats which were both classy and personal from Suzy; exotic turbans from Maria Guy; inimitably chic casual felts from René Descat; delicious droleries by Albouy; strokes of genius from Agnès, and lastly, Madame Legroux, that poetess of the hat, which acquired an indescribable subtle enchantment when it passed through her hands.'[22] Far from blocking this creative spirit, the occupation acted like a stimulant. If certain great names gave free rein to their imagination while staying within the limits set by elegance, less prestigious craftsmen sometimes verged on extravagance during these four years. Hanging gardens, birds' nests, enormous monuments, or dolls' hats, headgear sometimes assumed unexpected forms. 'Today,' Colette notes, 'there is not one woman of taste who in the safety of her home does not find sensible words to condemn the strange creations with which fashion wishes to crown her.'[23]

Perhaps this riot of shapes and materials should be regarded as appropriate compensation for the misery of the time! Wearing a medieval-style hood or a 1900-type hat would be a way of cutting oneself off from reality and taking refuge in the past. Political and economic crises had sometimes generated surprising clothing reactions, particularly in accessories like hats. Barely emerged from the Terror, the Merveilleuses, the ultra-fashionable women of the Directoire period, invested enormous effort in achieving a studied elegance in their dress and headwear; they had a marked preference for antiquity. During the period 1940–4 the creative exuberance of headgear can be explained as the diffused manifestation of a revolt against the harshness of the times. In 1945, some fashion columnists[24] had no hesitation in justifying this attitude, interpreting it as a premonitory sign that in the near future France would shake off its chains and drive out its enemies. A rather over-optimistic view of reality, unless it were a re-reading of events after the victory.

It all began soberly enough. The winter collection of 1940 suffered greatly from the pressure of events that turned the everyday life of the French upside down. If a few sophisticated designs continued to exist, intended for people who had time and money or worn with brio by artistes like Danièle Darrieux, the bulk of the productions at the outset met the demands of a clientèle that was suffering from the cold and inclement weather and that had of necessity to travel by foot, bicycle or metro. All this explains women's obsession with practical designs. It caused *Figaro*'s fashion columnist to write in November 1940: 'Wisdom has got as far as hats . . . which have at last returned to a becoming and pleasant shape. No more ridiculous headwear tipped over the eyes, which so many women wore to astonish rather than to please. They are going to gain by this sobriety.' Felt hats ruled supreme in all sectors: brown, red, black and bottle green, with conical or pointed crowns. They had a band of ribbon or muslin, even of plain or tartan wool, matching the scarf worn around the neck. Toques that fitted closely round the nape of the neck, and artistically draped turbans were very successful. They framed the face but the hair at the back of the head was often covered by cascades of fabric or pieces and loops of ribbon.

In December 1940, when he showed his collection at Lyons, Marcel Rochas unveiled his inspirations, including a 'red velvet toque on which a large meshed red veil was skilfully ruffled'. In Cannes, where a branch of Parisian fashion grew up, two designs were voted in by the clientèle wealthy enough to afford them: a black jersey cap enhanced by the head of a fox, and a draped turban ending in a mink's tail. Throughout 1941 and until 1942 customers went mad about a model of a turban signed Albouy. Made from tartan wool, it covered the nape of the neck and ears and was crowned by a birds' nest from which the heads of two little ducks peeped out.[25]

The severe cold explains the breakthrough of the innumerable versions of the hood, which had already begun in 1939–40. The most practical one (which people could knit for themselves) was made of two pieces of woollen cloth, one black for the outside, one light for inside. It was tied under the chin and was worn with everything. When lined with fur it assumed a totally different appearance, 'evoking a vast snow-covered landscape'. The latest thing in hoods came from Patou, who made them in luminous shades of cashmere, such as sapphire blue or champagne. A smaller version of this headgear made of silk was worn in the evening. It was clearly inspired by the lace 'mantillas' from Spain. A great milliner, Madame Agnès, raged against women who no longer wanted to wear a hat for fear of spoiling their curls. In order to reconcile masterpiece and code of elegance she suggested a black felt headband with clusters of small bows in the same fabric sewn on to it, together with foliage or feathers.

From the great milliner's headband to the everyday turban was only a short step, and many women made the transition. They adopted this hat, which was not really a hat at all, because it offered the indisputable advantage of being easy to make. All you had to do, explained Violette Leduc,[26] was to take a cotton or flannel foulard or plain kerchief, fold this piece of material in two, then wind it round your hair. For want of a hairdresser and for convenience, Simone de Beauvoir took to this very fashionable headwear, which suited her very well.[27]

With the introduction of the first policies for clothing that seriously restricted the range of their wardrobes, women looked around for something to counterbalance their enforced prudence. They turned to their milliners, who became accomplices in their desire. Many in fact gambled on the creators to bring a touch of grace and imagination to their outfits. What did it matter if costumes were a little tired or shoes a year old? In this world of shortages it was up to the hats – which symbolized the art of creation at every period, however difficult – to set the fashion of the times.

So well did the milliners understand this that they succeeded in overcoming the difficulties of supplies and offered their clients a collection spiced with a touch of eccentricity. The fashion was for small hats, often matched with fine, coloured veils, made either of lace or wide-meshed tulle. Small veils, but also ribbons, fruit and birds made charming hats, which the Germans, somewhat taken aback, admired, and which bystanders made fun of. (Walking in Paris in October 1941, not far from the Opéra, Ernst Jünger offered his companion a hat: 'a pretty design, as big as a humming bird's nest and with a green feather on top. It was amazing the way in which this pretty lady seemed to grow and change in this new headdress. In fact it must be said that it was not really a hat, but an ornament.')[28]

What a practical fashion. All you need is a small straw hat to which you add anything that is at hand just before you go out: a few flowers taken from a vase, a spray of lilac, pansies or tulips, or perhaps some fruit plucked from the fruit bowl . . . A final touch in front of the mirror and you have a hat that you can change every evening.[29]

Extravagant, touching, bewildering, disarming, skilful, provocative, fascinating, flourishing . . . are all these adjectives sufficient to describe the new season's hats? A milliner asked me if coming down to earth in matters of fashion was not 'a return to the soil', to what is most pleasing in nature . . . All the hats are decorated with flowers. Hanging gardens! minute gardens where the optimism of flowers in full bloom is concentrated.[30]

In this spring of 1941 the streets swarmed with these beds of straw, hung with fruit, all the more mouth watering because strawberries, grapes and tomatoes were beginning to become scarce. What could one say about 'Temps des cerises' ('Cherry season'), with a red velvet ribbon, made chic, young and luminous by two fat black cherries? And oh, the temptation of those strawberries placed on a bed of foliage that decorated that little straw hat inevitably named 'La cueillette' ('Fruitpicking'). Tipped forward, putting the nose at peril, balanced as if by a miracle, these small hats were sometimes worn by women of taste and, as that pitiless observer, Colette, commented, made one think that they 'lose their reason the moment they enter their milliner's boutique'. 'There is no other explanation for the phenomenon whereby a woman of taste who arrives full of circumspection and critical faculty goes home with a balloon of violets on her nose, a cascade of printed ribbon at the nape of her neck, a pillbox full of balls of silk across her right eye, and one of those veils that make a lasting impression in the metro, a turtle-dove hovering.'[31]

The fact was that, from 1941, hats had become the only 'dressy' item for a majority of women, so much so that some of them sometimes thought that all they had to do to look smart was to place one of those preposterous masterpieces on their heads. Some milliners – and not the least of them – disregarded the restrictions and made hats from Albene taffeta or rayon.

Elsa Schiaparelli describes how everybody in New York noticed her when she wore hats that had come from Paris via Buenos Aires. It was, she says, their first glimpse of Paris fashion, so unlike anything they were used to seeing.

> One of them, made of heavy brown velvet, looked like the hat I wore as a child . . . The other, perched high, was all veils and blue and yellow wings . . . The hat was a sensation, and I realized what an act of courage it had been to flaunt it in public when an article duly appeard in *The New York Sun* under the title, NAZIS PUSHING PARIS FASHIONS.[32]

Whether it was to defend a cultural heritage much coveted by the Germans or a desire to show that, whatever happened, *haute couture* was the stronger, Mme Agnès went ahead doggedly.

> If we are short of felt, silk or exotic straw for our models,' she claimed, 'I make do with bits of string . . . Look at this one, shaped like a diadem: it is made of cottonwool. This next is made with a hank of raw wool, sheared and dyed, held together by a hairnet. What do you think of this felt riding hat, 'Bleu Agnès'? The back of the crown is cut in strips, the ends of which circle round.[33]

Another was made of genuine shavings of West Indian hardwood, dyed blue and clouded over with a veil of the same colour. Jean Dunand, a master craftsman, agreed to make and lacquer the wood shavings. They had all the flexibility of ribbon, were easy to sew and, what is more, were waterproof. Thus was born a new fashion, destined to adorn the heads of the ladies of Paris. 'Alice Cocéa, Mila Parély and Madame Van Parys were among the pretty women who are wearing these new creations,' explained *La Semaine* on 25 June 1941, with a photograph by Philippe Vals to support its claim. The creations of Agnès and her colleagues kept their status, but they were copied with varying degrees of skill by local and provincial milliners. Consequently, there were hats and hats. 'The one that set the whole metro laughing', in the words of a contemporary Montmartre song writer, was not always a hat of the highest fashion.

Some found astonishing a burgeoning fashion to wear feathers, called 'knives', standing straight up from the hat:

> Where do they find those dreadful, ill-proportioned hats which try to prove their elegance by one or two enormous feathers aggressively planted at random or where their height seems most striking? How does a woman dare to walk about equipped with such a lightening conductor? . . . Marvellous hats can be made with feathers, but for that you need talent.[34]

No matter! The 1941–2 collection was a pyrotechnic display of new ideas.

Madame Le Monnier offered 'convertible hats'. A large, flounced detachable veil placed on a small, discreet, skilfully draped crown turned it into an elegant hat, and the addition of a clip or a pin gave it a dressy touch for the evening. In the large hat department were the little girl designs of Comtesse de Ségur, all made of felt. Rose Valois offered her clientèle pretty crowns in pale blues, pinks and yellows, hung or veiled with lace and black tulle. Clients were certainly surprised to learn that the raw material of these ravishing concoctions was nothing but blotting paper! People found the idea pleasing and elegant ladies snapped up the models. The whole world of 1900 was evoked by a large crumpled hat made from newspaper from d'Albouy. By adopting these newspaper toques 'shown in *Comoedia* or in *Paris-Soir*', every individual could advertise his opinions via his daily paper. Suzanne Talbot, on the other hand, took refuge in the past and drew the inspiration to compose her gold-entwined hoods from the Middle Ages or the Renaissance.

As the seasons came and went it seems that a great deal of research into craftsmanship was diverted into hats. Except for the cyclists who turned their back on headgear and created a fashion entirely of their own (bare heads, a predilection for tartan, shoes with flat heels and sling bags), the large majority of women were always loyal to the hat, however insane! 'Relatively small (in 1942), round like a pill or narrowed to an oval, crowned with flowers, plates of petals, fruit, birds' nests, gauze cabbages and chicory in a diadem, they defy all convenience . . . Whether they imitate lampshades, nurses' headdresses or those of fatted calves, pen wipers, clowns' hats';[35] in short, even if they were ridiculous, they were still appreciated because they formed part of the code of good manners.

In November 1942, the Committee for the Organization of *Haute Couture* had to limit the use of fabrics going into the production of women's hats. 'With the aim of respecting the creative spirit that characterizes the profession, the piling up of fabrics is allowed on condition that the total length of rationed fabrics, used in the production of a finished hat must not exceed the permitted length.'[36]

Despite the prohibitions, hats grew larger in 1943, climbed dangerously high and were characterized by a considerable volume of trimmings. According to Sacha Guitry, 'these tall heavily decorated hats, perched on top of women's heads, are pulling them towards the sky'. The fashion was for velvet and lace hats in the shape of aeroplanes, for felt hats with wide brims – in the style of a musketeer or perhaps a postilion. Still just as crazy, in 1944 certain women had such a clutter on their heads that many were refusing to wear that sort of monument.

However, for four years, those who intended to remain fashionable demonstrated an astonishing faculty for obeying their milliner. Hats were a consolation in an unsmiling period, unless, choosing to make them a farce, they were a means of mocking the occupier, a sort of provocation in the face of the world. Hats were 'lords of the day'. Many people agreed that 'over-dressed women with their feather-brained apparel look as if they want to snap their fingers at the Germans' – the main instrument of which was the hat.

Jacques-Henri Lartigue stressed the importance of headgear in the unremitting struggle in which the limited circle of fashionable women engaged to attain so-called elegance.

> The battlefield is Maxim's, the weapons are hats, veils, hair, clips and earrings and a thousand complications which make me split my sides laughing. The acknowledged champions are: Geneviève Fath, Annette Van Dem, Yvette Lebon, Jacqueline Janet, Gaël d'Oncieux. Yesterday, Cocteau told me that before the revolution women adopted improbable coiffures. How much more are we going to have to take![37]

In 1944 the French were not alone in their concern at the disturbing size of headgear and the proliferation of bad taste that accompanied it. The Germans waxed indignant. They emphatically informed Lucien Lelong[38] that a stop had to be put to the extravagant use of material; decency and strict economy must be respected. In response, Lelong tried to explain that 'these exaggerations do not emanate from the houses which launch fashion, but rather from amateur milliners or else from *couturières* who re-use fabrics from individual wardrobes in order to drape round crowns which are as inaesthetic as they are voluminous'. The Liberation put an end to these important and fundamental discussions.

During these years, when a textile ration card was indispensable if you wanted to dress up (except for the men and women able to pay the high prices of the black market, or the minority who were dressed by the *grands couturiers*), new clothing practices appeared, linked to circumstances. As it was quite hopeless to renew one's wardrobe every season, clothes first assumed a practical and utilitarian aspect, which each individual tried to embellish in his or her own way. The only exception were the hats, the last refuge of unbridled fantasy. They took on an unexpected prominence, as if fashion, that incorrigible and capricious mistress, was exploiting her power and seeking to diminish the clothing shortage. Hats may possibly have symbolized the wish to flee from the difficulties of daily life, but they were also a demonstration of insolence that did not go unnoticed by the Germans. As Elsa Schiaparelli explains so well, 'the hideous headgear, tormenting, heavy, and unbecoming – all denoted a Paris convulsed and trampled but still possessed of a sense of humour and, in order to defend its real inner self, intent on putting up a front that purposely skimmed the edge of ridicule'.[39]

–5–

Fibranne, Rayon and Ersatz

Although production of traditional textiles fell perceptibly because of the implementation of the terms of the armistice – which provided for heavy deliveries of wool and finished products to Germany – artificial fibres[1] like rayon and fibranne (spun rayon) made rapid progress. As nothing else was available, fashion and *haute couture* had to adapt to them and use them when they had exhausted their pre-war reserves. Once again, press and propaganda acted as transmission points, urging consumers to familiarize themselves with these new, attractively-named fabrics, and publicizing the best achievements of the *couturiers*.

Once the shortages were confronted, everything happened very fast. Because imports had been banned, wool from Australia, cotton from the United States and silk from the Far East could no longer get through! Their absence was resented all the more because France was an occupied country living under the shadow of the terms of the armistice. In a report sent to head of state Maréchal Pétain on 6 August 1940, the Secretary of State for Industrial Production, René Belin, made it compulsory to declare 'stocks of all textile raw materials as well as skins and hides', in order to ensure a rational distribution and eventually to regulate use.[2] A first step towards implementation was made within the framework of the 16 September 1940 decree which limited the sale of textile materials.

However, the occupying forces had definite opinions on the subject of natural and artificial fibres and intended to lay down guidelines without delay. On 16 August 1940 Gauleiter Kehrl, 'Führer of the German textile industry' came to Paris especially to establish the foundations of a manufacturing project for the French textile industry.[3] In addition to securing the contribution to the military needs of the Reich, one of the 'aims of the plan is to place the clothing of the French population and that of the German population on the same footing, and to achieve a common system making it possible to economize on natural raw materials, either by reducing manufactured goods, or by using substitute raw materials, such as artificial fibres'.[4] In front of the leading figures in the various branches of the textile industry (including Maggy Rouff, whose attendance had been specifically requested by Hartman, the man responsible for textiles in the administration of the occupied territories), and Bichelonne, whose presence the occupier had considered necessary, Kehrl, accompanied by officials from the Majestic,[5] had no hesitation in unveiling his plan.

In Germany, all the available wool was reserved for the military, civil needs being met solely by artificial fibres. However, 'the quantity of wool per head of inhabitant, placed at the disposal of France, is greater than in Germany, where annual consumption has been reduced to less than 30 per cent of normal requirements.'[6] Production in the two countries had, therefore, to be synchronized so as not to create inequalities between them. The division had to be based on existing stocks and not on needs; but there was a possibility that it might even be necessary to introduce clothing coupons in France.[7] For the moment, the plan provided for deliveries of wool, cotton and jute to the Reich: 'As of 25 June 1940 all existing stocks of textiles in the occupied zone are placed at the disposal of the Germans, either as wartime seizures or as requisitions.'[8] However, the 'textile Führer' admitted that it was essential to keep the French factories running in order to avoid social problems and unemployment; to this end, it was agreed that France would deliver finished or half-finished products to the German authorities. Lastly, it was necessary that French industry, in order to meet the clothing needs of the population, be directed as soon as possible towards using larger quantities of artificial fibres than in the past.

A few months later, a programme for the textile industries in France had been worked out by Gauleiter Kehrl and the industry, represented by the administrative officer Jarillot. A note on the Franco-German textile plan, written by the French authorities on 25 January 1941, mentioned 'exports of raw materials and manufactured products to Germany and deliveries to the army of occupation to the value of more than 5,000 million francs.[9] As a trade-off, [the plan] included a promise to deliver wood pulp or artificial fibres to a value of less than 1,000 million. Wool, cotton and jute would be delivered to Germany or converted on its behalf in France', as a certain number of enterprises would be working to execute German orders.

In the face of the disproportion between the value of the deliveries made to the Reich and what the Germans were prepared to give in return, Yves Bouthillier and René Belin hesitated to give their consent. The occupying authorities then let it be known that if the plan was not adopted 'they would completely wash their hands of French industry in occupied France and would seize all existing stocks'.[10] The French delegates then decided to yield rather than have the arrangement forced on them. In return, they obtained from the Germans the concession that 'no requisition or massive purchase of raw materials would be effected outside the plan'.

In the first year the convention, which Jean Bichelonne signed with Dr Elmar Michel on 1 February 1941, proved disastrous for wool: Germany received a large part of the shorn wool, in addition to all stocks in the occupied zone, which robbed France of the greater part of its production, at the same time as it was delivering a considerable quantity of manufactured cotton products to the army of occupation.

Confronted with the almost total disappearance of traditional textiles, industrialists were forced to turn towards artificial fibres. The Kehrl plan indirectly resulted in the expansion of a hitherto undeveloped sector: fabrics manufactured from a wood pulp base, which in 1938 had accounted for a mere 7 per cent of French textile consumption. Their production involved a simple process, barely developed in France, which needed the help of chemists to implement. The 'cellulose' that was used for the manufacture of rayon and fibranne was obtained from pine, fir or poplar trees; it was delivered, fully prepared, in the form of sheets. After chemical processing, these were placed in 'chippers', which reduced them to white flakes; these in their turn were converted to 'viscose'. At the end of a series of processes, this semi-viscous pulp emerged as fine threads that, when twisted together, formed rayon thread capable of being woven. Fibranne was nothing more than viscose and acetate rayon presented in the form of threads cut into equal lengths and gathered into 'wads', similar to those for cotton or for wool. In April 1941 the General Committee for the Organization of the Textile Industry, in agreement with the Ministry of Industrial Production, officially decided to reserve the term 'rayon' for 'continuous rayon threads' and adopt the term 'fibranne' for cut rayon fibres.

In France, four mills, including the factories of Vaulx, Bezons and Calais, were able to produce cut rayon, perhaps some 5,000 tonnes annually. Following the decisions agreed with the German authorities, production of fibranne had to be raised to 15,000 tons and divided solely between the 'wool' and 'cotton' sectors, as it was intended for the manufacture of a substitute for wool and cotton.

A group of Lyons silk manufacturers,[11] hit by the shortage of silk, protested against this decision, arguing that they had achieved some very important advances in creating artificial fabrics imitating wool even before the war, such as 'flesa albène', for example. It was on these grounds that the group claimed its share of raw materials. A. Dubois and Novetof were the most aggressive firms involved in the protest. Through the intermediary of Colcombet, an industrialist married to a German woman, they presented Hartman with different samples of 'flesa', which did in fact look very much like wool. In autumn 1940 they even organized a show of coats and dresses in Paris for the benefit of the German authorities, in the hope that they would relent. The fabrics used on this occasion were exclusively made from substitute products, but the cut was the work of the *couturiers* Marcel Rochas and Maggy Rouff, who had made it a point of honour to produce chic designs of relatively contemporary style. Kehrl was convinced. He agreed to make an exception, the silk sector obtaining a grant of 2,000 tonnes of cut rayon, which it was supposed to divide among manufacturers. The aim was to make available to consumers, with minimum delay, fabrics manufactured with a viscose and acetate base to replace pure wool.

The establishments that were subject to the exception had to be industrialized and able to produce standard cloth (130 cm for a dress length, 150 cm for a coat); the Germans reserved the right to inspect them to ensure that they were working properly and that nothing was wasted, in anticipation of the merging of the weaving mills.[12]

To appease the German authorities, Edmond Dubois proposed the formation of a company, Soportex (Société centrale pour les textiles de remplacement de la laine), in which some dozen fashion houses would have a place: Bianchini-Ferier, Barioz, Colcombet. 'What was being attempted at Lyons was a first try at real organization of the textile industry, with a production plan, the centralization of certain processes and the pooling of creations.'[13] The firms would receive the raw material, plus a production programme laying down broad guidelines for their use. Of standardized production, 75 per cent would be similar to the German fabrics, but 10 per cent would be reserved for use in the latest fashions, and 15 per cent would be unrestricted. Colcombet was specially charged with encouraging the *grands couturiers* to increase their use of the new textiles. The presence of Jean Barioz (head of the silk sector and of the Office de Répartition de la Soie) among the recipients of fibranne was sharply criticized by his less fortunate competitors, who accused him of having pulled strings to be selected.

In November 1940, an agreement was reached, independently of the Kehrl plan, between the German industry represented by the ZKR (Zellwolle- und Kunsteiden-Ring) and the French producers of artificial fibres. With government consent, a company, France-Rayonne, was set up with a capital of 500 million francs,[14] encompassing the Comptoir des textiles artificiels, the Soierie lyonnaise des textiles and various secondary mills, the Germans taking a 33 per cent share. ZKR agreed to let France-Rayonne benefit from its experience and its material, and to provide or arrange to provide the cellulose required for a fibranne factory (to be set up in Roanne), while still wanting France to pass on a certain percentage of imported wood pulp to Germany in the form of rayon and fibranne. It was agreed that Dr Schieber, in charge of artificial textiles in Germany, should go to Roanne in March 1941 to examine the conditions for the resumption of work at the premises. He would be accompanied by the head of the artificial fibres sector, Ennemond Bizot, and the German administrator in France, Dr Mömm.

According to a note addressed to the Armistice Commission at Wiesbaden,[15] a cartel of the artificial thread industries embracing some twenty artificial silk firms was formed in France for the first time. The majority of the companies constituting France-Rayonne were in Paris, the factories being situated in the north or in the Alps region. The whole affair became common knowledge. Officially the emphasis was placed on the drive for modernity which the artificial fibre industries were making, and on the assistance given by the Germans (who had pledged to deliver 81,000 tonnes of wood pulp under the contract):

> Through the very extensive forests situated in the free zone, France must establish an important and modern cellulose industry on the model of the German industry which will

pass on to it the product of years of research and experience, enabling it to produce quality products immediately and at minimum expense . . . Collaboration in this area will not be a passing commitment. It must be viewed as the beginning of continental Europe's collaboration in supplying raw materials and organizing production.[16]

In the short term, repercussions were felt in the field of fashion, where every-thing was mobilized to urge women to turn to the most unexpected substitute products, including the new materials brought in to replace traditional textiles.

Today's fashion is a series of riddles. For example, one wears ravishing overcoats, easy on the eye and soft to the touch, which look as if they are made of angora and which are not. They look like fur, but there is none of that around any more . . . No more guessing: it is marabou. But as the marabou is an exotic bird and as the blockade affects even down, presumably swans, geese and other farmyard animals must have been baptised marabou after their death . . . If the war goes on much longer, we will have learned to use these substitute products so well that when real wool or real leather come back, people will think they are the new ersatz.[17]

The race for artificial textiles lay open: before the war France produced 27,500 tonnes of rayon and 5,000 tonnes of fibranne. Production was expected to expand considerably, raising fibranne in particular to 50,000 tonnes, to everyone's benefit. Jean Guénin, responsible for the manufacture of women's clothing, explained to the public the consequences for clothing: progress had been made in improving the quality of the new fabrics as far as warmth, strength, waterproofing and crease resistance were concerned.[18]

After that, an unending stream of articles, lectures and exhibitions sang the praises of these substitute products to the public. 'The forest has been denuded to clothe you', was the title of a report on rayon and fibranne which appeared in *Pour Elle* in 1941:[19]

In the past, every animal that was created was available [to clothe us]. Today all that has changed. By depriving us of natural raw materials, events have turned the established order upside down . . . However, put your minds at rest. What is real and positive at the present juncture, are rayon and fibranne, mainly extracted from cellulose.

The same article drew up a balance sheet showing 'that a tree trunk of 100 kilos yields approximately 60 kilos of fabric and, depending on the width of the fabrics obtained, 265 shirts or 80 dresses or 37 coats'. No word of course about the flaws observed in the new fabrics and, in particular, the fact that they shrank dangerously when washed.

At the end of March 1941, *Le Figaro* launched a major investigation on a theme dear to the hearts of its male and female readers: clothes.[20] 'How will we be dressed tomorrow? mulberry tree cloth? nettle cloth? glass fibre or hair-cloth? rabbit wool or horsehair? The craziest things have been said on this subject. They provide the optimist with an attractive argument but have little relation to reality.' But this was not the real question. More to the point was the inventory of resources: 'Where are the woollen, cotton, silk and rayon industries? What can they still contribute to our wardrobe?' The answers were clear. Stocks of cotton were exhausted and were not being replenished in the absence of imports from America and Egypt. Shortages meant that wool was lacking and silk production was reduced to a minimum. It was therefore necessary to use rayon – before the war used almost solely in the production of artificial silk goods – in the production of new fabrics. Sooner or later, it seemed obvious 'that a standardization programme had to be conceived and implemented if people want to be able to dress in rayon fabrics'. The conclusion followed quite naturally: no-one should be surprised if, on the one hand, the Reich took the lead as the main supplier of cellulose considering its great advance in the field, and if, on the other hand, it brought equipment, processes and 'considerable financial co-operation' into the country. A hope was born: in the race for artificial textiles, France, which had started last, was benefiting from its competitors' advances, and it was doing so with help from Germany.

Lectures were given by experts in both the provinces and Paris where the meetings of the 'Maison de la Chimie' gave much prominence to recent discoveries and their applications to clothing. Under the title, 'In Doctor Faust's laboratory', Charles Reber, a journalist who had returned from Germany, revealed to his readers how the German population had solved its clothing problems thanks to ersatz products. The women were currently wearing dresses made of artificial wool produced from cellulose, their jewellery was made from some material imitating Bohemian glass, and their bags were manufactured from the stomach of an ox. As for the men 'out of uniform, they are wearing sealskin breeches and ties made of salmon skin'.[21]

At the same time, the first tangible results were made public, and people were allowed to judge some items for themselves. In July 1941, an exhibition devoted to the new fabrics was held in the Petit Palais, at the same time as the Exhibition of European France.[22] Two bodies participated in it, one German, the Deutsche Zellwolle- und Kunsteide-Ring, the other French, France-Rayonne. On show were the multiple applications of rayon and fibranne, from tarpaulin to the most delicate lingerie in 'ladderproof' or hand-knitted material, as well as furnishing fabrics, blankets, and so forth, and finally every type of clothing: work clothes and dresses, even the uniform adopted by the Red Cross, all made of fibranne. The *couturiers* showed their latest creations in these new fabrics. Lucien Lelong offered a costume in very beautiful hounds' tooth checked wool and fibranne cloth; Robert Piguet, a coat, Hermès, a ski suit in fibranne and cotton; Anny Blatt, delicate lingerie; O'Rossen showed a man's suit in fibranne.

According to *L'Illustration*,[23] which reported this exhibition, one stand (the hosiery stand) illustrated perfectly the new achievements, which would one day form part of the everyday wardrobe, because exhibits included 'a thick, soft pullover knitted in light and fluffy rayon thread; underwear in fibranne and angora jersey; pyjamas made of lined fibranne; fibranne socks and gloves, and nylon stockings'. Advertising now emphasized how 'up to date France was'. A purpose had been found for every textile thanks to efforts made over recent years, 'well before severe restrictions had made it necessary to seek substitute products'. Of course, they were still a far cry from German innovations, including the 'cows' wool' shown at the Leipzig fair in spring 1941, which scored a triumph and was given considerable space in the French press. A large place was given to the textile and particularly the ready-made clothing industry, but *haute couture* was not totally absent. Of special interest was a rainwear exhibit consisting of gaiters, cape and hat, made entirely of transparent synthetic rubber.[24] The impetus was set. For example, a visit to the German technical exhibition at the Petit-Palais gave the milliner Agnès the idea of using 'fibranne wool' in her creations. She found this new textile so valuable because of 'its suppleness, its resistance, its reactions to dyeing' that she had no hesitation in composing some fifty designs for her collection entirely in fibranne. And, she added, 'It is a great success which proves in practice, the excellence of the combination: French creation, German production.' A hat by the famous French milliner, made entirely of fibranne, was shown at the Leipzig Fair.

In the provinces, Grenoble, Lyons and Toulouse devoted a considerable part of their annual fairs to achievements in French cloth production. The stands of the Comité général d'organisation de l'habillement et du travail des étoffes were veritable hotbeds of propaganda, stressing the advances achieved 'in solving the difficult problem of clothing the French population with a stock of raw materials cut by two-thirds'.[25] One of the discoveries of 1941, angora thread, had become a valuable accessory. As well as the classical bed-jacket, 'it can be turned into a supple felt for headgear, into the fake sealskin coats so popular with elegant midinettes and into warm linings'. At the International Exhibition in Lyons in October 1941 the Valisère stand showed a selection of knitted fabrics as well as samples of fabrics made from fibranne. The same exhibition, a year later, showed what progress had been made. Thanks to substitute products, the clothing industry had gained ground even if quality did not always meet expectations. 'La galerie 20' offered visitors a room displaying 'finely cut dresses, suits and coats, full of inventiveness, with ingenious details and made with consummate skill'. They were made from amazing fabrics: one that was worthy of comparison with wool cloth was actually of more modest origin, it was composed of 75 per cent rabbit fur and 25 per cent fibranne. As the problems facing the creators of fashion became more complicated (reduction in permitted lengths, difficulties in obtaining thread and gros-grain, disappearance of wools and silks), wholesale dress production developed and was always prepared to experiment with the new products on offer. A textile exhibition took place in Lille, Roubaix and Tourcoing in March 1943, showing the public the fruits of the work of the Société de recherches et d'applications textiles.

If the optimistic forecasts published in the professional journals devoted to the latest discoveries were to be believed, winter 1943 would see the triumph of rayon and the widespread use of fibranne. In fact, by that date the quality of the fibres, at least at the experimental level, had perceptibly improved, thanks in particular to the results achieved by the Laboratoire d'études et de recherches de la fibranne attached to France-Rayonne. The latter described fibranne as 'the ideal textile'. 'The possibility of producing it in a range of diameters varying from the fineness of natural silk to the coarseness of horsehair is one of the original qualities of this new textile.' Experiments showed that it offered a considerable number of possibilities in clothing techniques: fibranne could be spun by itself or in a mixture with any of the natural textiles and was therefore open to a wide variety of uses. The combination of medium and fine threads produced a fabric that looked like wool. The introduction of a proportion of wool, however small, had a considerable influence on the quality of the fabric; over 50 per cent and it looked like pure wool.

However, these qualities, recognized and tested in the laboratory, were not put to widespread use in practice. A note from the Direction des fibres artificielles dated 19 October 1943 listed 52 grades of fibranne and acknowledged considerable efforts to improve its resistance by 25 per cent, but it emphasized that it was indispensable that research continue in order to remedy the fabric's undue shrinkage after washing.[26] It is interesting to note that the problem was only solved in the 1950s and 1960s.

From autumn 1942 onwards, a few textile manufacturers offered a range of products that were unanimously praised by the fashion magazines: they were soft to the touch, they came in pretty colours, they hung well, they looked good. 'How far has the composition of these fabrics moved on from the past? Not for us to reveal it here, but we can at the very least set your minds at rest on the quality of the mixtures employed.'[27] Let it be known! Women could stop worrying! Their elegance was safe. Those who feared that they would never again be able to wear anything but drab and standard outfits now had the means to choose and handle beautiful fabrics. 'Here are plain woollens . . . those made of wool and those which only look as if they were. We will not fear the cold with a casual coat made of diagonally woven, soft and heavy Duvetine.'[28] 'Labbey, Colcombet, Rodier, Moreau, Lesur, Ducharne, Coudurier, Chatillon and others remain worthy of their reputation; there are beautiful new creations everywhere for costumes and coats, created in classical colours, tartans, checks, imitation fur, goatskin, and breitschwanz . . . which will not only make pretty clothes but, in the hands of milliners, hats as well.'

Fabrics that looked so much like silk they could be mistaken for it included satins, jerseys and crepes of every sort – Moroccan or moss pebble weave, faille, matt and lustrous velvets, and above all the ripple silks called 'Astraline', gold and silver metal threaded material to make blouses and dresses. The prize for innovation went to 'three original creations: "Triklidou", "Jolibab" and "Doussalba". They feel and look like wool, and their satin-like back will enable wearers to make some charming combinations. As for afternoon gowns, they offer an infinitely Parisian suppleness and chic with "Givremousse", with a satin back and ribbed material labelled "Côte Bérénice".'[29] These fabrics probably came from the group of Lyons manufacturers of silk and rayon fabrics who had obtained the right to go on creating materials for *haute couture* alongside their standard production. The fashion journals welcomed the blends that had successfully transformed silk into a material so closely resembling wool that it could fool even a trained eye.

From 1941 onwards, fashion seized upon ersatz. 'Difficulties of supply have always been one of the strongest stimuli for creators. There is no lack of this stimulus today . . . It seems that its influence has even extended as far afield as America . . . The ersatz dress is currently "the last word" on the other side of the Atlantic.' In everyday life it became hard to avoid these new materials, which were also the delight of caricaturists and song-writers, since they were far from perfect.[30]

What did women think about these new fabrics with their alluring names? Opinions were divided according to age and income. Questioned by a journalist commissioned to investigate the use of the new materials, an elderly lady praised the practical aspects and cheapness of rayon, but complained that a dress made of that material creased easily, was not sturdy enough and did not keep one warm. But its biggest failing, in her eyes, was its lack of resistance to water. This view was not shared by a young woman of renowned elegance who stated that she wore nothing but the new fabrics. She pulled out of her wardrobe at random a white Moroccan crepe gown intended for dressy occasions, a floral one that was almost totally crease-resistant as it was made of acetate rayon, a blouse in Albène piqué, scarves . . . The fact was that she had the means to spend freely, and so was able to buy from the best fabric firms, whose high quality creations only a minority could afford.

As there is no substitute for experience, Andrée Morane, who wrote the women's column in *Paris-Soir*,[31] agreed to take part in a test: 'to tell the real from the fake'. She was presented with a collection of samples of ersatz in which one piece of woollen cloth was included. Her task was to find this piece. 'Feel, smell, take your time and tell us which is the woollen cloth.' After she had taken a piece of beige herring-bone 'woollen' cloth out of the parcel, followed by a navy-blue stripe, she opted for a mottled grey, a man's cloth type, only to learn that all these fabrics originated from rayon.

Some housewives confessed that caution led them to follow the recommend-ations of their favourite magazine to the letter and to use all sorts of means to reinforce these synthetics to make them serve the same purposes as woollens. The elegant ones used matching items, such as a rayon alpaca coat, which became very warm when a quilted spotted foulard lining and revers were added to give it the comfort and solidity of a woollen garment. The practical ones quilted an Albène cloth jacket either with kapok or with the remains of an old fur coat, but these new materials gained ground more by necessity than by any real popularity.

Economy was the order of the day and this could not be achieved without a number of drastic measures, such as those concerning the use of certain fabrics and the fixing of certain lengths,[32] or the standardization of designs in order to save raw materials. Large-scale manufacturing programmes were economical, intended in the first place for freed prisoners and agricultural workers who were promised imitation corduroy velvet.

In 1943–4 curiosity value was fading. What only recently made people laugh had become intolerable. Reality took over. The hosiery trade, which had looked so promising at exhibitions in 1941, was in full crisis. A visit to the workshops in Troyes showed the problems facing industrialists in the manufacture of underwear. 'The substitute materials (which some people no longer hesitate to say do not easily replace cotton, silk and wool . . .) sometimes hold surprises; there is underwear that stretches or shrinks in all directions when it is washed.' Growing labour shortages and a scarcity of substitute products suggested a gloomy future, which this particular journalist is no longer trying to hide.'[33]

The mail sent to the Maréchal's office included innumerable letters of complaint calling for warmer and, above all, sturdier clothing; naïve missives penned by a hard-working, often rural, female population asked the head of state to intervene on its behalf and to take account of its everyday problems. Propaganda did not let up in the face of this discontent. In spring 1943, so-called 'national' socks made entirely of fibranne were put on sale in Paris to a great burst of publicity. Customers were few and far between but they were skilfully photographed in the shops and the prints were reproduced in the press with appropriate commentary: 'In the last few days, four Paris department stores have displayed and put on sale hosiery "articles nationaux" which the public has welcomed. These "articles nationaux", woven in fibranne, wear as well as the fine articles of pre-war days.'[34]

In Vichy at the end of December 1943 the president of Linvosges gave a lecture on artificial textiles. The 'Le Paris' cinema was packed, said the report. At least 400 people came to hear the speaker. The talk was accompanied by a film entitled *La Magie du fil*, which showed the secrets of the manufacture of rayon and fibranne. 'Anxious to fulfil the expectations of a public[35] whose supposed interest in the new fabrics is not satisfied, the Trampus agency wishes to gather material on "nilon" (sic) and would like a factory to be named for its investigation.' The Ministry of Industrial Production directed it to the Etablissements Rhodiacéta at Vaize. Despite these initiatives, the gulf widened between the producers of artificial fibres on one hand and their discontented users on the other. However, in 1944 the Direction des Fibres Artificielles acknowledged that the fabrics lacked stability when they were wet but added that 'the chemists have not finished their work yet.'

Faced with the shortage of traditional textiles, and while awaiting the promised arrival of rayon and fibranne on a large scale, the government used all sorts of measures to encourage research into any substitute product able to make up for the shortfall. In November 1940 an industrialist, Robert Le Vaux, had sent a note to the Secretariat of State for Industrial Production explaining a process he had devised in his factory at Breteuil 'for converting Spanish broom into a thread that replaces flax and hemp thread in every case'.[36] Although the technique was perfected, its inventor explained, the raw material was lacking.

Six months later Robert Le Vaux was authorized by the Minister of Agriculture to go ahead and attempt the systematic cultivation of Spanish broom in the South of France. 'The present shortage of textile materials makes research into substitute fibres essential. Among those currently under study and on the point of passing from the experimental stage to that of practical implementation at the industrial level, broom fibre is one of the most interesting. This fibre can replace flax, hemp, cotton and even wool.' In August 1941 a 'new fibres' group was created within the framework of the textile organization. A law of 11 September 1941 made it compulsory to gather broom. But a year later the industrial production of this fibre ran into serious problems and the factories at Dolomieu and Mazamet assigned to process it failed to yield the expected results. The fabrics obtained from a broom base were unusable; mixed with wool, the fibre was just about usable in the manufacture of blankets.

'Will we be wearing reeds from Provence tomorrow?' *Le Matin* asked its readers in summer 1942, when it suggested an investigation into the new fibres.

France has allowed itself to lag behind its more active neighbours: we know the enormous efforts Germany has made in this field; Italy's achievements have been such that it currently meets all its needs; while we are dependent on what the outside world can pass on to us. Where will we find something to fulfil our vital needs?

Answer: in plants. After flax, hemp and broom (which was rapidly seen to be more suited to manufacturing rope and cable than textiles), great hope was placed in the great reed (donax). Its length gave it a suppleness that was valuable for textiles and conclusive experiments had already been carried out. 'A company has been formed, the Société francaise de la cellulose; before the year is up, it will produce the woven reeds that we will wear.' The construction of a factory was even contemplated, but tangible results were slow in coming.

Ideas burst out in all directions. Gathering pine needles as a means of manufacturing wool was one of the schemes mooted, but this ran into a manpower problem.

Bean stalks had their devotees: the story went around that on the platform of Luçon station in September 1942 'hundreds of carts of stalks were stored and pressed into rectangular bales before being loaded on to wagons and sent on to a factory'. Experiments with ferns were rapidly abandoned. A certain Georges Normandy unsuccessfully suggested 'planting sisal agaves on the hundred thousand hectares of lands from Saintes-Maries-de-la-Mer to Menton which were unsuitable for any cultivation'.[37] According to him, apart from 200,000 tonnes of paper pulp, this could yield a very considerable quantity of fibres directly usable in mills. Cultivation of marsh mallows was advocated because 'that plant provides an excellent fibre suitable for uses varying from string and rope production to fabric of every sort'.

All these new fibres were on show at the Toulouse Fair in October 1942, when wax mannequins exhibited a series of frocks, coats and costumes made from marsh mallow or broom. The organisers saw the crowds which gathered around these stands as a sign of future success, confirming the vitality of the new processes.

Someone also had the idea of using hair.[38] A report that appeared in *L'Œuvre* in January 1942 stressed that research pursued over a period of several months into using this material as a textile fibre had been successful. 'Several factories in the Lyons region are producing a variety of products today that justify high hopes, although they have not yet entered the commercial field.' 'Fabrics and footwear are made by splitting hairs,' added *Le Matin* jokingly during the same period. A few months later, a decree of 27 March 1942 ordered that hair be collected from hairdressing salons (between one and three kilos according to location). 'Cyclists go to the hairdressers and pay 4 francs a kilo for all the hair that is cut off. It is reckoned that Paris can supply 30 tonnes of hair a month and that the whole of France can produce 200 tonnes.'[39] Processed in a factory in Calvados near Condé-sur-Noireau; cleaned and incorporated in fibranne (20 per cent), they produced a mixture that was carded mechanically, then spun. The fabric obtained (piloïta) was used to make slippers, gloves and even handbags, a godsend for cinema advertising.

Before the war a woman could say 'I have nothing to wear'; now she asserted, 'I can't find material any more'. Not surprisingly, these hard times saw a return to the practice of ancestral crafts. Many an amateur bent over a small weaving loom she had constructed herself and produced her own fabric. 'Make your own clothes', *Le Figaro* advised its female readers, recommending the design of a tweed jacket that only needed 500 g of plain wool in a dark shade and 500 g of assorted wools.

People were encouraged to rear silk worms. German propaganda put pressure on some major women's magazines to publish a story about a small German village where the whole population was involved in sericulture. In November 1941 *L'Art et la Mode* praised this initiative, ending its article with the words: 'We in France might be inspired by the prowess of this little German town'.[40] In actual fact, the German example made no converts, since the benefit provided by natural silk was derisory for everyday dressing and it was almost exclusively reserved for fashionable creations.

Theatre and cinema turned to ersatz to produce its costumes. During the shooting of his film *Les Visiteurs du Soir*, Marcel Carné came up against the impossibility of finding the velvets, satin or brocades in which he wanted to dress his leading characters. In the end, one of the assistants found a small tailor in the Rue de Passy who had a stock of pre-war fabrics that he planned to dispose of at an exorbitant price. The transaction took place but the price was such that substitute fabrics were used for the crowd scenes. Marcel Carné lamented:

> Made of glass fibres and similar products, they have neither the softness of velvet nor the sheen of satin. They are also thin, light and lack firmness, and this shows . . . From afar they give the impression of richness comparable to that of the principal actors; close-ups implacably destroy these illusions.[41]

As a result of the shortage of leather, footwear with wooden soles was, as has been seen, increasingly in general use. According to professionals, one cubic metre of wood could make 160 pairs of soles for clogs or 175 to 200 fancy soles or 50 pairs of wooden shoes.

The proliferation of ersatz or substitute materials for soles called for regulations, which appeared in the course of 1942.[42] It was decided to reserve the name 'texoïd' for all imitation leather or hides backed by human, animal or vegetable textile fibres. This term applied neither to imitation skin and leather with a cardboard or paper base, nor to products hitherto labelled artificial leathers or synthetic leathers, which were called 'syndermes'. Progress could be assessed at an exhibition of substitute products that took place in Paris in October 1943; a variety of footwear designs were shown, as well as a wide choice of articulated soles:

- Artiflex soles, a series of sheets of hard wood (beech trunk) 2 cm thick, assembled with a slight gap between. The joint between sheets is held fast by one or two metal bands.
- Isoflex soles, composed of thin sheets of wood, cross-cut, flexible and sound-proof (according to the publicity).
- The Smelflex, one of the most popular.

On the lines of what was being done to meet the shortage of skins in Germany, there was also an attempt to tan fish skins, but it ran into major problems because of the scales. People rummaged in abattoirs for the guts of animals, which they turned into bags. Ox bellies were popular because of their solidity.

Cosmetics also had to be adapted. The big names in beauty products warned people who used lipstick against malpractice. Manufacturers had no supplies of either eosin or carmine, two products that came from America. Cocoa butter had disappeared. At the same time, perfumers fell back on wax candles as a substitute material but met competition from candle merchants who snapped up available stocks. An unexpected consequence of the shortages was that the perfume factories in Grasse and Cannes were not able to continue to work outside the local flower season because of lack of communications with Madagascar or Bulgaria where they obtained their precious essences.

To make everything with nothing or almost nothing, to try to replace the irreplaceable: such was the headache facing the creators who made do with a greater or lesser degree of *brio*. What is rightly called the 'spirit of Paris' endured, symbolized by the shop windows where the mannequins were clad in paper, where the bows were made of rayon velvet, the drapery of acetate.

France benefited from technical help from Germany, where great strides had been made in the innovative field of substitute products. The example of the France-Rayonne factory demonstrates this. Modern in concept and implementation, it functioned partly with German capital and technicians, which ensured it a definite technical advance, but at the same time put it in a vulnerable position. France-Rayonne was prey to sabotage by the Resistance, which refused to accept the idea that a German factory – even a partly German factory – might function on French soil to clothe the population. By choosing this course of action, the Resistance fighters also prevented Germany from benefiting from part of the production.

Spectacular advances occurred in these four years, to the point of revolutionizing clothing, which showed a perceptible movement towards substitute products. The explosion in artificial textiles in the 1950s and 1960s had its roots in this period of misery. The impetus came from the Direction des Fibres Artificielles. The consequences were important. A considerable leap forward in the field of ready-made dress production on the basis of these new textiles was visible after the war.

Norms were imposed not only on the manufacture of fabrics but also of shirts and lingerie. Leaving the realm of experimentation, large-scale implementation began.

The practice of using fibranne to replace missing wool supplies would remain. Although the luxury industries and the *couture* houses returned to the traditional materials after the Liberation, they had to reckon with the artificial or new fibres – even the vilified broom, study of which was mooted again in 1946.

Tenue d'abri, Winter 1939–1940. Design by Robert Piguet. (Photo: Roger-Viollet).

l'après-midi,
Champs-Élysées

Fourrures Max. — Longue veste en écureuil lustré. Chapeau de G. Orcel en velours.

Paquin. — Manteau de velours, col et poignets de renard. Béret en velours de Paquin.

FOURRURES MAX   PAQUIN

l'Élégance
chez soi

J. Lanvin. — Robe en armure de soie ; piqûres matelassées.

R. Piguet. — Robe en crêpe mat brodé d'or.

J. LANVIN   R. PIGUET

A day in the life of an elegant woman (*Images de France*, October 1942).

à l'Exposition

Bruyère. — Robe en lainage garnie de ganse de tissu finement travaillée. Col en velours « épinglé », comme le chapeau de Bruyère.

Mad Carpentier. — Manteau souple et drapé en lainage velouté de Ducharne. Chapeau en feutre et jersey d'Agnès.

BRUYÈRE   MAD CARPENTIER

de Six à Huit

Worth. — Robe et jaquette en soie brochée noire. Gilet indépendant en même tissu blanc. Chapeau en panne, de Worth.

J. Dessès. — Jupe et boléro en velours bleu de Coudurier Fructus Descher, blouse de marquisette brodée de paillettes du même ton.

WORTH   J. DESSÈS

Jacques and Geneviève Fath: the designer and his wife (1939). Photo: Seeberger.

Hats of different shapes (on the right is the Countess d'Oncieu de Chaffardon). Photos: Seeberger.

–6–

Haute Couture on German Time

From 1940 to 1944 the Germans took a close interest in *haute couture* and its various branches, attracted by its brilliance and worldliness, which brought them right into the heart of fashionable Paris. But above all they wanted to appropriate an art whose know-how was traditionally linked to French culture. This interest was in fact dangerous. Heavy clouds were gathering. Fashion was threatened in its very essence because it remained one of the rare fields where, despite the defeat, France was superior to Germany. The prestige and influence of French fashion remained intact, hence the conquerors' efforts to hem it in.

For a long time, the storm smouldered. Unhappy to see their country supplanted in this field, German women's groups protested vehemently against the '*diktat*' of French fashion, accusing Paris of wanting to run the show. The all-powerful Bund Deutscher Frauen (BDF) even called for 'liberation from the tyranny of Parisian *haute couture*'.[1] The government of the Reich wanted to crush its rival. At the end of July 1940 five German officers showed up at 102 Rue du Faubourg St Honoré, home of the Chambre Syndicale de la Haute Couture, where they were met by the secretary, Daniel Gorin. They came to seek information on the situation. A few days later, the German authorities forced their way into these premises looking for documents on the creation and export of designs. They helped themselves to everything in the filing cabinet relating to overseas buyers.

On August 14, at a Franco-German meeting planned to take place between M. Kehrl, textile 'Reich Führer', and the French representatives of the same sector, M. Hartman, in charge of textiles for the German administration of the Occupied Territories, asked that 'Mme Besançon'[2] (Maggy Rouff) be present, 'because,' he explained, 'the *couture* industries in particular are at risk of being hampered by the future regulation of textiles, and consequently it would be useful to hear from one of its spokesmen'.

The same month, a group of representatives of the Arbeitsfront, plus some German officials, visited the President of the Chambre Syndicale, Lucien Lelong, and revealed the Reich's decisions. 'Parisian *haute couture* will be integrated into a German organization with headquarters in Berlin and Vienna.'[3] French ateliers would supply the specialized workforce, and the creators of fashion would be moved from Paris to Vienna or Berlin, where prominent positions would be kept for them. The great Paris houses would thenceforth be deprived of their 'unfair' monopoly, which no longer corresponded to the needs of the new Europe of which Berlin, not Paris, would be the cultural and artistic centre. It was time to change places. A German French-language paper made no bones about the plan: 'Until now Paris has been the focus of the world in the realm of fashion, but the creators of the Seine have been clouded in their judgement of what is really beautiful, good and appropriate . . . Parisian fashion must pass by way of Berlin before a woman of taste can wear it.'[4]

Lucien Lelong's answer came loud and clear: 'You can impose anything on us by force but Parisian *haute couture* will not budge either as a whole or bit by bit. It is in Paris or it is nowhere.'[5] It was not within the power of any nation to rob France of the creative genius of fashion, which was not only a spontaneous explosion but the result of a tradition nurtured by a body of specialized male and female workers trained in a number of crafts. Although the German representatives appeared somewhat shaken, they let it be understood that Berlin was not ready to give in. One of them suggested that Lucien Lelong go to Germany and explain his point of view. Before agreeing, he met with his colleagues from the Chambre Syndicale at the end of October and informed them of his conversations and the threat looming over *couture*. 'The Germans,' he explained, 'want to seize a prestigious, eminently French, industry and steal a workforce which is unique in the world.'[6]

With the approval of both the Minister for Industrial Production and his peers, the *couturier* left for Berlin in November 1940 determined to defend French interests. Basing his argument on the fact that the Germans regarded fashion as a cultural activity, he claimed that each country had the right to create its 'own' fashion. Confronted with the men responsible for the textile industry who wanted an exchange of workforce and above all the organization of an Ecole Supérieure of *couture* in Berlin staffed by French experts, Lelong stated once again that the designers and workers would not be able to produce anything if they were removed from their familiar surroundings. It was up to German fashion – undergoing radical changes at that time, since the *couture* industry was being nationalized – to prove that it could make its mark without any influence from Paris.

Finally, with other things on their mind,[7] the Germans abandoned the plan to centralize the fashion trade in Vienna and Berlin. French fashion remained autonomous, preserving its own personnel and its own way of life.[8] But from that moment on it was buying time. The conqueror's calculations were clear. For the moment there was no need to abolish French *couture* with the stroke of a pen. It was better to let it play a secondary role, which would gradually lead to its collapse because, deprived of external outlets and quality material to enhance its creations, its opportunities would shrink and it would suffocate and die.

From then on, all Lucien Lelong's skill was mobilized to enable *haute couture* to survive, even if that meant a certain amount of cooperation with the Germans.

His primary idea was to make the concrete achievements of fashion as widely known as possible. At a time when textile rationing was threatening to bring Parisian *couture* to an abrupt halt, he thought it was essential 'to bear witness to its vitality, to demonstrate that French creations remain worthy of their past and that they intend to safeguard their future.'[9] In addition, in spring 1941 French fashion was not only subject to behind-the-scenes attack from the Germans, but it was the target of sharp criticism in the American press, which had no qualms about forecasting its disappearance, as is shown by this extract from a New York paper reprinted in *Les Nouveaux Temps*: 'American women who for years turned to Paris to discover the trends in dress are no longer looking in that direction. The artistic creation which flourished in the Rue de la Paix is dead.'[10] The leaders of *couture* were quick to reply. They initiated a publicity campaign on behalf of the luxury industries. Using radio, cinema and fashion journals – carefully chosen for their circulation in France and overseas – it stressed that French creation continued unabated.[11] 'We will let people know that all our quality industries are still alive, producing and creating. We will demonstrate the part that Group 1 industries (*couture*, fashion and jewellery) play in French business, and the importance of their national and social role. Our propaganda efforts must safeguard the diffusion of French fashion and maintain the prestige of those who inspire and create it. Our Group 1 industries represent as a whole "the train of quality", with creation as its driving force.'

In a letter of 6 March 1941 to M. Jarillot, head of Textiles and Leathers, Lucien Lelong asked for approval and an adequate budget to implement the plan.[12] Where the press was concerned, the aim was to obtain increased space and more pages devoted to the fashion houses, as well as some technical improvement in the presentation of designs in the issues of April, May and June 1941. Publications were selected for their aesthetic quality and their luxury clientèle (*Images de France, L'Art et la Mode, l'Officiel de la Couture, Votre Beauté*), or because they were homemakers' journals, 'interesting media', with a wide circulation and popular with the provincial public (*Modes et Travaux, La Femme Chic*). Overcoming the obstacle of German censorship, this propaganda campaign allowed *haute couture* to advertise its presence and to publicize the designs from the collections via photographs and press reports. Even *La Semaine,* known for its friendly attitude towards the occupier, devoted an entire report in its issue 38 of April 1941 'to the models of France', subtitled: 'The new spring gowns show that French taste lives on'. In *Votre Beauté* , an article entitled 'Smiles of Paris', by the reporter Lucien François, set the tone. He praised the spring 1941 collection highly:

> It has been proved yet again that in France nothing really perfect is produced unless it has to overcome all the odds. It is a long time since we have seen such elaborate collections, so refined in detail, so subtle in cut, despite . . . The *couturiers* have

– 87 –

performed miracles of grace, of creation, of rejuvenation, of invention, despite . . . Despite what? Despite the shortage and rationing of raw materials, despite the disappearance of the foreign clientèle, despite the limitation on the number of models . . . Despite the gloomy times, the Parisian creators were expected to do as well as usual; they have done better.[13]

La Femme Chic, a magazine which was very popular with provincial *couturiers*, reserved several special pages in its April issue to the collections of Jeanne Lanvin, Marcel Rochas and Jacques Fath. Lucien Lelong showed a collection 'in which the designs contain all the shades of the Paris sky, all the flowers of the Paris gardens. In a word, his creations are Paris in a nutshell.'[14]

At the same time, some of the dailies allocated increased space to fashion columns and carried a series of articles on the need to preserve *haute couture*. Similarly, *Les Nouveaux Temps*, countering American attacks (according to which French *haute couture* was now switched off) stated that 'this year the trend for the new fashions is still set by the French *couturiers*'. Best proof of this came from a radio report recorded in the *couture* houses by an American in Paris, Miss Carmel Snow, who paid homage to the designs created purely to save the honour of Paris.[15] Lucie Hirigoyen, who was in charge of the woman's column in *Le Matin*, defended fashion in lyrical mode. '*Couture* fulfils a considerable social function: not only does it represent the soul of France, the brain of Paris, but also the taste and skill of its craftsmen . . . Paris, France have a prestige to safeguard, a racial heritage to stand up for.'[16]

The publicity had been a success as it had allowed *haute couture* to display its work and hold its ground at a time when it was seriously threatened by American[17] and German competition.

The *couturiers* defended themselves against attacks, conscious that it was not only a question of safeguarding a heritage but also of practising their art. Even if the gowns and costumes were intended for only a tiny minority, what really mattered was that they were designed at all, because they were the guarantee of the taste and prestige of France. What mattered above all else was to demonstrate that, despite the constraints of shortages, despite the weight of the occupation, *haute couture* still occupied first place in the world, and that it formed an integral part of Paris – on the same footing as the capital's finest monuments. A few well-known journalists and writers had no hesitation in offering up their talents for the cause. The writer Colette recalled the narrow confines within which fashion is born:

The Paris of *haute couture* is really only a village. It begins at the Concorde bridge and ventures along the rue de Rivoli. Its grand canal flows along the rue de la Paix, washes both the place and the avenue de l'Opéra before a capricious loop returns to the boulevard, and skims the Madeleine; a considerable tide has washed over the faubourg Saint Honoré, the length of the Champs Elysées.[18]

In the front rank of the propagandists throughout these four years was the indefatigable Lucien François, who seized any pretext to defend the *couturiers*. A small anthology entitled *Cent Conseils d'Elégance*, which he published in 1942, contained not only the rules of good taste for the use of society ladies, but a few pages devoted to defining the role of Paris and *couture*. If the most subtle creations were born in Paris, it was because that city was at the heart of a highly civilized past. 'Served by the influences of a town that is more refined than any other, by the inspiration and choice of the most cultured women in the world, by the spirit and hands of the best craftsmen, the Parisian *couturiers* are incomparable.' And he did not hesitate to warn, in veiled terms, those who would like to appropriate such know-how or 'transfer' it elsewhere. 'But only a few seasons away from Paris, the most gifted of them seem to lose the happiest elements of their art.'[19] In *L'Eloge de Paris* he returned to the theme, extolling *haute couture*, 'the exporter of Parisian taste': 'Nowhere else does a woman find more ardent servants to her charm. Not just the Parisian lady . . . but women the world over: that woman who makes the most sensational entrance into the grandstand of the Catalan arena on the Sunday of a grand corrida, no less than her sister for whom the top Chicago food canner works his fingers to the bone.'

All these ideas were also expressed by Maggy Rouff, herself an expert and the author of an essay on *La Philosophie de l'élégance* in 1942. In the chapter on the *couturiers*, she likens them to 'an extremely sensitive and delicate engine'; its components could, if necessary, come from outside, but it absolutely had to be assembled in Paris. 'Even when construction is complete these machines are not exportable. It is a fact that in a foreign country the machinery runs amok, so that instead of dresses it produces rubbish or nothing at all.'[20]

This all went to prove that the capital, that favoured place of quality and excellence, contributed to the formation of a melting-pot in which fashion was forged. Germaine Beaumont threw herself into the battle, emphasizing how, like a rose, the dress worn for one day was both ephemeral and immortal, sustained by an immemorial culture that remained invincible in the midst of defeat.

> Such a little thing, so light and yet the sum of civilizations, the quintessence of equilibrium, of moderation, of grace . . . because a Paris gown is not really made of cloth, it is made with the streets, with the colonnades . . . it is gleaned from life and from books, from museums and from the unexpected events of the day. It is no more than a gown and yet the whole country has made this gown.[21]

Greatly hampered by the shortage of raw materials, the leaders of the Chambre Syndicale strove to convince the French authorities to agree to special regulations on behalf of a prestige industry that made a large contribution to France's reputation. The industry behind Parisian *haute couture* was a driving force that stimulated and generated a considerable number of the small businesses working for it (embroiderers, leather workers, jewellers, footwear specialists). If it were brought to a halt, a large number of skilled workers would be condemned to unemployment. But it was the arguments put forward by Lucien Lelong and Daniel Gorin that carried the day: production of *haute couture*, they reasoned, represented a minimum of materials for a maximum of workforce; that being so, a contribution representing a tiny subtraction of 0.5 per cent from all textile stocks would be enough to secure reduced but adequate activity on the part of *haute couture*.

Understanding the usefulness of maintaining, even within the strictest limits, a branch of production on which the reputation of French quality was based, the textiles distributor, Robert Carmichaël, agreed to a relaxation of the law of 11 February 1941 that introduced a system of ration cards. As a result, some *haute couture* houses, referred to as 'authorized houses', were assigned a rigidly fixed allocation of materials (60 per cent of 1938 wool consumption) and could continue to sell clothes to their clientèle without coupons.[22]

The press gave the following explanation for these regulations:

> Textile rationing would have greatly restricted Parisian *couture* if the law had not been relaxed in its favour. Before crying out at the injustice, one should give a moment's thought to what the luxury industry represents. By permitting *haute couture* to go on with its work, a whole economy and a highly qualified workforce can be maintained, thus preventing not only unemployment, but also the loss of skills and confidence in the craft.[23]

When clothing coupons were created in July 1941, a creative-*couture* ration card was sent to buyers of *haute couture* with strict conditions attached: a deduction of 50 per cent of the points on the individual's clothing card, a deduction of the letters A and B, which were essential for the exchange of two old garments for one new, and the payment of a tax. However, permission for this exception from the law also had to be obtained from the Germans. Originally they fixed the number of *haute couture* houses at thirty. 'Thirty *couturiers* have been chosen and authorized to continue their creative work. They will only use 50 per cent of the fabric that they used before the war.'[24] Faced with this decision, the leading figures in the *couture* world stressed that there was a social and professional need to extend the privilege to smaller, even medium-sized, houses. Negotiations began with the occupation authorities for the extension of the list, which after much discussion was increased to 85 in June 1941. The occupying power continually tried to reduce the quota of privileged houses, challenging its very principle. In November 1941 the figure was no more than 71; it fell to 47 in March 1943, and then stabilized at around 54 from September 1943. Despite this, the relaxation of the law saved *haute couture* from disappearing, because 100 tons of raw material a month was enough to keep 97 per cent of the workforce, or 12,000 women, employed. It also made it possible to preserve a form of production based on seasonal collections as well as their sale to a specific clientèle. In spring 1943 the Vichy government filled in the gaps in the system by rearranging the statutes of the profession on the basis of a decision by Jean Bichelonne. Thenceforth, ready-made dresses, dress-making and *haute couture* had to obey to precise criteria.

As was to be expected, the system aroused envy. Hermès and Lanvin, which had branches in the provinces, wanted their branches in Nice and Cannes to enjoy the same privileges. Jean Jardin[25] even offered to lobby the head of Groupe-creation, but without success.[26] In Tours a revolt broke out among *couturiers* who loudly demanded the same privileges as their Parisian colleagues, arguing that they too had great difficulty in surviving and that, without help, all provincial creativity would come to an end. Their case was also rejected.

The introduction of rulings that were favourable to Parisian *haute couture* (the institution of a creative *couture* ration card, the allocation of a percentage of raw materials) was accompanied by strict regulation of the composition and present-ation of the collections. In 1941–2 couturiers were not allowed to produce more than 100 designs (this fell to seventy-five in 1942, then to sixty in 1944) and had to observe a discipline of economy from the moment of conception. In effect the provisions of the regulation

1) limited the proportion of designs using fabrics containing wool;
2) fixed maximum lengths of fabric for each type of these designs, taking into account as fairly as possible the specific needs of creation and the work on order.[27]

The purpose behind these decisions was, first, to prompt creative fashion to use the new textiles, but also to prevent the special rulings taken in favour of *haute couture* from going beyond certain limits. Compulsory dates were fixed in spring and autumn outside of which *couturiers* could not present collections in private or public or to the press. In addition, to protect certain craftsmen from redundancy, it was decided in 1942 that every collection must comprise a minimum of:

a) one design containing lace,
b) one design made entirely of lace,
c) one tulle design in which the fabric is the main material and not merely decorative,
d) 10 per cent of designs must include embroidery. For at least two of these models the embroidery must be made a dominant feature (art. 6).[28]

A maximum length of material was set for garments made in woollen cloth (3.25 m, and 1.40 m wide, for a gown; 4.25 m, and 1.40 m wide, for a coat; 3.75 m for a costume); if a garment exceeded these lengths, the deviation had to be justified.

Lastly, the *couture* houses had to keep a register in which they entered the number of the design, its type, the references, the description and length of the fabric used, and the customer's name. The register was available for inspection. Lucien Lelong was very aware of the difficulties that these authoritarian measures created, but hoped that they would also have beneficial consequences, as challenges to the creators' ingenuity and talent for research.

The propaganda and the relaxation of the law served the *couturiers'* immediate interests and helped to keep German acquisitiveness at bay, but the head of the creative-*couture* group also wanted to preserve the future at any cost. *Haute couture* constituted an asset that had to be put in apparent cold storage, in order to be defrosted at the earliest possible opportunity. When faced with the German prohibition of French exports, Lucien Lelong chose to react indirectly. He organized a fashion show in Lyons in the free zone in March 1942 in which some twenty *couturiers* participated. He explained the reasons behind his actions in a letter to M Jacques Deligny, director of the Comité d'Organisation du Vêtement in February 1942:

> There will be nothing spectacular about these shows . . . What we are trying to do is to meet the wishes often expressed by the *couturiers* in the free zone and by the buyers themselves, by giving them access to the ideas which they need and of which they are deprived. In this way, Parisian *couture* is making the gesture of solidarity which the *couturiers* in the non-occupied zone are constantly demanding.[29]

Lelong hoped that the show would be a means of reaching part of the neutral international clientèle: Swiss, Spaniards, etc . . . In order to divert German suspicions, he placed the exhibition under the aegis of Secours national, and made it seem like an artistic event. A gala was arranged in which Serge Lifar participated.[30] Nevertheless one considerable problem remained: obtaining 200 passes for the *couture* personnel, the models and a troupe from the Opéra. After sounding out Dr Mömm, head of the textile service, who showed no great enthusiasm, the *couturier* turned to a Frenchman, the Prince of Beauvau-Craon. The Prince organized the 'Round Table Lunches' at which some twenty French personalities and the same number of Germans from the world of trade and industry met regularly from February to October 1942. One purpose of these meetings was to bring a variety of people together, giving them the chance to settle their minor differences in a friendly way. Lelong asked the Prince to invite him to the next meeting, planned for February 1942 in the salons of the Ritz hotel, Place Vendôme, and to seat him next to a German administrative authority from the Majestic so that he could talk to him. This made it much easier to obtain a pass, but at the Liberation Lelong was to stand trial as a participant in the famous 'Round Table Lunches'.[31] The case ended when the charge against Lucien Lelong was dismissed, but it showed how far some leaders of industry would go to safeguard the future of their sector, even if it meant compromising themselves with the Germans in the process.

On 6 March models, *couturiers* and personnel, representing nineteen well-known houses, took a train to Lyons and crossed the demarcation line between occupied and non-occupied zones without mishap. Several newspapers publicized the event, backed up by photographs.[32] The Parisian dailies captured the departure of the 'ambassadors of charm' on film, and *Marie-Claire* dedicated to *haute couture* a report entitled 'Paris visits her twin sister, Lyons. Place Vendôme expands to include place Bellecour'.[33]

In order not to shock people who were not in a position to treat themselves to luxury designs or even simply renew their wardrobes, the plan was to avoid all excess and to grant entry to the reserved enclosure only to buyers and *couturiers*. Furthermore, the Comité d'Organisation du Vêtement ordered that it be specifically stated that houses showing collections were sharing the costs. Three hundred to 350 professionals from neutral countries – Switzerland, Spain, Portugal, Turkey, North Africa – thronged the Lyons Palais de la Foire, and the exhibition of designs, hats and accessories was a success.

> The general style [of the collection] tends towards simplicity, without the slightest trace of eccentricity: the line is straight, the waist in its rightful place, the shoulders very wide, the fullness, where there is any, is gathered in the front or at the back. The great innovation are the 'basques', the long, very clinging tunics which almost all the *couturiers* have adopted. Some refinement of detail can be noted but without excess. Here, it is moderation that reigns, harmony, and that inimitable simplicity in which Paris attains perfection. [This is the proof that] Paris fashion makes light of the problems and retains its rich powers of invention through thick and thin, ready to bloom again as soon as circumstances permit.[34]

As the Germans virtually prevented *haute couture* from exporting its production by reducing its textile allocation, the *couturiers* sold ideas for gowns, paper or cloth patterns, on the spot. The scheme succeeded perfectly. On his return, Lelong was summoned to the Majestic by the German authorities responsible for clothing (probably Dr Michel and his assistant Dr Mömm), who were well informed and took him to task for misleading them and, in passing, reminded him that Berlin, Vienna and Italy reserved the sole right to fashion shows in the European capitals. Observers from Germany asked to be shown the collections. Their brief was to decide whether the time had come to deal the death blow to an art that was proving decidedly too robust.

Despite all their efforts to destroy an awkward rival, the Germans had achieved nothing. They had been not been able to fathom the secrets of the crafts so that they could appropriate them. Visiting the atelier where Jacques Delamare and his mother Noémie Fromentin painted delicate flowers on velvet or silk, a group of German industrialists demanded to be shown the tools needed to produce these miniature masterpieces and to be given a detailed explanation of how to achieve such marvels. Waving her hands in front of the stupefied spectators Fromentin finally said: 'These are my most valuable possession'. They left without uttering a word.[35]

Nevertheless, they did not give in. Instead they redoubled their efforts to take hold of *couture*, this time by indirect means. They could, for example, be found taking a close interest in a closely related area, such as fashion journals. A large fashion publishing house, Editions Gustav Lyon, already existed in Berlin before the war. As the agent for Europe of a company called La Mode Artistique,[36] it edited and printed fashion catalogues in French, including *Idéal Parisien, Paris Chic, Toilettes Modernes* and *Favorites*. The business, headed by a French Jew, Louis Joseph, owned a considerable number of branches throughout Europe, in Vienna, Munich, Milan, Brussels and Paris, from where they published inter alia *La Coquette*, a monthly journal under German influence. In 1938, antisemitic legislation forced Louis Joseph to leave Germany and to put his commercial interests in the hands of 'trustworthy persons'.[37]

Obviously the occupation offered a springboard for the Germans to increase their hold on the French branch. Under cover of La Mode Artistique, which had become a limited company established at 5 Rue Mayran in Paris and now distributed some fifty titles, the Germans set about producing fashion journals that plagiarized French fashion. When they were not trying to poach French model makers and dress designers, they were borrowing their ideas and designs.

In 1940 the journal *La Coquette* continued to be printed in Paris with photographs taken in Vienna and designs executed in the capital. On page four it described itself as a 'French magazine for the whole world published in Paris'. (The same journal appeared in German under the name of *Modenschau*.) From 1941 the name of the publication changed to *La Femme Elégante*. Other magazines – *Mode Idéale, Elites, Juno* – were sold in France and abroad, stating that they were 'printed in Vienna (Germany)' on the first page, and with the name of the Managing Director, M Bilcard, Ed. Gustav Lyon, Paris-Berlin, on the cover. (The publications were still being distributed in 1944, when they bore the name of a new printer, Primo Semini, located in Zurich.)

A business claiming to offer a Paris *couture* and fashion service was set up at 111 Rue Réaumur and took over the distribution of the German continental press during the occupation (hence its name Conti-Press). Some slightly misleading publicity in 1943 proclaimed that the most famous fashion experts worked for Conti-Press publications, distributed throughout France, and that these publications were the emissaries of good taste. For example:

Smart, Smaart, that word means spruce, spick and span, well-dressed, chic, elegant. All these qualities appear for your delight in this fashion publication distributed by Conti-Press. Designs that are attractive but in a quiet, stylish, almost sober key, which is the real characteristic of chic elegance, of the fine turn-out so dear to our good French citizens.

On several occasions – in May 1943, and again in July 1943 – when the Paris fashion magazines could not reach the southern zone, the company managed to obtain authorization from the ambassador, Fernand de Brinon,[38] to distribute journals such as *La Viennoise Elégante* and *La Mode Favorite*. It is interesting to see the cautious tactics adopted by the authorities, who were disturbed when now and then they saw, as a subtitle, the comment: 'Too explicitly German in origin'. In July 1943 they demanded that the words be withdrawn so as not to hamper sales to French male and female readers. (This explains why *La Viennoise Elégante* became simply *L'Elégante*.) The tone and the contents, however, left little room for doubt about their origins, as in the following example plucked from these journals:

We do not relish the useless extravagance and frippery of an over-frivolous fashion, yet the creative imagination remains intact. Its elan only slightly restrained, it sets out on a new path more adapted to our times. Here fashion yields to the magical command of restrictions, but does not abandon the graceful elan of the silhouettes.[39]

Or again these descriptions of designs: 'Youthful summer dress, in two tones of dotted crepe, light-coloured or dark coloured, with an extended yoke over the centre front'.[40] And 'This gown, made of a pretty silk fabric, shows a little cape which falls on to the back, its folds held in place by bows on the shoulders.'

Whereas the Germans facilitated the circulation of their own publications, they strictly limited the number of French fashion journals. The wish to supplant the French in the art of fashion drove them to extend their hold over the women's press, which was subject to the general system in force and had to obtain permission from the German censor to be printed, a permission granted with greater or lesser speed depending on the individual case. Month after month the paper allocation fell until a point when some titles were forced to cease publication. *L'Art et la Mode*,[41] one of the oldest *couture* magazines, which reached a very specialized public, was the first to file a request to come out with the Propaganda Staffel service (15 July 1940) – and to obtain it. In return, the Germans obliged it to print the captions to designs in German; the editor agreed, but suggested that these captions also appeared in French and English on account of her very large overseas readership (English, American), which gave rise to endless discussions. Much envied because of its presentation and its 'Americanized' look, *L'Officiel de la Couture et de la Mode*[42] obtained permission to appear only in February 1941. A real shop-window of *haute couture*, the magazine was closely supervised, and was suspended in May 1941, then again in May 1942 for not being sufficiently amenable. Moreover, on three occasions it was obliged to insert advertising on behalf of German milliners. Thus, the January 1942 issue contained an advertisement for a famous milliner, 'Wittmer & Co', established in Berlin, Ritterstrasse 46–47. Lucien François's magazine, *Votre Beauté*,[43] succeeded in preserving its independence, but only at the price of several suspensions for refusing to publish German propaganda. Not content with applying constraints, the Abteilung department resorted to more subtle means to tighten its stranglehold on the women's press, as it was doing with the Parisian press in general. Dr Hibbelen was given the task of discreetly forming a group of companies with a financial interest in the publication of magazines.

In this respect their attitude to magazines with large readerships, such as *Modes et Travaux* and *Le Petit Echo de la Mode*, is very revealing. They proposed financial collaboration on very favourable terms. Deaf to these appeals, E. Boucherit at the head of *Modes et Travaux*, was subjected to repeated harassment, but he did not give in. A similar attitude can be sensed among those responsible for *Petit Echo de la Mode,* which strove to maintain a strict neutrality. Other titles did not demonstrate the same scruples. Such was the case, for example, with *Dimanches de la Femme* and *Notre Cœur*, which came under German control.

Lastly, the occupier tried at all costs to seize French companies which published fashion patterns. It tried to approach Editions Marcel Daubin, which preferred to wind up its affairs rather than collaborate.

Propped up by the fashion editors and journalists, *haute couture* managed to avoid all the traps. Even when Lucien Lelong was no longer in a position to reproduce his publicity coup of spring 1942, an album reproducing the Paris creators' designs was published in Monte Carlo with infinite care and widely distributed abroad. (Three volumes later appeared at six month intervals: in spring 1943 and spring and autumn 1944.) The Germans retaliated in February 1943 by prohibiting the publication of photographs of designs. Meanwhile, two tendencies appeared in the ranks of the conquerors at this point in time. Whereas people in Berlin continued to think that German fashion would eclipse French fashion, in Paris the authorities appointed by the occupier began to understand that the Berlin experiment had failed and that Parisian fashion was surviving all the problems it encountered. From this they concluded that the really clever thing to do would be to allow it to continue in order to turn the export potential of the Parisian *couturiers* to the benefit of the German economy when the time was ripe.

Haute couture's situation deteriorated further in February 1943 when it was theoretically forbidden to use any form of publicity. Lucien Lelong was warned that Berlin had given the order to close the fashion ateliers altogether. By employing evasive tactics he succeeded in obtaining a reprieve. Forty-seven houses had a right to continue their activities – half the previous number – while awaiting a definitive ruling on their fate.

To this end, a meeting was arranged in Paris between Dr Schilling and Jacques Deligny, who since July 1942 was in charge of the Comité d'Organisation de l'Habillement et du Travail des Étoffes.[44] On 14 April 1943[45] the two men met in the Majestic. Schilling's position was clear: given that almost all the Berlin *couture* houses were closed, it would be difficult to make it known to these businesses that the Parisian *couturiers* remained open, unless the latter agreed to accept a change of direction. It was high time they made a useful contribution to the European economy – for example by expanding their exporting activities to countries such as Sweden, Spain, Italy and Portugal.

The Germans therefore considered forming a 'continental consortium' in Berlin, a trading concern that would take over items of *haute couture* produced in France for resale overseas. An overall plan would be drawn up for the ateliers integrated into the scheme and a cloth quota fixed annually. At Deligny's request, Dr Schilling confirmed that the Parisian *couture* houses would be able to continue to work for their special clientèle to an as yet undetermined, but probably tiny, degree. The discussion also touched on the problem of the fashion journals: all except two were banned in Germany so what possible reason could there be, Schilling demanded, for maintaining this type of publication in France when paper was becoming increasingly scarce? Deligny successfully pleaded the cause of the low-price magazines, which contained patterns that were simple to make up, on the grounds that they played an irreplaceable role serving the general public. Before they parted, they once again went over the use of the minimum amount of fabrics to make *haute couture* designs, the occupier significantly complicating the task of the creators, who were up in arms in the name 'of the principle of freedom of inspiration'.

A year later, in May 1944, when German towns came under heavy Anglo-American air raids, Berlin suggested making the French *couturiers* work for the victims of the Allies' bombardment.[46] On 25 July 1944, the Germans let it be known that because of the lack of valid proposals from the French for clothing the German victims, they had decided to reduce the purchasing power of each creative *couture* card to two items. In addition, they required French fashion, merged with Viennese and Berlin *couture*, to participate in the promotional exhibition in Stockholm planned for July 1944. That would have been well and truly the end of independent French *couture*. In August 1944 the extreme limit of the arguments, delaying tactics and refusals had been reached.

Like a large number of French industries, *haute couture* was subject to authoritarian rulings, such as the requisitioning of manpower. Some large footwear factories,[47] which guaranteed a production programme for the Reich, were able to preserve their personnel intact when threatened by these measures, because they benefited from a form of protection from S. Betrieb.

The fur sector, where the majority of businesses were Jewish and employed less than ten wage earners, presented the occupiers and their spokesmen with a dilemma. The Germans needed fur craftsmen because they were the only people who knew how to make the jackets, gloves and warm clothing indispensable for the soldiers fighting on the Russian front. Hence the decision taken by Inspector Rieger of the Rüstungskommando at the end of September 1942 'specifying that, by a special decision of the Sûreté department, Jewish workers in fur businesses are assured of their position', that is to say, protected on condition that they were not in contact with the public. The following examples illustrate the matter: 'I the under-signed Compagnie Franco-Canadienne de Fourrure et Pelleteries, 15 Rue de Paradis in Paris, certify that I have employed Monsieur Woda, living at 43 Rue Piat in Paris, since 13 March 1942 in the capacity of a home worker for the production of rabbitskin waistcoats ordered by the Wehrmacht Beschaffungsamt'. Or again: 'I the undersigned Hélène Jiday certify that Monsieur Maurice, residing at 191 rue Lafayette, works for me on a product destined for the German authorities. This worker is not in contact with the public.' In March 1943, 325 furriers were freed from the Drancy concentration camp in order to work for the Germans.[48] The *couture* workshops were more vulnerable because they did not work directly for the Germans. In February 1943 the *couture* houses received individual summonses from the German employment offices, which sent them a questionnaire on which they had to list their male and female staff. The size of the staff reduction was determined in an arbitrary fashion by each employment office. Some were fixed at 10 per cent, others at 80 per cent. Lucien Lelong prevented all the houses returning their lists and embarked on discussions both with the employment office of the Chamber of Deputies and those in Rue Scribe and Rue de l'Université in order to obtain a blanket reduction of 10 per cent. He refused to hand over the lists unless he obtained satisfaction. In the event, the requisition of manpower from *couture* never exceeded 5 per cent.

On another front, the creative *couture* group succeeded in avoiding the scheme aimed at merging businesses by citing two solid arguments, developed by Daniel Gorin, Secretary General of the Chambre Syndicale: first, its artisanal nature and, secondly, its high proportion of female workers: 'Our group is essentially artisanal, a proportion of 87 per cent . . . The aim of the merger is to economize on raw materials (coal, electricity). But as production by our group is carried out by hand and individually, it only consumes a minimum of power . . .'[49] In short, these industries presented to the highest degree the characteristics quoted in the list of features that qualified for exemption from any merger: 'low consumption of materials in relation to the workforce employed' and 'production of luxury items being assured of a dominant place on the world market'. In the end, the Germans acknowledged that the working conditions of 'the manufacturers of made-to-measure clothes' rendered useless any scheme to organize production. However, businesses making ready-made male and female clothing were affected by the merger;[50] in particular, businesses managed by Jews and those that used tailors working from home. 'The image of the little Jewish tailor . . . was the target of calls for relentless extermination. The small family workshop set up in a concierge's lodge . . . was eradicated from the production scene . . . a considerable reduction ensued . . . both in women's clothing and men's suits: "the industry which produced twenty million items in 1938 delivered no more than 5,800,000 in 1943."'[51]

Although there is plenty of information on the overall conduct of *haute couture* during the war, and particularly on its relations with the occupier, it is more difficult to discern the attitude of individual houses during the same period. The Germans undoubtedly tried to give privileged status to one or other of them on an individual basis. This formed part of their general strategy to infiltrate everywhere they could. How were their advances received? Archive documents and evidence show that there were 'degrees' of understanding between the two parties. They ranged from polite refusal to full and entire cooperation and, in between, a minimum of compliance.

Thus the designer Alice Barton, better known as Madame Grès, opened her own atelier[52] in 1942, borrowing from her husband, the painter Serge Czrefou. From her very first collection she exasperated the Germans, who wanted to close the atelier, outraged by the patriotic nature of the blue, white and red gowns they saw filing past. Moreover, the designer defied the prohibitions that imposed strict rules on lengths of fabrics and hardly bothered about the restrictions. In the name of freedom of inspiration she was determined to stay faithful to the skilful draping on which her fame was based. In January 1944, the Germans ordered the house of Grès – 1 Rue de la Paix – to be closed on the grounds that it did not respect the regulations in force.[53] It reopened in March the same year on condition that it abandoned the technique on which the value of its creations was based – which limited its margin of manoeuvre.

Another *couturier*, Cristobal Balenciaga, of Spanish origin, and a refugee in Paris since 1936, was also subject to close surveillance and had to give up practising his art. After the Spanish ambassador intervened, he was able to resume work in 1944. Noteworthy was the attitude of their colleagues who, out of solidarity, gave them part of their cloth quota to enable them to show their collections.[54] As for Anita de Pombo, known as Anite of Spain, she fled, just in time to escape arrest by the Gestapo.

New houses opened or re-opened, directed by former heads of ateliers. One such was Marcelle Chaumont. After a long period working with Madeleine Vionnet, who left at the beginning of the war, Marcelle Chaumont created her own *couture* salon at the end of 1940 at 19 Avenue Georges V. She showed a great deal of courage in continuing to produce in the difficult conditions, supported by some of Madeleine Vionnet's staff that she managed to gather together after the liquidation of the atelier. With no money, no publicity and with synthetic materials and an under-fed workforce, she did her utmost to keep the standard of designs high. Two models, Antoinette and Marcelle bore the heavy responsibility of showing the collection to its best advantage.[55] Marcelle Dormoy, also a former member of the Vionnet team, followed the recommendations of Lucien Lelong, who in 1939–40 had advised *couture* to settle in Biarritz in order to be able to maintain contact with the outside world. Returning to Paris, she resumed activities at 22 Rue de la Trémoille. Working in the spirit of Edward Molyneux, the designs she produced were simple but in good taste. She was one of the very first to launch 'robes-culottes' cut from the modern fabrics, like the djersamix from Rodier. Many talented young designers – who would certainly become great assets after the war – passed through her workshop, bringing her their sketches. They included Alice Le Bris-Lehmans who joined in 1942.[56] The *couturière* dressed several actresses, including Edwige Feuillère and Lise Delamare, and also worked for the cinema.

A few big names, like Schiaparelli, Chanel and Molyneux, ceased part of their activities during these four years. In June 1940 the *couturière* known as 'the Italian' left for a tour in the United States from which she returned in January 1941, but only for a few months. Her house remained open under the management of Countess Haydn.

> Work was going on in an infinitesimal way . . . The French were working to keep themselves and their families and their country alive, thus following the oldest instinct in the world. If they had stopped everything and if the Germans had turned France into a vast cemetery, what good would that have done? Either you kept the door of your business open, or you threw your people out of work. As for the doors of your private home, that was a different matter.[57]

By May she was to be found in New York with a *couture* house in her own name.

Although Gabrielle Chanel closed the atelier in rue Cambon, at least the perfume and accessories boutique remained open! Before the war, the capital of the prestigious trademark had been divided up as follows: Mademoiselle Chanel, 10 per cent; the Wertheimer brothers, 70 per cent; and the Bader-Galeries Lafayette group, 20 per cent. Totally absorbed in her liaison with a German officer, Hans Günther von Dincklage, called Spatz, 'Mademoiselle' no longer bothered about couture and travelled a great deal.[58] When the laws that eliminated Jews from all the economic life of the nation were decreed, she tried to recover the perfume company, which she had given over to the Wertheimer brothers. In April 1940, however, the brothers had left France for the United States and had given full powers to represent them to their manager Petit-Barral. A contract for sale to Félix Amiot was completed. 'Nevertheless, it seems that at the time of the transfer of the capital of the house into non-Jewish hands, Mademoiselle Chanel tried to regain control of the firm which bears her name with German support. This seems to be demonstrated by a note from the Ministry of Finance which mentions the nature of the relations between the occupier and Chanel.' Chanel's attempt to recover the business failed because of the presence of Félix Amiot, who held the largest share of the capital.[59]

No qualms of conscience embarrassed the young Jacques Fath, who had just started up in 1939. Called up in 1939–40, the *couturier* re-opened his house in 1941. He moved to 48 Rue François I in August that year and employed a skilled staff drawn from other Paris houses that had closed for various reasons. The number of his workers increased from 176 in 1942 to 193 in 1943 and then to 244 in 1944.[60] What mattered most to this talented creator was to practice his art and to sell. It was unimportant who bought. The main thing was to do business, even if it was with the occupiers or with traders on the black market. He and his wife were at every Franco-German gathering and made themselves conspicuous by their regular attendance. Madame Jacques Fath, Geneviève, was very pretty. She was repeatedly photographed at the Longchamp races in June 1941. She posed for the cover of the magazine *Pour Elle* in March 1942. Jacques Fath did not hesitate to join the Cercle Européen, a group that collaborated with the Germans, and his wife was not far behind as she maintained business connections with the German purchasing office set up in Rue Vernet in Paris and headed by a certain Zalhoum. Jacque Fath's creations were reproduced and discussed in both the French and German press. On 2 May 1941, for example, *Je Suis Partout* warmly welcomed the house's productions.

Maggy Rouff's position was ambiguous. She was very attached to the defence of her art and of tradition, but on several occasions the Germans claimed that she was the only reliable spokesperson, which suggests that there was at least a certain compliance on her part. Moreover, it is known that these gentlemen proved very assiduous in their attendance at her boutique when she showed her collections.

As far as Marcel Rochas was concerned, all the evidence points to his opportunist attitude towards the occupier, to whom he made innumerable pledges. On 15 October 1937, the German magazine *Die Dame* described him as 'the youngest of the Parisian *couturiers*, with square shoulders, suntanned, with shiny black hair and sparkling white teeth'. *La Semaine* on 3 April 1941 devoted an illustrated article to the man it called 'the prince of Parisian *couture*': Marcel Rochas. When the Jews were forced to wear the yellow star, he no longer greeted even good customers and friends because they were Jewish and crossed the road to avoid catching their eye when he chanced to meet them in the avenue Montaigne.[61] It was rumoured that his dearest dream was to open a *couture* house in Berlin. In all other respects, however, Marcel Rochas stood out as one of the most gifted designers of his generation. In 1942, inspired by Mae West, he produced the famous bustier (long-line strapless top) that went round the world. In 1941, he was also the first to create a cinema department. He took part in Jean Cocteau's film *L'Eternel Retour*, for which he dressed Madeleine Sologne. Danièle Darrieux, Jacqueline Delubac and Micheline Presle were among his most loyal clients. In 1945 the house employed 200 women workers.

Maggy Rouff and Marcel Rochas were the only *couturiers* to present a private show of designs cut from the new materials to high German dignitaries in November 1940. No comparable actions are attributed to Jeanne Lanvin, who was content with minimal relations with the conqueror.

As for the *couturier* Jacques Heim, his name was enough to make him a target. He was put under strict German surveillance. 'This Jewish businessman is very actively engaged against the army of occupation and travels around freely,' comments a hand-written note dated July 1941 and preserved in the dossiers of the Majestic,[62] and an investigation showed him involved in spreading Gaullist propaganda and owning two business houses, one in Paris – 13 Avenue Matignon – the other in Biarritz. The conclusion recommends 'arresting the *couturier* and his family, moving them out of Paris and putting them under house arrest in a small village 200 or 300 kilometres from Paris.'

In addition, in December 1940, a short paragraph appeared in *La Gerbe* mentioning that 'the house of Jacques Heim is no longer a Jewish house', which was an indirect way of explaining that the creator had become a victim of the aryanization laws[63] – an operation intended to eliminate 'Jewish influence' from the economy – and forced to give way to a provisional administrator, an aryan. Being Jewish, he was forbidden to do business. And the journalist concluded: 'Madame Jacques Heim has a very aryan profile. She is also charming.'[64]

In the luxury trade, aryanization was a practice that caused little shock. Some people profoundly hoped for what they call 'cleansing'. François Ribadeau-Dumas, for example, wrote in November 1940: 'France will be saved and will be rebuilt by elements that are intrinsically her own; the essentials are French blood and the French brain. The moment the foreign houses are closed, and the more than questionable Jewish houses disappear, the atmosphere of the Parisian luxury trade will be purified!'[65] In these circumstances it is not surprising that this manoeuvre succeeded.

Closely linked to *haute couture*, with which it maintained very close relations, the fur trade was quick to become the target of German greed. The clauses of the armistice of 25 June 1940 gave the Reich the right to demand delivery of a considerable portion of the stocks of furs and skins in France, and the occupiers were more than ready to do just that. They were not embarrassed to exercise this right. The German

Jeanne LANVIN

Maggy ROUFF

PAQUIN

Lucien LELONG

Taken from *Nouveaux Temps*, 17 March 1944.

delegate of the Occupation authorities with special responsibility for this area –
Dr Hollander from Leipzig – seems to have been well informed: he valued total
French fine skins and leather at 500 million francs, which allowed him to make
enormous demands. In the end, after some discussion, he lowered his claim to 50
million then to 40 million francs. An agreement was concluded on 3 December
1940,[66] whereby Germany pledged to make no further requisitions of fine furs after
this delivery. As for rabbit skins, the conqueror estimated production at 80 million
skins, of which he demanded half.

The fact remains that the fur trade, more than any other business, was open to
compromise. What can one say about the attitude of a certain great Parisian house

which, almost as soon as the Germans arrived in Paris, offered the wives of dignitaries in office some twenty fur coats? What is one to think of the purchases that one Monsieur Maerz, an accredited German, made quite freely in his capacity as exclusive buyer, acting on behalf of his compatriot furriers? He faced French negotiators prepared to sell at any price and whose turnovers[67] clearly proved that they were not troubled by scruples (their sales more than tripled between 1942 and 1943). The deliveries were made to the house of Simone Vita, 19 Avenue de l'Opéra, which centralized purchases, organized the dispatch and made payments. How can one describe the conduct of certain establishments, including Révillon and Toutmain, which agreed to make fur waistcoats for the German army on the Eastern front, thus helping to equip the enemy – and doing so in June 1942 when the French population was vainly seeking means of shelter against the cold of the coming winter, and when propaganda frequently repeated the need to make sacrifices.

Lastly, considering the large number of Jewish furriers[68] settled both in Paris and in the provinces,[69] the racial legislation operated to the full in both the occupied and in the free zones, to the advantage of a very small number of privileged individuals often positioned in the structures of officialdom. Some people found the disappearance of certain fur houses regrettable; many others regarded it as a measure of the healthy state of the industry, as this quotation from the professional press shows: 'Present circumstances have made more than one French furrier understand that they had been exploited by undesirable elements with a genial smile, accompanied by a plentiful and pleasant lunch.'[70] A number of provisional administrators owned large fur houses. The house of Renel, for example, 5 Avenue Victor Hugo, had been bought on behalf of the company belonging to Roger Binet, president of the Comité d'organisation Pelleteries et Fourruress.[71] Jean-Marie Révillon[72] administered Fourrures Brunswick, 63 Boulevard de Strasbourg,[73] and a large number of other establishments. Their names, as well as those of André Reynié and Léon Cassier, appeared frequently as administrators.

In the Alpes-Maritimes, in Nice, more than thirty establishments were provided with temporary administrators. Although certain businesses were the object of fictitious sales, most had been sold openly and legitimately. Significant in this regard is the example of the house of Toutmain. The business went through the aryanization process in both Paris and the provinces (Marseilles, Nice, Vichy). The Paris staff was investigated. It consisted of 83 persons: '6 department managers or senior employees, 41 employees and 36 male and female workers'; or 74 aryans, four Jews and five cases of 'questionable origin'. Care was taken to state that the Jewish staff had no contact with the public. The case of Madame Carpe, a saleslady, aroused some discussion; dismissed at first, she was reinstated because she had lost her husband in 1914–18 and her son during the 1939–40 war. The temporary administrator wrote to the Commissariat Général aux Questions Juives about her case, stressing that she had no resources other than her work and had asked to be reinstated in a department where 'she would have no contact with the public'.[74] Significantly, the houses of Révillon and Toutmain suffered a great deal of sabotage organized by the immigrant resistance movement aimed at reducing their production. At the end of the day, the Germans were actually the winners at every level: on one hand the furs were sold to their compatriots at cost price and, on the other, they recouped the product of the sale on the grounds that it was enemy property.

This survey would not be complete if it failed to mention the importance of the black market, which involved such enormous quantities of goods that even the men responsible for the Peaux et Fourrures sector were worried. In January 1942 one of them gave a figure of 1.5 million skins and demanded counter-measures in vain.

But furs were not a unique case. Other raw materials used in the luxury industries were involved in underground deals that often were not squeaky clean. This was the case with silk, which felt the full force of the shortages because of the halt in imports from Japan and Italy. Before the war, consumption reached 2,000 tonnes; subsequently it barely amounted to 180. But, in June 1940, at the request of Marshal Gœring, a commission for purchases intended for Zentraltex in Berlin was set up in Paris under cover of the concern 'Les Fantaisies Textiles'[75] situated at 15 Rue du Helder. It was instructed in particular to carry out purchases of high-priced textiles (natural silk, squares or scarves, lace). The commission proceeded to Lyons where it operated completely undisturbed for several months, seizing large quantities of merchandise. When, in June 1941, Robert Carmichaël was informed of the situation and asked for an inquiry, he was told by the German in charge, Hartman himself, that the director of the Comité d'Organisation of the silk sector, Jean Barioz, was aware of the transactions and had not protested. Moreover, 'these sales are regular sales since they do not involve rationed materials nor have they been the subject of exemptions from the law on the part of the Vichy government'. It was left to the authorities at the Majestic to specify, 'It is difficult to exercise supervision since the suppliers figure under reference numbers.' Only the German orders made in May 1941 to the houses of G. Fortier and Rodier and the Establissements Colcombet are known. In fact, nearly forty enterprises were involved in the matter.

Like the whole French economy, the luxury enterprises were brought face to face with the Germans. Quite often their attitude was characterized by compliance with the occupier, in the hope, they explained in 1945, of ensuring some, albeit reduced, activity for the profession. It was certainly difficult in this period of the occupation to run a business without serving German interests; nevertheless, it was one thing to be forced to adopt this option, another to create it. This was the whole problem. Roger Binet at the head of the Comité d'Organisation Pelleteries et Fourrures, and

Roger Ribes, who ran the Comité d'Organisation du Cuir, said in their defence that they did everything to delay the seizures ordered by the Reich being carried out.[76] They were rather quick to forget that at the same time they did not hesitate to conceal certain practices, in particular the German orders – the one, for example, that the house of Hübner in Berlin placed with the French furriers in March 1942 – to the point where it might be suggested that during this period there was a sort of 'international ring of the wealthy' motivated solely by profit.

Every attitude therefore co-existed in *haute couture* as it did in French society in general. It recalls the modes of accommodation which Jacques Sémelin speaks of and which Philippe Burrin has explained at length.[77] Lucien Lelong chose the path of minimal cooperation to safeguard the cultural heritage of his sector as well as its workforce, and this was acknowledged in 1945 by the judgement that acquitted him. Other *couture* houses openly put their bets on a German victory and made a lot of money, profiting from every occasion without scruples. On the other hand, some continued to work but resisted in their own way by taking no notice of German directives. Between the two, the moderates held on for better days, contenting themselves with a minimum of cooperation.

–7–

Fashionable Paris Dresses Up

That *haute couture* managed to survive during these dark years while everyone or almost everyone condemned it was partly due to skilful propaganda directed at its clientèle. Despite some reservations, the efforts made from the time of the armistice to urge society ladies to respect that 'elitist code of distinction' called fashion was not ignored for long. In spring 1941 many of them were once again heading for their *couturiers*, where they were joined in the following months by a 'new clientèle', self-serving and with its base in the black market.

The first trends of the winter 1940 collection were barely known before advance signs appeared that society life was resuming. Even though fashionable Paris was still dispersed by the flight to the south, and many had not returned to the capital, André de Fouquières, arbiter of elegance and the life and soul of fashionable receptions, welcomed the reopening of the race-course at Auteuil on 12 October 1940. It would, he wrote in *Une Semaine à Paris*, 'spur on the blossoming of *couture* and fashion, which has supported thousands of craftsmen and apprentices'.[1] And, as in the finest pre-war days, the enclosure and grandstands served to show off the latest creations worn by models from the great *couture* houses, even if they now had to share the limelight with German officers and German women in uniform (known as *souris grises* – grey mice), who were particularly numerous in this milieu.

Of course, the newspapers did not fail to report this very successful event, nor to print photographs of the designs on view (mink or beaver fur coats, astrakhan toques, elegant hoods) shown to best effect by their graceful wearers. If the gossip columnists regretted the absence of certain famous race-going couples, detained elsewhere, they acclaimed in passing the incomparable chic of Geneviève Fath, both wife and model of Jacques Fath. Life also returned to theatres and concert halls, but here fashion did not benefit from the anticipated results. Their clientèle was attracted by the practical side of the collections, but seemed to be holding back from its more sophisticated aspects. Restaurants and theatres were reborn into Parisian life but were hardly an excuse for model parades. Evening dress had vanished into thin air. Music halls and cabarets had reopened at the request of the authorities of the Majestic, but their tables were in the main occupied by Germans. To their great delight, the 'Alcazar' (rechristened the 'Palace' by the conquerors),

'Tabarin', the 'Folies-Bergères', the 'Casino de Paris' and many others offered strip shows.

New plays were advertised daily, intended for Parisians as well as for the occupier. Some women reacted negatively: 'Is it appropriate,' they asked, 'when the current atmosphere is spreading gloom and it is fashionable to search one's conscience, is it appropriate to continue to "dress up"?' In other words, was a somewhat studied elegance acceptable at a time when the Germans were triumphant and the population was beset with difficulties? 'Yes, yes, a thousand times yes', answered the men and women who contributed to the creation of luxury gowns and hats, while the fashion journalists joined forces to remove any remaining scruples.

The days of austerity were over: 'elegant women have played with poverty long enough'. 'The well-to-do have not been so affected [by the disaster], since many ladies can still be seen in restaurants, theatres and cabarets. They are not worried about not being smartly dressed. These are the ladies I blame,' wrote Lucie Hirigoyen 'because they are following a trend which is not for the best and which is harmful to themselves and to all of us.'[2] The new France did not imply that French women should abandon their legendary charm and chic.

Lucien François struck the same note when he waxed indignant at this attitude, which was so disastrous for the luxury industries. One had to turn one's back on the 'snobbery of the pennyless'. 'An end to make-believe! no more sackcloth which imitates silk, lamé which counterfeits wool, wool which pretends to be cotton, no more shapeless dresses in trying to be plain.'[3] Those who had the means must resume their social role, which was to be well dressed. By so doing, they would enable the creative designers to survive. Informality, just about tolerable in these hard times, was quite out of place when it was a question of going into society. The advice to women who were going to dine at Maxim's or attend a first night at the theatre was to don outfits of irreproachable chic. 'The room must be a pretty salon where elegance meets elegance', following the ritual to which fashion subjects women. The client who does not have to bother her pretty head with money matters must continue to dress to order. It is her duty to do so in order to help the craftsmen and also to prove to the whole world that the art of couture is still alive and still richly inventive. 'Before the war, most society ladies dressed, chose hats and wore jewellery in accordance with Paris fashion: therefore, stylishness has, by the force of circumstance, now become an economic weapon. If elegance were to run dry it would be the end of the prestige of French creations.' Hence the paradox: the harder the times, the more important it was to continue to 'act as if . . .'

In one circle the gloom was short-lived. After an intermediate period of general self-inflicted guilt, when everyone followed the example of the Maréchal and his government in seeking answers to the causes of the collapse, blaming, among other things, general carelessness; and following a withdrawal into virtuous hypocrisy, life carried on as it always had done. The backcloth of the defeat and occupation did not radically upset the habits of a minority of elegant ladies because their way of life or extensive connections, or both together, spared them these kinds of material contingencies.

Some film stars whom the defeat had momentarily driven from the capital, could not wait to get back to Paris. One of the first to return was Corinne Luchaire, followed by Cécile Sorel and others, all of them consenting with good grace to be patrons of the galas and receptions in aid of good causes, which flourished under the best of pretexts. A new Franco-German élite took shape and filled the leading roles, quickly becoming one of the favourite targets of *haute couture*. There is absolutely no doubt that 20 December 1940 marked the official resumption of social events. On that day, 2,000 people attended a grand gala held at the Opéra in aid of Maréchal Pétain's Entraide d'Hiver and presided over by Fernand de Brinon. Prominent Paris personalities were invited and large numbers of elegant ladies were advised to come, 'the presence of women, as beautiful as they are warmhearted, contributing without a shadow of doubt to the success of that hour of benevolence'.[4] People may have been told to avoid flashy luxury or excess, but it was still agreed 'that a full-length gown with long or short sleeves proves indispensable for this type of reception'. This was still the rule at the beginning of these dark years! Lucienne Boyer was resplendent in a violet velvet gown decorated with a fanciful crinoline. A great deal of effort was invested in hair styles: curls, a sea of waves topped by cock or ostrich feathers, aigrettes and a few birds of paradise. For the first time since the war there were women in evening gowns and men in coat-tails. The sale of programmes was in the hands of 'mannequins' from the Paris *couture* houses.

Soon, despite the difficult times, there was no shortage of opportunities to be elegant. Quite the opposite! Some people took pleasure in maintaining, quite artificially, a fashionable life style, which, as a side effect, favoured the blossoming of fashion and frivolity. To celebrate the publication of the hundredth issue of his paper *Les Nouveaux Temps* on 11 February 1941, Jean Luchaire invited Paris high society to a cocktail party. He also asked German personalities: his life-long friend Otto Abetz (who sent a representative), Achenbach and Dr Schleier. 'Some of the most beautiful and most elegant women in Paris are there. What could be more natural at a reception where one can meet the ambassadors of *haute couture*: Jeanne Lanvin, Marcelle Dormoy, Agnès, Paquin, Marcel Rochas, Jean Dessès, Jacques Fath?'[5] The assembly also included Mmes Nard and de la Marlière, M. and Mme Steve Passeur, M. and Mme Dubonnet, M. and Mme G. Paul-Boncour, as well as several artistes: Arletty, Alice Cocéa, Suzy Solidor, Odette Moulin, Eva Busch, Francine Bessy. If Jean Luchaire was counting on this reception to consecrate the success of his paper in political and social circles, his daughter Corinne had other ideas. Her main aim was to attract attention. That day she was wearing a long, full dress which stood out because of its style. It was cut by Marcel Rochas, her favourite *couturier* who, 'in maintaining traditional French elegance, does not hesitate to make creations which amaze the occupier while still safeguarding Paris fashion'.[6]

In spring 1941, the reopening of the racing season at Longchamp, where sport and elegance traditionally mixed, acted as a starting signal for the spring collections. The most prominent society ladies mingled with the models in the enclosure. Geneviève Fath, in a navy blue gros-grain costume with white dots, was photographed from every angle. Featured on the right-hand pages of the women's magazine *La Femme Chic* were the Comtesse d'Oncieu de Chaffardon, a client of Maggy Rouff's, who wore a black crepe gown, the Baronne de Beaufort, dressed by Germaine Lecomte, and the comtesse de Monjour in an ensemble by Balenciaga. This time it really looked as if everything had returned to normal and that the calls issued by the fashion magazines had been followed by action. If the gossip columnists were to be believed, the pace of the social round had even accelerated. The same old faces appeared again and again dressed up afresh to listen to music and to watch a new play.

> A few days ago it was Mme Paul Morand who was entertaining, then Mme Dubonnet, as well as the duchesse d'Harcourt. Yesterday, the comtesse Etienne de Beaumont opened her beautiful Paris garden . . . The company was select: Mme Jean Larivière in black, lit up at the neck by pearls, was wearing a small hat covered in hand-painted silk. The medium: the front page of a daily paper with photographic news coverage . . . The Comtesse Marguerite de Mun, also in black but crowned with a large white straw . . . Mlle Delubac had come 'dressed-up' in the pre-war sense, in a very beautiful outfit, a striped silk coat reminiscent of the robes in a Watteau painting, and adorned with resplendent jewellery.[7]

As spring gave way to summer, 'the Paris season' was born again. The Centre d'Échanges Artistiques et de Culture Française, of which the Comtesse de Cossé-Brissac was president, organized fortnightly concerts of French music. Every Friday during the months of July and August galas attracted a select company to the Grand-Palais. The Golfer's Club opened its doors once a week for elegant teas. Chic was not dead: receptions, dinners at Maxim's, outings to cabarets, charity galas and theatrical first nights formed part of the social whirl of those ladies of the in-crowd who were not afraid of attracting attention. Soon these privileged people were applauding the same performances together, and frequenting the same luxury restaurants, where they found themselves among their own sort. 'Maxim's tops the list. In the cloakroom, Arletty spots Sacha Guitry's panama amidst the verdigris caps . . . Raimu is also there, as well as every famous artiste, businessmen, new or old, etc. that Paris holds . . .'[8] High society rubbed shoulders with Germans: the marquis de Castellane, the marquise de Polignac, Otto Abetz, Jean Luchaire,

Louise de Vilmorin . . . Alice Cocéa confided in her Mémoires: 'During the occupation I could not refuse two or three invitations to the German embassy. Once there, I met almost all of fashionable showbusiness Paris, bound like myself by certain obligations that theatrical servitude imposes: E. Feuillère, M. Jamois, M. Bell, Dullin.'[9]

One of the soirées held in summer 1941 was exceptionally successful. It was organized by Maurice Chevalier in the Ambassadeurs restaurant and presided over by his Excellency ambassador Scapini. The proceeds were earmarked for charities dealing with prisoners of war. Some 596 places were laid and more than 1,000 applications from would-be spectators turned down. The public was hand picked: Serge Lifar, Tino Rossi, Giraudoux, the famous Miss, Yvette Lebon, Elina Labourdette in a long gown, Ginette Leclerc, dressed completely in white. In the glittering assembly a few (Mistinguett) women (almost always the same ones) attracted attention by their stylish outfits: Corinne Luchaire, Jacqueline Porel, and Mme Ribadeau-Dumas (the wife of the director of *Une Semaine à Paris*) whose hat made of mauve tulle violets was much admired. On stage, one of the stars of the show wore a Lucien Lelong creation: a moiré taffeta skirt with white spots topped by a heart-shaped bodice.

Little by little, to the great relief of the luxury industries, elegance triumphed – that 'true class elegance, the only type appropriate today, where hat, gloves and gown form an inseparable trilogy'.[10] Some Parisian women could not bear to be seen wearing the same outfit at two consecutive soirées. It is true that a large number of them had no need to worry about whether or not there were coupons left on their clothing cards, but only about discovering the new trends in fashion. On the pretext of helping economic recovery, fashion's order of command advised women to appear 'dressed up' and, with the help of skilful advertising, it was obeyed. Place those two words, 'Paris' and 'fashion' side by side and no more was needed to evoke elegance, proclaimed *Marie-Claire*.[11] *Haute couture*, as anyone could see, was very much alive and always riding high. The luxury industries kept their leading role. The products of fine lingerie, of glove making, of custom-made footwear were proof enough.

At cocktail time the gilded youth gathered at the St James nightclub and with them came an element of folly and provocation. Ultra short flounced skirts, peasant blouses or fichu bodices made up the uniform of the young girls who assembled there. As always there was the inevitable display of hats, one of which, named 'Vitamines', was greeted with some mirth. This was a small boater topped with two carrots, two radishes and five red pimentos, all balanced on miniature artichokes.

The most successful charity cocktail parties always took place at the St James, acme of Parisian elegance if ever there was one. That given in November 1941, and presided over by the Duc de La Rochefoucauld in aid of soup kitchens, was original. A turkey was put up for auction and raised the fabulous price of 10,000 francs. 'I do not know who will eat that turkey but he will be able to boast that he is eating the most expensive turkey in Paris and also the most elegant', commented a female journalist, 'because these auctions have gathered the season's prettiest hats and prettiest dresses around this farmyard animal.[12] Which shows,' she concluded, 'that charity does not exclude elegance!'

Fouquet's almost resembled a fashion parade, so chic was its clientèle. In passing, one could identify a ravishing light brown woollen costume by Worth worn with a pale blue blouse. A little dress by J. Lanvin in fine navy blue cloth enhanced by a row of red and white beads drew murmurs of approval.

Literary salons, somnolent till then, began to open up. The tea parties of Comtesse Pierre de Segonzac and Baronne de Dietrich were renowned for the welcome they gave to artistes. 'One fashionable Parisian salon is Florence Gould's, American through her husband, who sumptuously entertains the world of literary Paris.' Florence's 'Thursdays' were very popular because they gave writers the opportunity to eat properly and to rub shoulders with a variety of personalities. On the second floor of 129 Avenue Malakoff, the hostess welcomed French and Germans. 'Giraudoux, Cocteau and Marcel Jouhandeau were among the regular clientèle, as well as Gerhard Heller and Ernst Jünger.'[13] 'The latter is the guest most sought-after by hostesses because in addition to his talents and his elegance he has the quiet charm of genuine opposition to Hitler.'[14] All in all he was the symbol of a successful occupation.

Marie-Laure de Noailles and Marie-Louise Bousquet, two ladies renowned for being leaders of elegance, opened the doors of their apartments wide for glittering receptions where the 'Franco-German' elite of Paris crowded together among paintings and a well-stocked buffet. Both were famous 'hostesses' of fashionable Paris. Marie-Louise Bousquet was editor of the French edition of *Harper's Bazaar* (a fashion magazine); a very elegant lady, she entertained in her apartment in the Place du Palais-Bourbon. Soirées at the home of the princesse Murat were equally cheering.

Creative *couture* missed no occasion for publicity. At the Exposition de la France Européenne organized in the Grand Palais on 24 June 1941, it was represented in a '*Couture* and Fashion' section, as requested by the Comité du Vêtement. It was a diversified company, grouping together the various creative industries and dedicated to the workforce, which had become the primordial element at a time when raw material was restricted. The whole thing was in line with government guidelines. The event took place against a backcloth, 'Les Moissons' ('The Harvests'), symbolizing nature, the French soil, source of inspiration and life. There were no mannequins, but simple stands on which muslin and lace fabrics were placed. Everything was prepared and created on the spot under the direction of the painter Cassandre and with the co-operation of dress designers and dressmakers.

Lucien Lelong invited high society to the opening, as well as the world of *couture* (Jacques Fath, Jeanne Lanvin, Germaine Lecomte); personalities included the Princesse de Polignac, the Comtesse de Chambure and M and Mme Dupré, but also Dr Michel, director of the economic services of the Militärbefelshaber, F. Sieburg, representing Abetz, and Dr Mömm. The press devoted considerable space to the event which celebrated 'the apotheosis of French taste' in the framework of European fashion.

With the 1941 autumn and winter collections a new image appeared and made its way into practically every *couture* salon: 'Through the grey air of Paris, despite the earnest secrecy which prevails in every fashion house, there sprung a common inspiration for a more noble, more ornate gown, a small miracle immune to copying and made by the most poetic hands in Paris.'[15] Gone were the straight dresses – their simplicity made them all too much alike. Fashion offered a choice between the 'barrel-shaped' gown and the 'amphora' line. Fairly short skirts were gathered in by scallops and pleats, and hips were emphasized and further enhanced by drapery. Gathers were everywhere, in close-set rows or a single line; it was the gathering which determined whether the fullness in the front, at the back and on the sides should take the form of flares, paniers or pockets. A wealth of work, a wealth of decoration, everything alive with imagination, because fashion was truly poking fun at logic! The atmosphere of the times called for penitence and fashion did not hold back from enriching the heart of its creations.

In winter, black was predominant, corresponding to a wish for sobriety and to the gravity of events. However, gowns were always decorated with hand-made trimmings. Velvets were everywhere, as well as furs, which gave warmth to these austere fabrics. An afternoon gown by Jacques Fath, 'Marché noir', symbolized this trend: it was made of black wool with a black velvet appliqué motif embroidered on black tulle on the bodice. Jeanne Lanvin's collection was an enchantment, with draping over the hips producing that 'amphora' silhouette that clients considered so elegant. Blacks, greys and browns were mingled with a geranium red and a luminous green. The collection was classical in its use of sumptuous embroidery. It was often inspired by the Renaissance, and added a floral theme to the gowns, whether in fabric, gold or silver thread, precious stones and a contrasting shade of silk. Marcel Rochas, Maggy Rouff and Lucien Lelong combined practical sense with Parisian chic. Their collections contained many costumes and simple dresses, but also brilliant inventions that enabled the Parisian lady to be 'invisibly' chic in all circumstances. These dual-purpose gowns could be worn at any time of day because all they needed to relieve their sobriety and make them irresistible was an accessory (trimmings, velvets, ribbons).

'If the theatre or a dinner require you to go out in the evening, a lighter blouse and a hat will add lustre to the outfit, but above all it is in the details of a collar, in the jewellery, and in the colour of gloves that the subtle difference between day and evening wear will be revealed.'[16] So Charles Montaigne's ensemble for restaurant and theatre struck exactly the right note. Made of black wool and with a pleated skirt, it had an over-blouse fringed with jet and a cape of the same fabric edged with 'flame' duvetine.

Another formula consisted of creating outfits of refined elegance, which were concealed under plain coats. Once the coat was removed, the outfit was revealed. This was the triumph of lamé suits and fine jersey dresses with a V-neck by Anita de Pombo. Marcelle Chaumont, 'pleating wizard', was one of the rare designers to retain a severe and harmonious style which her loyal clientèle appreciated. They included the Princesse de Faucigny Lucinge, Madame André Citroën, the Marquise de Polignac, Madame André Dubonnet, and the actresses Marie Marquet and Françoise Rosay. Schiaparelli, on the contrary, did not hesitate to transform her sober black dresses by adding irridescent incrustations, colours, gems, and spangles, a secret of her own. Jacques Fath, most eccentric of the couturiers, chose to show his summer designs to a glittering throng gathered at a soirée at the 'Bagdad' in June 1941. The success of the 'amphora' line[17] was already confirmed; now viewers at the soirée had the chance to discover the 'sultana' line, a skirt that climbed back to the knees following the lines of oriental trousers.

For several months women kept faith with the cumbersome gowns decreed by fashion. In September 1942, Marcel Rochas decided the time was ripe for change. His one-piece gown, clinging to and revealing the curves of the figure, was one of the most sensational innovations of the season. The shoulders were drooping, but were held in place by a bustier. This was the signal for genuine change. Winter 1943's fashion was dominated by femininity and moderation: 'Gone were the sloping shoulders, forgotten were the constricted waists and over-padded hips, outmoded were the little-girlie skirts. Colours are obeying this new taste for restraint. These are smoke grey, mouse grey and dark brown.'[18] Fullness was slimmed down; there was a movement towards a tapered figure. As for hats, small or large, month in, month out, they were impressively bold, alive with flowers, feathers or ribbons and remained as much the indispensable complement of the elegant woman as her accessories: gloves, umbrella, bag.

All the artistes involved in the fashion industry emphasized creation and the combined efforts of the whole atelier, which turned every design into a real masterpiece of workmanship. Reverting to tradition, the *couturiers* strove to meet the wishes of a clientèle that was regaining a taste for fashionable life. As in the past, each change of season saw the birth of new trends to respond to the expectations of a minority of women and the life they were leading.

But Paris did not have a monopoly on social events. In Cannes, La Croisette had become the centre of elegance for the free zone. A few film stars, wealthy idlers and rich Jews, who had sought refuge there, combined to maintain a fashionable life. Worth and Jacques Heim chose the casino and the floor of the 'Ambassadeurs' as a framework to show their most beautiful designs. They set a fashion for casual outfits – short linen skirts worn with long jackets – but ended their parades with the traditional procession of evening gowns in tulle, embroidery or in diaphanous lace encrusted with brightly coloured spangles.

Soon summer 1942 brought its share of receptions to the Côte d'Azur. A wedding took place at Cannes to which the fashionable aristocracy thronged: the marriage of Mlle de La Force with the son of the duc du Praslin. The guests gathered for a frugal lunch after the ceremony.

> The majority of the generally elderly men are wearing morning coats. The women . . . are extraordinary. Some seem to have stepped out of an ancestral portrait; others, like Mme de Villeneuve-Bargemon, are extremely elegant. Still others look like huntresses, despite their pearls and feathers. A world one might have thought submerged by the times has just resurfaced, while at Stalingrad, at El-Alamein . . . I am dazzled[19]

confided Philippe Erlanger, ex-head of the Service d'action artistique at the Ministère des Beaux-Arts, who had sought refuge in Cannes.

An open-air production of *A Midsummer Night's Dream* in July 1942 at the home of the Comtesse Pastré[20] in Montredon, was greeted as a cultural revival and a manifestation of elegance. The play was put on by professionals plus a few amateurs, including Mademoiselles Borelli, de Barante, and Edmonde Charles-Roux. The Comtesse had spared no expense and presented an unforgettable entertainment with the cooperation of Christian Bérard.[21] He improvised the stage costumes directly on the actors, draping them in velvets and satins. 'When it was noticed one day that stocks of these materials, unobtainable in Marseilles, had run out, the lady of the house had the hangings of valuable ancient fabrics that still cover the walls of the abandoned château', torn down to complete the project.[22] Owing to either a desire to provoke or to a mad excitability, at the end of the ball that concluded the evening, the order was given to destroy the costumes so that no trace of the play remained and so that it would be remembered as if it had been a dream! Reported among the spectators were several evening gowns which were not only 'in honour of the hostess but also a triumph over easygoing casualness'.

'There are no more grand dinners, there are only quite small ones, but this does not prevent people dressing for them, quite the contrary, and the gowns are in inverse proportion to the scantiness of the repast.'[23] It is true that in the provinces during the summer of 1942, a few young women were still wearing long gowns to entertain or to go out in the evening. Light muslins, white tulle dresses and taffeta skirts had no other purpose but to prove the existence of fashion. The thrifty took their pre-war formal outfits out of the wardrobe, while the resourceful used the cretonne from floral curtains or from bedspreads to have pretty, slightly gaudy, dresses made. The main thing was not to lose face when going out. There was also in fashionable circles a certain type of dignity to which many people clung.

The prestige of Paris fashion was such that provincial *couturières* jumped at the chance to organize private shows of their collections, to which they only invited professionals. In autumn 1942, the hotel 'Europe' at Aix-les-Bains was converted into a *couture* salon and welcomed an impatient crowd that had travelled not only from Marseilles, Nice and Toulouse but even from Madrid and Barcelona. They were able to admire the Bruyère, Grès, Lanvin, Lelong and Maggy Rouff collections. A tradition had been created: in 1943 shows reserved for professionals were held in Lyons and Nice. They brought the latest innovations from the capital to the provinces, which jumped at them.

A change is noticeable from February 1943. News items about *haute couture* did not totally disappear from the papers, but they became rarer and photographs of designs were no longer printed.[24] If indeed the unveiling of the collections was mentioned at all, the emphasis was placed on problems of supplies, which were genuine, and on the need to adapt. There were fewer entertainments. 'Because of the lack of lighting and also the curfew, evening life has come to a halt: no more grand receptions, no more first nights reserved for the elegant; with the uncertain fortunes of the current period, the night-time cabarets are attracting a totally different clientèle.'[25] The courage, determination and art of the *couturiers* who succeeded in reviving creation was acclaimed. Simplicity was the dominating principle: the silhouette was stripped of excesses which damaged the overall harmony; Lucien Lelong launched a costume composed of a short clinging skirt and a jacket with long basques, lined throughout with fur. In April 1944 the Carven collection was inspired by the Middle Ages. Spring 1944 saw the flowering of bright dresses. Despite the tragedy of summer 1944, despite all the difficulties, the collections came out, ingenious in their search for lines and materials.

Creative *couture* was growing ever closer to the fashion of everyday living.

One question is still difficult to clarify: that of the clientèle for *haute couture*. Apart from its regular customers, what category was it aiming at during this particular period? Without claiming to produce a definitive explanation, there is some evidence that can provide a few hints. First and foremost the number of '*couture* ration cards' in circulation, requested by women as special purchase permits. These permits, which only the group *couture*-création was entitled to issue, carried the proviso that the recipient surrendered half the points on her clothing card and her right to exchange them and, above all, paid a surtax.[26]

In 1941 there were nearly 20,000 of them – not a large figure at first sight but one that involved a very clearly defined group, because the clientèle essentially comprised wealthy women, living in Paris or in smart suburbs such as Neuilly and Versailles. More revealing, the percentage of *couture* cards that the Germans reserved for themselves was very low: only 200 cards were claimed by the authorities at the Majestic.[27] This demolishes the legend that the *couturiers* primarily dressed the wives of dignitaries posted to Paris. These women were no more than a fraction of the total and certainly not a majority (although Otto Abetz's wife, Suzanne, of French origin and ex-secretary of Jean Luchaire, proved a frequent customer of Schiaparelli). On 15 April 1944 there were no more than 13,629 recipients, but the number of cards reserved for Germans always remained unchanged at 200. Moreover, the category of young girls (16 to 18 years old) among the recipients, seems to have been large enough for the authorities to have provided an additional classification relating to them. If there had only been a few dozen they would probably have been lumped in with everyone else.

The first impression to emerge from the assessment of this clientèle is that its sociological composition was heterogenous.

The world of show business almost always belonged to the privileged elite that had the financial means to continue dressing as it did before the war. The price of gowns soared spectacularly: from 3,000 francs to 5,000 francs. From Corinne Luchaire and Mistinguett to Alice Cocéa and Cécile Sorel, the war brought no abrupt end to the aura of elegance surrounding these women. On the contrary, they remained the target for criticism, which all the papers reported. 'They lived through the occupation with minimum concern and a certain carefree spirit.'[28] On her way to Paris, the famous 'Miss' hit the headlines when she came with only a few dresses, four hats and two or three pairs of stockings. What should she do when the capital more than ever demanded an irreproachable chic? 'Mistinguett sent her maid to the Côte d'Azur, whence she returned that week with all the cases from her wardrobe and some twenty decorative hats.'[29] While waiting, the artiste scoured the milliners and *couture* salons.

> There was a crowd (and some very beautiful outfits) at the inauguration of the theatre which Touchagues decorated for the Palais des Beaux-Arts in the avenue de Tokyo. Suzy Solidor, very elegant in a magnificent mink jacket with three-quarter length sleeves dominated the scene from the height of a bar stool.[30]

We know, through chance confidences, that Corinne Luchaire's favourite *couturiers* were the houses of Jacques Heim and Marcel Rochas; that Jeanne Boitel, one of the most elegant Paris actresses, was dressed both in the town and on the stage by Molyneux, who created magnificent gowns for her; that Elvire Popesco swore only by Maggy Rouff. The same was true of Madeleine Sologne, who changed gowns three times a day. The charming Danièle Darrieux ordered by the dozen the dresses that she took on her overseas tours.

A few male actors, well known for the popular parts they played on the screen, did not object to their female counterparts being dressed by the *couturiers*.

Noël-Noël confided to a reporter that *his* favourite gown came from Nina Ricci, appreciating its sober line and discreet elegance. Jean Tissier, for his part, acknowledged that fashion was important because it allowed wives to spend their husband's money. Having said that, what he wanted for his own wife, right down to her casual outfits, was the label of Robert Piguet. War or no war, Sacha Guitry did not relent: *haute couture* remained an indispensable weapon of female seduction, and his fourth wife was a loyal client of Jeanne Lanvin and also of Piguet. The wife of Steve Passeur, a journalist and dramatist popular at the time, missed no chance to be seen when the collections were shown. And as her position allowed her to live comfortably (the couple occupied a suite at the Ritz), expense did not bother her.[31]

The wives of certain Parisian collaborators and journalists, like Françoise Luchaire and Mme Steve Passeur, or political personalities, like Mme de Brinon, the daughter of Pierre Laval, and Josée de Chambrun, who had to keep up their position in society or who attended Franco-German receptions, also formed a distinct and limited circle, which had its entrées to the *grands couturiers*. This was also the case with the wives of certain high officials or big industrialists who were photographed in formal dress at private views or receptions. Georges Dubonnet's wife, renowned for her legendary chic, was a case in point. Like the Steve Passeurs, the couple lived permanently at the Ritz, which throws some light on their life style.

Also very revealing is a document from the accounts of the newspaper *Paris-Soir* preserved in the German Archives from the Majestic. This is a contract concluded in July 1941 between the daily paper and Lucien Lelong 'concerning an exchange of services'. Under this agreement, the *couturier* had to supply gowns to four people to an amount not exceeding 12,600 francs, in return for which *Paris-Soir* and *Paris-Midi* would give him free publicity during the second half of 1941. According to the Germans who financed the paper, the clauses were scrupulously respected. In any case, the names of the parties involved, whose dresses came from Lelong, stand out in black and white on the document: they are Mme Brunet, described as publicity agent for *Paris-Soir* and as a loyal and frequent client of the 'famous *couture* house' in Avenue Matignon; Mme Morin, sister-in-law of the paper's temporary administrator; a certain Mme Fischer (who was none other than the singer Vina Bovy, Eugène Gerber's mistress), another of the *couturier*'s regular customers; and a fourth woman, Mlle Peret who was supposed to be a protégée of a fairly senior employee of *Paris-Soir*. However that may be, each of these ladies received an outfit to the value of 2,500 to 3,000 francs![32]

This category also covers the companions or mistresses of men who made money under the Germans. Szokolnikoff, under cover of a 'Société commerciale de l'Océan Indien' ('Trading Company for the Indian Ocean'), Rue du Faubourg-Poissonière, supplied the occupier with food, and pocketed the handsome profits.

His friend, Elfrieda T., known as 'Hélène', was well-known for her elegance, owning no fewer than twenty fur coats. She was not unique.

At the other end of the spectrum, Maréchal Pétain's wife was scarcely renowned for her clothes. Some pictures of her were so unflattering that the censor had much to do before he handed out permission to print photographs. Vichy had had its moment of glory; now it sank beyond recall and *haute couture* no longer flourished there.

A section of Parisian high society and the aristocracy, which had frequented the *couture* salons in the past, also resumed its customary routine, returning to the classic elegant round of exhibitions, race courses and fashionable restaurants. In 1942:

> the collections are very well attended. Jean Larivière and the Duchesse d'Harcourt are chez Lucien Lelong, who always directs his model parade himself with authority. At Jeanne Lanvin's, the usual crowd of mothers from the faubourg St Germain gather with their gaggle of young girls to marry off. At Maggy Rouff's, Mme Besançon de Wagner, very elegant in a black dress, greets Renée Saint-Cyr, Vina Bovy and Ginette Leclerc.[33]

Jacques Fath's was the meeting place for eccentric youth. In March 1943, *Les Nouveaux Temps* had no qualms about painting a picture of a typical Jacques Fath customer. She was an elegant lady who wanted to be very stylish. 'The women he dresses are resolutely of one season, with no need to cling to the traditions of their past.'

The fashion magazines,[34] current in 1941 and 1942 published photographs of Paris fashionable society, mentioning its clothes and sometimes its *couturiers* (and this is true up to February 1943, when the Germans finally banned the distribution of photographs of French fashion). It can therefore reasonably be deduced that the majority of the elegant women shown in these pictures were well and truly holders of the *couture* ration card. However, this does not mean that all these women belonged to the new Franco-German elite. Some of them probably did not have any scruples about attending the places which Serge Lifar recalls in his mémoires: 'Maxim's and Le Racing, those two shrines where one finds young embassy aides, young German officers, young girls and young women, from society and artistic Paris'.[35]

But it is important not to forget that among these society ladies was a fringe who were to know the horrors of deportation for showing rather too strong an antipathy to the occupier, or for joining the Resistance movement. This was true of Odette Fabius,[36] who worked for an information network: well established in the circles of the upper bourgeoisie into which she was born, her elegance was irreproachable. This did not prevent her being entrusted with all kinds of missions, for which she made use of her social connections. She appears in Vichy, trading precious stones on behalf of her immediate boss Colonel Alamichel with the jeweller Van Cleef, whom she had known for a long time. On one occasion when she was arrested she was wearing a Lanvin suit. She herself gives a strange example in her memoirs, the case of a highly placed relative whom she was surprised to find in the camp at Ravensbrück. Questioning the unfortunate lady, she was astonished to learn that she was aryan by origin but married to Philippe de Rothschild. She had been arrested and deported because she had refused to sit next to Mme Otto Abetz at a showing of a collection at Schiaparelli's in 1944, ostentatiously changing her seat. This simple act had been sufficient motive for her deportation.

If all these elegant ladies were linked by a taste for beauty, and were close to each other in wealth and the gilded life that opened the doors of made-to-measure *couture* to them, each had her own personal story. A few headline figures frequently recur, like the Princesse de Polignac, the Comtesse de Chambure, the Duchesse de Noailles . . . who attend the private view of the Exposition de la France Européenne, but also at Longchamp or at the gala at the Ambassadeurs. In this respect the racing reports published on the women's page of the daily papers are very useful because of the list of names which accompany them. On 11 June 1941, for example, *Le Figaro* reported:

> During recent meetings, many of which were spoiled by bad weather, some very pretty dresses and coat dresses in fine wool were to be seen. The dominant note was light grey. (There were designs by Jeanne Lanvin and Maggy Rouff.) White hats were numerous. The Duchesse de Noailles, Mme Herbert Fabry, Mme Mirabeaud wore jersey bands on their heads, while the comtesse Françoise de Ganay had a large black hat with a flat crown.

Some society events served as show places for Paris fashion. The wedding of Anne-Marie Besançon de Wagner (Maggy Rouff's daughter) to Jacques Bordreau on 13 June 1942 showed this to perfection. Apart from the people from the trade, the press was present, ensuring that the event was covered. We learn that the bride wore 'a ravishing gown of embroidered lawn and organdi' from Maggy Rouff's, and that six young girls in pink with sun bonnets formed her retinue. The guests were particularly elegant, like the bride's sister, the vicomtesse de Dancourt, in a multi-coloured floral crepe dress. Such events occurred in the provinces too. In Lyons, in January 1942, Mlle Paulette Pigeot married the son of Jean Barioz, President of the Syndicat des Fabricants de Soieries et de Tissus de Lyon (Union of Manufacturers of Silk Goods and Fabrics in Lyons).

Sometimes, a woman would agree to pose for the house that dressed her; this was often the case with milliners, rather less so with *couturiers*. Nevertheless, several examples can be found in *L'Officiel de la Couture et de la Mode de Paris*, where the March 1942 issue states: 'Mme Bruyère created this beautiful dress in ultramarine mat crepe, its pockets embroidered with sequin flowers, especially for Mme Jeanne Héricard.'

Living in a protected world, rich foreigners – South Americans and Spaniards – who lived in Paris during the occupation were regular customers of creative *couture*, which they warmly supported. Some considered this a duty to France, others believed that a life of luxury should continue despite the war. Their elegance made the soirées given by M et Mme Ernesto Estrada, an old Venezuelan family, in their residence on the Avenue Foch, much sought after. On several occasions the Chilean ambassador opened wide the doors of his legation. His guests were not only South Americans; big names from the Paris theatre were also seen there. Jean Hugo remembers a dinner at the home of Don Manfredo Sanchez and his wife Dona Bégonia where the company included Eluard. 'The hostess wore a long black crêpe de chine gown with unsymmetrical drapes, and her hair was coiled in blond curls, like orchids.'[37]

If only the clientèle of the great houses were still composed of those slightly decadent Proustian snobbish aristocrats, swearing only by Salvador Dali and James Joyce, who are to the *couturier* what the prototype aircraft was for the pilot; or again of those well-connected bourgeois ladies in whom tradition, clericalism and nationalism coexist happily with the cosmopolitan spirit, snobbery and aesthetic anarchy. Alas, if these latter pretend that they no longer dress, the others have taken refuge in châteaux lost among the horizons of Touraine or the burnt mountains of Provence.[38]

With some rare exceptions, the *couturiers* were left with 'the Harlequinesque parade of new money'. This came in two types: humble, timid lower middle-class ladies who scarcely dared to associate with a society hitherto unknown to them; and the 'queens of the black market', self-confident, furiously 'zazoues', mad about anything showy, and more than anything keen to prove that 'they had the cash'. They were known as the BOFs,[39] from the initials of the products, Beurre-Oeufs-Fromages (butter-eggs-cheeses), so precious at that time and the source of their new wealth. 'They arrive with pockets full of bundles of banknotes which they do not hesitate to place on the desk of the vendeuses. Their manners and language do not exactly match with the tone of *couture*.'[40] But no matter: they can afford the prices and have therefore bought the same rights as everyone else for themselves and their daughters.

These fat, very well-fed women . . . wiped their feet, embarrassed to walk on the luxurious velvet carpets of the salons . . . And when the vendeuse timidly named a price which to her seemed frightening and stressed the quality of the fabric, she was surprised to hear the customer exclaim in all innocence, 'Oh, it's less expensive than I thought!' Then they visibly gained confidence. They settled firmly and squarely down and brought their pals along. Life for them was good.[41]

The journalist Edmond Dubois reported a scene that was both surprising and typical of the period. A *couturier* saw a woman enter his salon. She had 'come to choose four dresses for her daughter at 8,000 francs a piece. The buyers were the wife and daughter of the salesman who had offered him butter for 300 francs a kilo at his back door.' And scenes such as this were repeated many many times. Thanks to their money, the *nouveaux riches* hoisted themselves to the summit of the social hierarchy and took on the external attributes of which they had hitherto been deprived. Meanwhile, some women did their best to battle against the prices, which were breaking all records. Two friends with the same measurements pooled their resources to buy a costume between them. They then took turns to wear it.

Despite the prevailing high prices, *haute couture* was doing rather well. From 1942 onwards it followed an upward curve and could count on a loyal clientèle. Sometimes so many people wanted to attend showings of collections that there was not enough room to admit everyone. On 23 February 1942, the management of Maggy Rouff had to apologize to the friends and customers of the house whom it had been impossible to let in to the opening of the collection because of the crowds. Be reassured, a notice in the lobbies specified, the collection would be shown every day.

Several sets of figures – for turnover and for the surtax paid by customers – prove that reports of good times for *couture* were not exaggerated. From 67,036,600 francs in 1941, turnover rose to 463,368,040 in 1943; it was still 202,739,000 in the first half of 1944. (Or, at today's prices, €1,760,350,412, €8,135,469,404 and €2,785,726,717 respectively.) The sums paid on behalf of the Fund for National Assistance (Secours National), followed the same curve: 3,351,830 in 1941, they reached 23,168,402 in 1943 and 10,136,960 in 1944 (or respectively €88,017,520, €406,773,470 and €139,286,473 at today's prices).

As draconian regulations reduced *haute couture*'s freedom to manoeuvre, the centre of elegance moved to the theatre and cinema, as the *couturiers*, not content with dressing the stars for 'around town', contributed to the production of their stage costumes, which was one way of staying in the public eye.

From Robert Piguet to Jacques Fath, from Jeanne Lanvin to Maggy Rouff, the list is long. The *couturiers* were not unemployed. The war had contributed to the rise of some ateliers which had made good use of the time to branch out into making stage costumes: Marcel Rochas, for example. Thanks to the theatre, Chanel's employees were able to find new jobs.

> The Paris *couturiers* have never put all their talent at the service of dramatic art as much as in these last years. They are not content with dressing some star or other for her part; they are also collaborating with the producer and author, adapting their viewpoint to the theatre and bringing the fantasies of their imagination, the refinement of their good taste and the virtuosity of their technique to the profession of costume-designer.[42]

Rochas went even further. In 1944 he actually appeared in the Jacques Becker film *Falbalas*. He took the part of a *couturier*, Blue Beard, who hanged the women he had loved in a shop window, dressed in the gowns he had created for them.[43]

For the *couturiers*, the cinema or theatre were a concrete means of proving what they were capable of doing despite shortages, as well as a way of spreading their ideas. Consequently, they gave free play to their talents. They surpassed themselves. A number of plays and films set their action in the past, which unleashed a riot of sumptuous costumes – at least for the leading roles, the others being forced to manage as best they could. With *La Main Passe*, a play by Georges Feydeau set in 1900, Robert Piguet did not take into account the orders regarding restrictions. He needed at least 10 m of cloth to make each of the gowns worn by the leading lady Jacqueline Delubac. Nothing but waves of lace and ribbon were worn with the enormous hats with veils; this was the time when parasols with birds' beaks, feather boas and veils, in short everything that the public could dream of, ruled supreme.

The nineteenth century and the 1900 period were very fashionable in the cinema and theatre; Alice Cocéa in *Clotilde du Mesnil* in which she played a young woman in 1885, wore a gown of candy-striped satin and black velvet specially created for her. These costumes indirectly contributed to the creation of some *haute couture* styles. In 1941, Worth was inspired by the 1900 fashion to create a very pretty bridal gown worn with long embroidered gloves from Hermès. He was not alone.

The influence of the historical cinema on dress fashion was irrefutable. The launch of the film *Pontcarral* resulted in the creation of the First Empire fashion with a double-breasted coat *à la* Pontcarral or a raglan Colonel d'Aubières coat. The Middle Ages inspired the creators throughout these four years, while the opening of the film *Les Visiteurs du Soir* reactivated the period, inspiring Jacques Fath to create costumes of the utmost beauty. For his winter 1941 collection, Lucien Lelong revived the hennins and the courts of love; anyone could identify with 'Troubadour', an all black model, or 'Gente Dame', a garnet velvet dress embroidered with small gilded lozenges.

Maggy Rouff and Jeanne Lanvin, the two great moving spirits behind chic on stage and screen, wanted to make something 'better than beautiful, better than brilliant, so that the effect of its charm would reach the audience beyond the footlights'.[44] One of their favourite stars, Jeanne Aubert, who played 'The Merry Widow', was a champion of elegance: awarded first prize for chic in New York in 1935, and in London in 1936 and 1937, she intended to maintain her image in order to please her public. 'I love to be all dressed up,' she explained. Other actors relied totally on these two creators. Jeanne Lanvin designed the costumes for Yvonne Printemps and also those worn by Arletty and Maria Casarès in *Les Enfants du Paradis*. In the play *La Ligne d'Horizon*, Elvire Popesco changed costume at least nine times, which almost amounted to a fashion show. All the outfits were signed Maggy Rouff, who also dressed Danièle Darrieux in *Premier Rendez-vous*.

Stage and screen played an educative role. They set the tone; they had to make an impression because it was through them that a style took shape and fashions were born. Stars needed elegance on stage but also in everyday life. 'There again, the *couturier* plays a primordial role since he upholds the grace of a woman who can do no less than be always ravishing, serving as an example to all her sisters',[45] who in their turn strove to copy her. There is no better propaganda than that provided by actresses when they took the models from the best houses in Paris on tour. Cécile Sorel in her travels in the provinces was a living advertisement for Maggy Rouff.

The war and the occupation complicated the *couturiers*' task by obliging them to undertake a certain amount of research and forcing them to use the new fabrics. Yet they did not bring the traditional elegance of a minority to an end. Receptions continued and with them the code of good manners, without which a society lady would not be what she is. For some people the daily routine scarcely changed. They ordered their wardrobes as in the past, sometimes so frenetically that one *couturier* had no hesitation in saying: 'The women made such a riot of colour that I am going to put them in black.' Other women, more affected by circumstances, were steadfast in the face of adversity and adapted. They got used to having one suit or one simple little dress, enhanced by unexpected touches. Sometimes detail was everything, which made it possible to be 'dressed up'. From 1943, only actresses had the right to wear long gowns; the domain of elegance in the pre-war sense had taken refuge on the stage and gave a public deprived of luxury substance for their dreams.

–8–

Vichy, Fashion and Women

The French government that came to power in 1940 imagined a total reorganization of the country. The foundations of society had to be rethought on principles true to the values that were said to have made France great in the past, such as respect for labour, homeland and family – values which the Vichy regime claimed the Third Republic had betrayed. In the task of 'intellectual and moral reconstruction' that the Maréchal urged the French people to undertake, the national revolution[1] attacked the roots of evil – love of pleasure – and blamed women in particular, accusing them of having neglected their duty through coquetry and egoism. A new portrait of woman now depicted her as wife and mother.[2] Under the banner of revival and sacrifice, the national revolution required a change of behaviour.

Whereas the misogynous discourse current in the inter-war period depicted women as capricious children, Vichy wanted France to be populated by women who were rational, serious and ready to make every sacrifice. This new ideal of feminine beauty was clearly reflected in fashion columns and fashion journals, perfect mirrors of such developments.

In the early days, in tune with the prevailing atmosphere, writers sought to understand the causes of the defeat. They turned again and again to the laxity of morals and the free and easy conduct that matched careless dress. 'Our country was sliding towards every sort of decadence', was the general diagnosis. Fashion came under attack for certain ill-favoured trends. The *couturière* Maggy Rouff – whose elitist clientèle was not affected by these remarks – decried 'the terrible pre-war slovenliness, carelessness, free-and-easy-ness', citing 'the decadence of customs' in the same breath as 'the emancipation of women'. Other, less well-known critics, took the same line. Because of their allegedly frivolous attitude, women were said to have contributed to the defeat. The image of the sophisticated *coquette* was incompatible with the renaissance of the nation and had to be changed. In this vein, Lucien François wrote:

We are passing through the most profoundly revolutionary period that France has known. The defe.. of our armies has opened our eyes to the weakness to which long years of a warped regime and lax customs have reduced our country. If we want to survive we have to change everything, clean up everything, purify everything. The distinctive feature of this revolution is that it is not only political and social but also, and above all, moral. And it is here that your role, the role of you women, can be immense.[3]

He had no qualms about writing the preface to a luxury women's magazine, *La Plus Belle Femme du Monde*,[4] in which he lauded maternity in the most worn-out stereotypes. Similarly, the editor-in-chief of *Votre Beauté* and 'the great Parisian experts in female aesthetics' 'added their voices to the programme of the National Revolution'. Because any moral reform had to start with the female domain, it was up to wives and mothers to show the way and to indulge in some serious soul searching: 'How in a France cut in two and in the presence of a future rendered increasingly gloomy by the prolongation of the war, could French women even consider following a fashion that respects neither decency nor propriety?'[5]

This Petainist discourse put the woman who wanted to be fashionable in a dilemma, for it meant that she saw herself either as a film star, wearing flashy clothes and showing off in a rather vulgar manner; or, as a tomboy, apeing men's mannerisms, 'right down to the cigarette',[6] cutting her hair and wearing very short, absolutely plain, shapeless dresses.

The Commissariat Général à la Famille attacked women who put coquetry before their role as mothers, and it mobilized opinion through the women's press, which formed an excellent channel for passing on information. In November 1941, government propaganda reached no less than 825 journals and did not mince words. Leaflets and posters saying things like 'The childless coquettish woman has no place in the city, she is a drone' were distributed 'among female staff and cust-omers in drapers' shops, shoe shops, and in fashion and hairdressing departments'.[7]

This was how the women's press posed the problem of woman and fashion, before handing out abundant advice adapted to the circumstances. 'France is no longer that dolled up idol demanding dances; she is now gravely injured and in need of constant care.'[8]

Judging from the fashion magazines, these appeals advocating change did not go unheeded. The natural gradually drove out the frivolous. Certain practices, then popular with the young and condemned by some moralists, were gradually abandoned:

> We no longer see skirts and shorts worn so short that they verge on nudity, no more bodices cut so outrageously low and open that they no longer conceal anything. This time the fashion is truly French and is not trying to emulate the trans-Atlantic style. And this is all the better because it is extremely beautiful and has regained all its very attractive, very fine gracefulness. Ambiguity is excluded. It is not in our character. Let us remain ourselves.[9]

The only alternative was 'to inoculate our daughters with love of decency and moderation, irrespective of whether a low neckline, underwear, skirts or hats are involved'.

Once again the question of women wearing trousers because the subject of debate, as this fashion was really seen as an expression of feminine emancipation. Many people regarded it as a step towards equality of the sexes: women tended to become more masculine and to copy men in many areas, forgetting their 'natural' role as a result. Trousers might be tolerated for cycling or for work in the fields, but women were strongly recommended not to wear them in public places. To make sure that they really understood how out of place this attitude was, the views of a popular actress and of a *couturière* were quoted and their advice carefully passed on. Both took a strong line. Arletty first: 'It is unforgiveable for women who have the means to buy themselves boots and coats to wear trousers. They impress nobody and their lack of dignity simply proves their bad taste.'[10] Marcelle Dormoy added: 'I am against trousers, which have nothing feminine about them. They do not leave woman her natural charm. I permit them as pyjamas. In any case be assured that the *couturiers* will never show trousers. We have too much concern for the French woman's elegance.'[11]

In practice, as we have seen, the habit of wearing trousers continued to spread. The wives of prisoners of war, for example, frequently delved into their absent husbands' dressing rooms to find something warm to wear, scarcely bothering about what people would say when they wore culottes. The fashion historian, Bruno de Roselle, explained that

These women, promoted to the role of heads of families, are consciously leaning towards simplicity and resourcefulness, and unconsciously towards emancipation. Since circumstances have forced them to take on a responsible role, by wearing trousers they are expressing their new role as heads of families which makes them the equal of man.[12]

All the same Vichy did not abandon the campaign against this borrowing from the male wardrobe and fashion did not escape its vigilant supervision. New norms gradually appeared, and woman escaped from the 'masculinization of female customs', which the adoption of short hair and cigarettes had made popular before the war. Escaping this 'danger' through an attitude considered more healthy, 'she rediscovers her place in the home and her role as mother in the sort of society that the Maréchal wishes to construct. Her body adapts to this retrieval of its natural function . . . Her breasts and hips "return" to normal, her figure ripened.'[13] Fashion followed suit.

'It is such a pleasure for me not to be dressing tomboys. Today private life is reviving . . . Return to the home is no longer only a political command,' declared the *couturière* Germaine Lecomte, 'it is a reality'. This 'reality' translated into dress. The time for eccentricities was officially over; now was the hour to turn towards greater sobriety. Whereas a few decades before elaborately decorated gowns were a sign of femininity, it now expressed itself by minimalism. Especially so as women, now mothers rather than seducers, could not leave the family home.

Because, according to Vichy, the family was the essential nucleus of society, the very foundations of the social edifice in which every individual had a function, the woman, guardian of the home, had to devote herself to her children. It was important not to divert her from this task and in particular to ban the unrealistic stories that could be seen in films or read in bad fashion magazines that led the young to take an interest in their appearance and their bodies. Young girls were invited to reflect on their future role as mothers and to prepare for maternity by avoiding everything that could turn them away from it. An official propaganda campaign was launched in May 1941 with childbirth as its main theme. Efforts were made to present examples in order to combat arguments put forward for not having children, namely women's careers, the desire for freedom, and also the fear of the physical consequences of pregnancy. Lastly, and this was quite new, the women's magazines gave more space to fashions for the expectant mother.

Propaganda emphasized the pernicious influence of American cinema, accusing it of having led astray a whole section of female youth. It noted that before the war, the American movie stars had often left their mark on the hairstyles or make-up of French women, diverting them from their primary mission in life. Now, thanks to the advent of the national revolution a reaction was setting in. 'Stay French! No more excessive make-up or platinum blonde hair. Be simple', it commanded. Some magazines seized on it. 'Andrée B. reminded me of I don't know which clumsy sketch where she played an American star,' wrote Suzanne Panne. 'She seemed so certain of her effect, so convinced of her resemblance that I took pity on her and decided to give her back her true personality, to recreate what she had never ceased to be: not a cheap Hollywood copy, but the simple and gracious young daughter of France.'[14]

Attacks came from all sides on the woman who was an '*objet d'art*', which the *couturier*, hairdresser, and beautician had hitherto created at will. 'This woman put on too much make-up, we have returned her to her true nature', ran a headline in *Votre Beauté*, using two photographs to demonstrate its claim. The first showed a 1938 French woman who was all artifice: 'The thick lips, a line for the eyebrows, the face hollowed by artificial shadows.'[15] It was nothing but a caricature of the American cinema. To make its strongest impact, this violently overbearing style needed to be accompanied by gaudy dresses and showy jewellery. In the other photograph, the beautician Fernand Aubry stripped the woman of her ultra-sophisticated look. She appeared with her own features, the outline of her lips was natural and her face discreetly made up. The contrast between the two photographs pointed to the renewal of France. 'A new style is born, of radiant women, scarcely made up at all and naturally attractive. In short, real women!' exclaimed Marcel Rochas. The make up respected the natural lines of the eyebrows. It was minute but so light, so really transparent 'that the face can register the manifold expressions of the soul'. 'We had begun to have our fill of those faces that all looked alike, of those false Garbos and would-be Marlenes. They have had their day.'[16] Neither mannequin nor statue, the woman of France was true to herself once more, genuine to the highest degree.

Vichy drew a picture of the ideal young French woman. It depicted her turning her back on outside influences. She was no longer solely concerned with her appearance and with expensive clothes. 'Our girls must be like fine fruit, healthy and appetising: not admitting the tiniest worm lest it cause damage.'[17] Down with those dangerously attractive fashion journals, with their colour pages and their modern presentation, where photographs were everything.[18] They tempted women and gave them a taste for luxury. Too often did the reader, full of 'advice' from her magazine, slide down the slippery slope of temptation. Columns about cinema stars and the way that artistes spent their time, stories of their beginnings and displays of their wealth, all turned young heads. Many a young girl had indeed dreamed of becoming a film star. They had tried to follow diets to keep their figures. Fortunately all that was over.

> Today, in this age of the national revolution, we are seeing a new type rising on the female horizon. One only has to look at the high school gates to see a whole [generation of] young girls amusing themselves in the streets and avenues to realise how things are, and how things are now is totally different from how they were ten years ago . . . Stockings have disappeared and been replaced by ankle socks, sensible shoes and a plain dress, leaving the body all the freedom that it needs. Bare headed and fresh-faced, breathing health and giving a clear impression of an engaging candour.[19]

The author's enthusiasm was slightly misplaced: the choice of 'ankle socks' and 'sensible shoes' was more often dictated by necessity than by any deliberate selection on the part of the wearer!

In both town and country the clothing worn by wives and mothers reflected the upheaval in their living conditions, while propagandists took the simplicity of dress to mean the reconstruction of the country.

Large numbers of these women were assuming new responsibilities. Apart from becoming heads of families, they were also replacing their prisoner husbands as heads of businesses and farms. They dressed in accordance with these functions; we have already seen a concrete example in the wearing of trousers. They had become more sober and more practical. The wardrobe of this new Eve constituted the very opposite of idleness and coquetry. In the fields, the athletic image symbolized by a young female farmer was held up as an example: 'boots, short skirt, brightly-coloured scarf round her head, sweater clinging to her bust'. Her dress showed her determination to adopt a life of labour that was very different and very busy. In town, the severely tailored costume was the indispensable companion of women who divided their time between children, queues and work. 'Their role of "devotion" accords to perfection with this discreet garb, which has become a sort of uniform.' It was the foundation of the female outfit. It came in several versions: casual with a half-belt; a smart variety, plain or striped, worn with impeccable blouses or shirts; a fancy genre, with a black skirt and bright jacket.

However, certain women's magazines in which fashion and face and body care played a primary role, did not think that beauty and coquetry needed to be entirely neglected. *Votre Beauté*, for example, refused to be 'the magazine for frivolous women' and intended to help the 'truly French woman' not let herself go. It was quite normal for her to feel sober and sad, but she must not, it stressed, give up authentic beauty that consisted of being true to one's weight and form. Aesthetic concerns had their place, as long as they were reasonable. *Votre Beauté*'s doctrine was equivalent to a philosophy for life: beauty 'is moral in the highest sense of the word, because it tends to better mankind through perfect health . . . If everything is harmoniously balanced it is better adapted to confront the underhand attacks of a cruel era.'[20] And it was left to the editor-in-chief to explain that current life gave women a thousand reasons to harden themselves to the war, which could enhance their beauty if they were properly understood.

'To be beautiful is also to be resilient: it is to prepare oneself to suffer the minimum hardship from privations, to tolerate the queues outside foodshops, to dispense with a maid, to have no difficulty in spending a hard winter in an ill-heated apartment.'[21] But none of this could happen without making an effort nor without renouncing idleness and negligence. This sort of beauty could not be bought; it was won by constant struggle.

In other words, there was a permissible brand of coquetry consisting of showing oneself to best advantage without exaggerated artifice. Let the young girls take pains with their hair, dress, and 'all the tiny details that go to make up feminine charm, while staying simple and ladylike, let them try to make the most of themselves; in short, let them attract men's eyes and sympathies. This is a law of nature.'[22] Moralists, even those with the best of intentions, were prepared to accept a contradiction.

Gone were extravagance and the loud and gaudy style. The majority of women had no use for evening gowns. Jewels sparkled only at the bottom of caskets. In view of the seriousness of events, the brilliant life of worldly society had to take a back seat as far as the majority of the population was concerned and give way to a simple existence declared by decree to be healthier.

The population discovered the joys of sport recently extolled by the Popular Front. Physical culture returned in full force. Vichy was obsessed with the idea of the physical decadence of French society and wanted to develop a sports policy. Most of the women's magazines agreed on one point: a cause of French degeneration was the result of forgetting and scorning the body. The national 'revolution' had to be made complete by 'the renaissance of the body of the French man' – the body of physical culture, not that of aesthetic affectation. Best foot forward!

The third was designed more specifically for women who, on holiday, helped to bring in the harvest. A large peasant kerchief on the head, a fairly full blouse over a short rayon skirt, espadrilles, and there they were, armed against the sun.

A gingham pinafore dress formed the basis of the last outfit suggested to readers. They were advised to wear it with clogs or knitted slippers. 'With a little blue and yellow check basque tablecloth you can make yourself this charming country dress. The high, chestnut-brown linen corselet gives the wasp waist look.'[30]

Some summer outfits were inspired by the regional costumes of the French provinces: the straw hats were borrowed from the vine growers of Burgundy, the pleated aprons from the women of Alsace.

For that other public, the public that had its clothes made to measure, the famous *couturiers* had no difficulty adapting to the taste of the day. In spring 1941 everything they showed had a bucolic charm and the names of the designs, basically garden dresses, were evocative. Cut from country fabrics – for example, *Zéphyr*, cotton, gingham, blue and white checked linen – these were simple outfits. '*Jacote* and *Colinette* were side by side with *Marion* and *Babet*. Beneath the neighbouring arbour, *Zéphyr* and *Romarin*. *Jardinage* smiled at *Ratissage* while *La Fête Villageoise* was to be found not far from *Vendanges*.'[31] Jacques Fath designed dresses inspired by peasant costumes.

Trinkets were also adapted to pastoral décor, while necklaces of cornflowers, marguerites and poppies were worn alongside the coats of arms of towns or the escutcheons of the principal regions, which could be sewn on to a coat or jumper. A white linen kerchief embroidered with a heart and a thatched cottage was the last word in 1941 fashion. As for jewellery, never before had it been so inspired by reality: an expensive ornament consisting of elegant peasants with emerald watering cans was very popular with the great Parisian jewellers. A cheap brooch aimed to be a dual symbol – of the conquered country and of the prisoner held far from home. It took the form of a map of France on which a heart was drawn with the words 'Tout pour lui et pour Elle' ('All for him and for Her', i.e. France). 'Jeanne Toussaint at Cartier created the jewel symbolizing the occupation, *L'Oiseau en Cage* (The Caged Bird), whose cage will open on Liberation, pinned on the revers of a patriot's suit.'[32]

To what extent was this government-sponsored fashion imposed on the public? Did the return to fashion of a type of beauty that tried to be the opposite of the artificial have any real effects? There are a host of questions with no easy or certain answers because of the wealth of conflicting pieces of evidence.

For example, from 1940 to 1944 the fashion for pastoral fabrics and for short peasant skirts was a reality. In the summer, women adopted this style for obvious utilitarian reasons: cycling dictated a practical outfit, while the shortage of material obliged them to raise hems as well as to make their dresses out of bedspreads or a pair of floral curtains, etc.

For the majority of French women in wartime, fashion was not synonymous with any catchword and was much more closely connected to the reality of shortages. For a woman to buy two scarves to make herself a peasant skirt did not necessarily imply that she subscribed to the 'return to the land', but rather proved that she was seizing an opportunity to dress at minimal cost, because the sale of these articles was unrestricted. Consequently, before concluding that there was a general fashion craze based on conviction, it should be noted that this taste was imposed more by necessity than choice! Once again, did people have the means to do otherwise? The style imposed was based almost exclusively on the woman's ability to build up her wardrobe. In the last resort, this was really the only imperative.

In made-to-measure *couture*, a few *grands couturiers* also yielded to the fashion for pastoral life and gave precedence to floral fabrics. But what was foremost in their minds when, like J.Lanvin, Schiaparelli and Grès, they strove to marry the three national colours? Was it patriotism, the wish to show they were French, or the return to the land urged by Vichy? According to a paragraph published on 3 May 1941 in *France,* a daily paper that appeared in London,[33] there was an element of provocation in such an attitude. Some people deliberately adopted this tri-coloured fashion in order to offend the Germans, who found it infuriating.

Another provocation came from the conduct of some young people, who loudly and ostentatiously advertised the fact that they were fed up to the back teeth with the national revolution. In summer 1941, a group of young town dwellers demonstrated in their own way their revolt against the absurdity of the war and the cloak of respectability that shrouded the country. It was at that time that the 'swings' and the 'zazous'[34] appeared. 'Swing' and 'zazou' (the two words are of American origin, and are linked to jazz music) were said to have crossed the Atlantic and were closely associated in Johnny Hess's song, 'Je suis Swing', which dated from 1939 and spread throughout France. Zazous recognized each other first and foremost by their eccentric dress and appearance.[35] In the male this inspired the following portrait:

> Hair brushed high, low forehead, vague gaze, small thin moustache, wet protruding lips, long legs, lithe walk with long strides, chest out. So much for the physique. Soft, tiny brown hat, striped shirt collar . . . gaudy tie with an ultra tight knot . . . long jacket covering most of the buttocks, trousers short, narrow at the bottom and loose at the knees, quite high turn-ups, white socks, suede shoes with quadruple soles, rolled-up umbrella with a long handle, gloves with an open-work pattern. So much for the clothes.[36]

Curiously, although at the time the phenomenon of fashion was primarily a female concern, it was the young men who set the trend here, perhaps because they were using clothes as a means of protest and also because they were making it a rallying sign to challenge the current situation, a sort of enrolment. Female zazous were less common but did exist and were equally eccentric. This description comes from *L'Illustration*:

> Animal skins on top conceal sweaters with roll collars and very short pleated skirts. Their shoulders are exaggeratedly padded in contrast with the man's drooping shoulders. Long hair falls in curls round their necks. Their stockings are striped, their shoes flat and heavy. They are armed with large umbrellas.[37]

The style that both boys and girls adopted was inconsistent with the rules imposed by the period when shortages and the return to nature were predominant. The jackets were almost always too long, the trousers quite wide, the skirts pleated, and the shoes flat and thick. It seemed that the restrictions did not affect the zazous; there was no leather but their shoes had triple soles and the girls were noted for their large sling bags.

They also mocked the regulation that came in from April 1942[38] concerning the manufacture of male clothing. It laid down precise norms and forbade, for example:

- backs with insets, box pleats, yokes, half-belts;
- pockets with insets or box pleats, except for military dress;
- flaps for patch pockets;
- likewise, the wearing of double-breasted waistcoats except for ceremonial occasions.

Zazous did not follow any of the regulations in force (clothing and shoe coupons), taking a mischievous pleasure in contravening them, even if it entailed resorting to the parallel market to complete their outfit. They resolutely stood out against the patriotic attitude towards clothing aimed at economizing on the use of cloth by paring it down to the last centimetre.

Their hairstyle was a basic element of their outfit. 'The male zazou's hair is curly, puffed out in front and long at the back. His female companion wears it long on her shoulders – never tied back – and very often platinum blond like the Hollywood stars.'[39]

As a finishing touch to their attire, many of them adopted dark glasses. The girls put on very conspicuous make-up, 'eyes ringed with blue eyelids, lips too red'.[40] This excessive use of cosmetics smacked of defiance: bleached hair and too much make-up like American starlets – and this at a time when such practices were widely condemned.

Their non-conformist attitudes to prevailing norms was severely criticized by the occupation press, but also by a large part of the public, who were annoyed by these new 'savages'. Their dress was the object of ridicule because it was seen as demonstrating negligence and a lowering of moral values. It was compared with earlier excesses: 'They are pale reflections of the dandies and the *merveilleuses* of the Directoire period.'

'Swing who can! In a jungle born of the defeat, these shifty little "Fauves", these firebrands in short trousers and long jackets, these "Incroyables" are only dangerous in the way that fleas are dangerous. They itch, they irritate.'[41]

But it was not only their clothes that were condemned. The zazous' amusements were also disapproved of. The fact that they danced to the sound of jazz music caused a scandal because it denoted a state of mind that the new regime constantly combatted: Americanism, laxity, idleness. The young zazous obviously had means, they apparently dressed without regard for expense and patronized cafés and dance halls. They were also opposed to the task of renovation in which the government was engaged and which was based on the labour of every individual, which is why the collaborationist press depicted them as henchmen of the Gaullists, as Jews and black marketeers. A favourite target of government propaganda, the zazou sometimes suffered physical violence. Certain collaborationist parties organized zazou-hunts, and if they happened to catch one of these young people, they taught them a lesson by cutting their hair, often using violence.

As a marginal phenomenon, the zazous did not belong to a specific social class; they were basically associated with a particular fringe of the population: the 17 to 18 year olds. They reflected a thirst for life in spite of everything. The zazous used all the resources of their imagination to dress themselves. It was a rebellion against the established order, but also youth winking at society, with the refusal to be like everyone else and the wish to attract attention. As Farid Chenoune observed, the zazou style brought about a small revolution in men's fashion under the influence of those who were already being called 'the young', over and above the divisions of class. 'The classic coordinates of elegance, which until now have been standardised and hierarchised, will henceforth meet competition from specific references to youth.' Did a youth fashion exist? *Adam* asked elsewhere in September 1945.[42]

Clothing also symbolized the hope of part of the population, just as the wearing of badges, the cross of Lorraine, and other things did. On 14 July, the national holiday, witnesses report that the three prohibited colours burst into spontaneous flower.

Some women seem to be rolled in flags. Louisette (Madame Guillotine) in her red and white checked dress and blue scarf was brought down from Belleville like a woman of the Republic . . . Everyone is hard at work spotting everyone else's inventions. What a lot of ridiculous efforts. One woman's blue shoes, white stockings and red dress. Another's red jacket, blue bag and white gloves.[43]

The police, who stopped a large number of passers-by on that particular day and took them down to the station for interrogation, did not get it wrong. This was a genuine rebellion, brought about with the means available and expressed through clothing.

An unconscious desire to provoke the occupier caused some young girls and young women to start wearing tartan after the defeat, for to do so was for some an indirect way of advertising their preference for Britain, a reminder of a country at war with the Germans. Michèle Bood was vaguely aware of this when she borrowed her brother's khaki scout's shirt to wear with a kilt. Jo Cardin wore a Scottish glengarry in 1940.

As for the men and women who were more deeply involved in the Resistance, their main concern was not to make themselves conspicuous. If their behaviour was too eccentric, it could cause them problems, even prove fatal. The wisest course was to melt into the crowd, and their clothes had to be absolutely free of any distinctive sign that would make its wearers noticeable. They chose the clothes, head gear and make-up recommended by the popular magazines.

Sometimes, feminine attraction became a weapon. Arriving at Lyons-Perrache station, Monique A., a pretty girl charged with the transport of Resistance newspapers, saw that there was a police barrier at the exit to the station. Her case was full of compromising literature. She could only accept the advances of the German officer who seized the aforesaid case in exchange for a rendez-vous which, needless to say, she never kept. A meeting with senior German authorities was part of the scenario that Lucie Aubrac dreamed up to save her husband Raymond, who was then in prison. So much was at stake that the young wife imagined a situation in which her outfit would play a part. To give credibility to her story of a young girl of good family seduced and then abandoned by her 'fiancé', she dressed with particular care. What she actually wore was 'a pretty large-checked rayon suit, big white porcelain marguerite earrings, and a little hat with a veil',[44] not to mention the lipstick and ring.

Some women members of the Resistance, whose general description was known to the authorities, thus rendering them liable to detection, used various stratagems to change their look. For them, hair dye was not a whim of fashion but indispensable camouflage. Men got by by growing moustaches and wearing glasses.

A young woman liaison agent from Lyons, restricted like everyone else by the clothing card system, remembers that, as she could not renew her wardrobe, she exchanged her own coat for a friend's, which she thought made her less vulnerable.[45]

At this time of shortage, any piece of cloth or the like was a godsend. When London parachuted arms or munitions to Resistance groups, the temptation to salvage the parachute cloth was too strong. Despite the danger involved, many women had no qualms about taking a piece to make themselves a blouse. On the eve of the landings, this even became a fairly widespread fashion in circles close to the Resistance. Coquetry overcame caution. As for the nylon stockings that members of the Resistance brought back from London, they constituted a risk for the women who wore them (for the same reason as did English cigarettes for smokers) because they pointed in an obvious way to the links formed with the British or the Gaullists.

The style that Vichy attempted to impose during these black years constituted a digression in the history of twentieth-century fashion rather than a true revolution. Of course, since cosmetics were scarce, restrictions dictated the law and women abandoned the artificial, symbolized by American filmstars, to turn more towards simplicity and the natural look. After the war, the habit of not making up in a sophisticated way remained. Soon, the ideal of feminine beauty would be incarnated by Ingrid Bergman, 'the girl with short hair, Gary Cooper's companion in *For Whom the Bell Tolls* who, it was said, did not need foundation cream since she washed her face with snow'.[46] The American star might have been obsolete, but the film retained its seductive power.

'Little Dictionary of "L'Homme Swing"', taken from *Toute la Vie*, 11 December 1941.

Of course, the classic little black dress enhanced by accessories, or the costume, formed part of woman's wardrobe, as well as casual outfits. But short peasant skirts and wedge heels would soon give way to longer dresses and stiletto heels, symbols of a regained femininity that Vichy had helped restore to importance. At the liberation, ex-model and photographer Lee Miller was captivated by the women she came across: 'Everywhere in the streets one sees superb girls on cycles or climbing on to tanks. Their figures seemed strange and fascinating to me, to me, who had come from utilitarian and austere England. Flared and full skirts with tight waists. The French woman's appearance has changed.'[47] For all that, the eccentricity or provocation that certain men and women showed, and that was so strongly criticized by those who supported the regime, was to set a widespread fashion. Even in fashion, the dark years were a turning point rather than a rupture.

Conclusion

Until World War Two, ways of dressing were part of a code of distinction. The elite determined the trends to which men and women were expected to conform. Although the main movements were reproduced in the glossy magazines, they were still the prerogative of a national and international privileged class. In reports of fashionable Paris receptions, the same people were almost always photographed, matched to different outfits. The other social groups 'copied' the designs shown as best they could with the help of their dressmakers or, failing that, made their clothes themselves. Whether women were wealthy or not, all were invited to follow a body of rules that, combined in a certain way, constituted fashion. For example, every woman, wherever she belonged socially, had to wear gloves, a hat and stockings for fear of contravening the rules of good manners that governed female conventions.

Even if fashion is primarily regarded as a social fact, it is also subject to the rules of the economy, which condition consumption and, consequently, creation. France, a large-scale consumer of textiles, depends on other countries for imports of wool and silk for its fabrics and of leather for its luxury trade. Problems begin when one of the links in the chain breaks. For five years the country experienced total upheaval because of the occupation. The disruption of traditional economic channels, German requisitions, scarcity of raw materials, and the black market imposed new norms that had repercussions for practices relating to apparel.

Those few years when France was occupied were only a short period when seen against the whole history of fashion. Nonetheless, the question arises: were they a temporary storm or the beginning of lasting changes? In other words, what has changed in that particular field? A society of shortages emerged, which gave birth to the reign of individual skill and imagination. At a time when the dictates of the *couturiers* forbidding such and such a colour, cut or fabric no longer carried any weight, a workaday trend developed that ran counter to fashion conceived as 'perpetual change' or 'constant self-destruction'. In fact, the equation 'fashion equals rhythm of buying to rhythm of wearing out' no longer proved true. Clothes were worn until it was no longer possible to wear them. Magazines, which formerly served almost exclusively to propagate or display luxury designs, became the mainstays of this workaday fashion, the motto of which was 'make full use of the means at your disposal', including the unfashionable. Side by side with reproductions of evening gowns, which served no purpose but to fuel their readers' dreams and provide an escape from everyday reality, the women's magazines dispensed advice and practical examples.

Haute couture, under threat because the Germans saw it as a possible challenge to National Socialist cultural hegemony, stood its ground against all odds. A specific piece of legislation – granted by the conqueror and constantly challenged – allowed *couturiers* to circumvent the system of clothing cards and continue to sell to their regular clientèle, except overseas. Certain *couturiers*, hoping for better days to come, were determined to defend a tradition of craftmanship with an elite workforce and were intent on preserving a cultural heritage by proving that *haute couture* was still alive. Throughout the whole occupation, thanks to the skills of its workers, creative *couture* never forgot the tricks of its trade, which made it inimitable and therefore immune to copying.

In practical terms, in order to continue to exist or to survive, the fashion houses had to establish more or less close relations with the Germans. These varied in extent. Sometimes, the conquerors attended collections, purchasing designs; sometimes they mixed in the same society circles as the *grands couturiers*, sat at the same tables, and so forth.

At the Liberation, when the time came to settle accounts, it may seem surprising that the 'épuration' (the purge) spared *haute couture* and its associated sectors. However, the question was seriously and paradoxically raised by Lucien Lelong, himself summoned to the Court of Justice for having attended the Lunches of the Round Table. In a letter of 25 October 1944[1] the Conseil de Direction de la Chambre Syndicale de la Couture Parisienne, through its president (Lelong), asked the minister of industrial production to create a commission to purge *couture*. The Minister's reply in November 1944 referred to the ordinance of 16 October 1944 'creating inter-professional regional committees for purging professional sections and an inter-professional national commission for *épuration*', these organizations being charged 'with ensuring the *épuration* of all persons participating in whatever capacity in the activity of an enterprise, who would have in some way furthered the designs of the enemy'. According to this ordinance, several motives for indictment were listed: apart from 'furthering the designs of the enemy', there was also 'hampering the war effort of France and its allies' and also 'the resistance efforts of the French'.

After consultation with the lawyers of the Chambre Syndicale de la Haute Couture it appeared that the Comité Régional Interprofessionel de l'Épuration de la Région Parisienne (CRIE) was really the appropriate body to receive the files on the *couturiers* and, in particular, section four, the textile section. But none of the 55 cases examined between 11 May 1945 and 21 January 1947 concerned *haute couture* and only one a ready-made clothing business. What was the reason for such a gap, such a lacuna? There, as elsewhere, it would seem that the lower strata took the blame for the rest, and that it was better to be a famous *couturier* than an employee. Madame X, a saleslady for Galeries Lafayette learned this to her cost; accused by a colleague of having been too nice to the Germans and having sold too well to them in 1940, she was sentenced to two months suspension from work. However, to have manufactured fur jackets for German troops on the eastern front was apparently not sufficient grounds to appear before the courts. In the same period, a great Paris shoemaker was summoned to appear by the Syndicat des Ouvriers de la Chaussure, 'accused of having furthered the designs of the enemy by supplying capital to an enterprise working for the Germans', the sentence meted out by the leather section of the CRIE banned him from acting as manager for a limited period. The manager of a famous fancy goods firm stood trial for having travelled beyond the Rhine but in the end the court declared itself unqualified to try the case and he was released.

Epuration varied from one sphere to the next. From motives inherent in the revival of the country, economic collaboration received scant punishment. In a devastated France it was hard, for example, to suspend businesses engaged in public works – most of which had participated in the construction of the Atlantic Wall – when the need for their cooperation in the work of reconstruction was so great. To prevent the great brands of cognac or champagne from resuming their activities on the pretext that their businesses had flourished during the war, was unthinkable because the state coffers were empty and only exports could help fill them.

In this context it is easier to understand the line of conduct adopted: an art such as *couture* carried considerable weight, economically and socially. The ruined country could not get back to work overnight, but everything that belonged to the domain of creation and good taste seemed to be directly exploitable and profitable. Jacques Deligny – who presided over the fate of apparel from 1942 – anticipated this when, invited to speak to a group of bankers on 25 May 1944,[2] he stressed the need to improve overseas trade after the war. And which textile industries did he propose? Basically the luxury industries, all those involved with exclusive fabrics and gowns – in a word, fashion, 'because it represents vast export possibilities.' 'For these industries to prosper, to be able to create, achieve and sell,' he explained, 'they need a generally favourable climate, a climate of order and also to a large extent benevolent care on the part of the authorities.' His opinion anticipated the stance that the country's leaders would later adopt.

The United States and South America, long deprived of the French 'label' or 'signature', waited impatiently for the resumption of relations with France. Here was a market to recapture, foreign currency to earn. It was up to *haute couture* to show its mettle and demonstrate that it had lost none of its talent. In such conditions how was it possible to oust the 'black sheep', those who had 'compromised' themselves with the enemy but whose professional ability was undeniable because they were creators in the full sense of the word? Furthermore, the workforce was intact and professional schools had even been created to train young girls in the trade. Everything could therefore get under way as before.

If the friendly countries were ready to resume relations with French fashion, Lucien Lelong had, in December 1944, to justify the position of Parisian *haute couture* in the face of what the Allies described as 'flagrant violation of the clothing rules imposed by the war'. 'I have just received copies of the regulations which limit the expenditure on clothing in England and the United States. And I now understand why certain journalists found that the Paris collections exceeded the limits.'[3] The President of the Chambre Syndicale de la Haute Couture demonstrated the mechanism of this 'excess', which the Allies found incomprehensible, showing the importance of this sector for France and for the whole world. For four years, he explained, we battled for 'creative *couture* to preserve the place it has always occupied in the eyes of the world'.

The best proof that war had come to an end can be found in a common achievement in which all the great names of *couture* participated: the Theatre of Fashion. Against an overall decor created by Christian Bérard, an exhibition was organized in the Pavillon de Marsan in March 1945. The very old idea of the fashion dolls who had in the past carried French creations to the whole world was revived. Some fifteen miniature theatres, designed by prestigious artists, provided frameworks for 170 small figurines dressed and coiffed by thirty-five couturiers, twenty-five milliners and twenty hairdressers. Seventy centimeters high, these wire dolls with plaster masks were made by Jean Saint-Martin, the inventor of wire mannequins, from designs by Eliane Bonabel and they were displayed in very different situations. For example, Touchagues reconstructed the place Vendôme, Douking, the Pont des Arts, Grau Sala placed 'the beautiful cyclist of 1945', dressed by Maud Carpentier, in a forest landscape. One of the most original compositions came from Jean Cocteau, who set his dolls, in formal dress, in the surrealist decor of a burned-out house. Lastly, Christian Bérard created a theatre. Out of every box leaned delicate faces crowned with everything and nothing: feathers, leaves, and so forth.

This fresh start for fashion was 'a real national mobilization' effort. It led Lucien Lelong to write: 'This is Paris and nothing but Paris: this theatre of fashion! its smile, its guts, its spirit, its charm.'[4] After being exhibited in Paris, these dolls sailed the world. We find them in London, Copenhagen, Zurich, Rio de Janeiro, ending up in New York. Throughout their travels these gracious ambassadors of fashion, demonstrated that the war had not stifled the *couturiers'* talent, and aroused murmurs of admiration. Those who had believed that the war would put a full stop to French creation were wrong. Paris fashion triumphed once again.

When the war ended, the phenomenon of fashion did not have exactly the same significance as in 1939. It was no longer the exclusive property of a wealthy class that could have their clothes made to order. Other trends were created, in particular 'a wartime fashion' in which street wear sometimes combined with the eccentric. Dressmaking ateliers sprang up in the Riviera, particularly Nice, heralding the advent of ready-to-wear clothes. In another few years these would supplant the 'hand-sewn'.

At the Liberation, women unconsciously yearned for a complete change of style. They wanted something different from their wartime uniform of fitted jacket and wedge heels. On 12 February 1947 the change was definitively confirmed. On that day, in front of the general staff of the fashion world – Michel de Brunhoff and the team from *Vogue*, Carmel Snow, the editor of *Harper's Bazaar* – Christian Dior presented his collection. The secret had been well kept. As the models walked past, unmistakable astonishment greeted the sight of the lengthened gowns and under-skirts. Applause broke out and the *couturier* was congratulated for his revolution, which Carmel Snow christened the 'New Look'. It was the triumph of a new femininity reflected in the skirts, full like corollas, and the tight-fitting bodices. Now the page was truly turned and the war really over; the New Look went on to conquer the world, and at the same time lent itself to multiple adaptations in which ready-to-wear clothes had an ever-increasing part.

Appendix I

Regulations for the Presentation of the *Haute Couture* Collections, Autumn-Winter 1942

Decision VI – A – 12
By the person in charge of the *Groupe de la couture et de la mode et de la parure, des vêtements sur mesure du Comité du vêtement de l'industrie textile.*

1) Composition and presentation of 'autumn-winter' and 'mid-winter' collections of *couture* designs.

2) Limitation on lengths of fabrics for designs and replicas in cloth containing wool.

The person in charge of the *couture*, fashion and decoration made-to-measure clothing group.

Decides

Art. I – Object
The present decision is applicable to businesses or parts of businesses that benefit from the special system of exemption from the general regulation of the sale of textile articles for domestic and clothing use.

Its object is to regulate the composition and presentation of the collections as well as to limit the use of fabrics containing wool.

Art. 2 – definition and composition of models and their reproduction.
Design and replica of design must be interpreted as:

1 gown (1 piece)
1 coat (1 piece)
1 cape (1 piece)

} skirt and jacket (1 piece)
1 costume }
} or skirt, jacket & blouse (2 pieces)
} dress and coat (2 pieces)
1 outfit }
} or dress and cape (2 pieces)

– 147 –

Art. 3. – Limitation on the number of designs
For the seasonal period between the opening of the autumn season and 31 December 1942 the autumn-winter and the mid-winter collections of each fashion house must not comprise more than a maximum of 100 designs, divided as follows:

autumn-winter collection: seventy-five designs
mid-winter collection: twenty-five designs

for the same period and for houses specializing solely in women's tailoring and casual clothes the maximum number of designs is reduced to thirty.

Art. 4. – Period for the presentation of the collections
The designs of the autumn-winter collection (seventy-five designs) cannot be shown in private, in public, to the press or to the fashion designers, before 24 August 1942 and after 24 September 1942.

These dates apply to the first presentation of designs by houses specializing solely in women's tailoring and casual clothes.

The designs of the mid-winter collection cannot be shown before 26 October 1942.

The 100 designs composing the autumn-winter and mid-winter collections can be shown simultaneously from 26 October 1942

Art. 5
The businesses defined in article 1 must make known the date that they have chosen for the presentation of their autumn-winter collection within eight days of receiving notification of the present decision or in the absence of such notification within eight days of its publication in the press.

They must make known the date they have chosen for the presentation of their mid-winter collection before 5 October 1942.

Group 1 will draw up a calendar of presentations and the press informed.

. . .

Art. 7. – Limitation on length of fabric for designs and replicas made up in cloth containing wool.
Definitive limits for designs created in fabrics containing wool and their replicas must not exceed the following lengths of fabric:

gown: 3.25 m (fabric width 140)
costume (jacket and skirt) 3.75 m (fabric width 140)
coat: 4.25 m (fabric width 140)

housecoat or pyjamas: 4.50 m (fabric width 140)
blouse: 2.5 m (fabric width 0.90), short sleeves
2.65 (fabric width 0.50), long sleeves

Justification for exceeding these limits must relate to replicas of a design for a particularly abnormal figure. This justification must appear on the register made available to the authority.

These fabric lengths include all details and accessories (pockets, facings, belts), unless these do not use fabric containing wool.

. . .

Art. 9. – Register of Designs
The orders in article 7 of the decision A.5 of the person in charge of Groupe I of the Comité du Vêtement, dated 22 July 1941 remain in force.

Art. 10. – Penalties
Any infraction of the present decision will expose its perpetrator to penalties laid down in article 7 of the law of 16 August 1940. In addition, the person in charge of Groupe I can request the head distributor of the Section Textile de l'Office Central de Répartition des Produits industriels for the withdrawal of the profit from which the perpetrator of the infraction benefits.

Art. 11
The present decision is operative immediately.

Paris, 19 June 1942

Seen and approved
Directeur responsable
du Comité du Vêtement
signed: Deligny

Person in charge
of Groupe 1
signed: L.Lelong

Seen:
Directeur des Textiles
et des Cuirs
Commissaire du Gouvernment
signed Jarillot

Appendix 2

Discussion Majestic/Monsieur Deligny
14 April 1943
Monsieur Dr Thomas was present at this interview which was held in the office of Monsieur Deligny (8, Rue de Richelieu)
FUTURE STATUS of HAUTE COUTURE
Monsieur Dr Schilling noted, and M. Deligny associated himself with his remarks, how desirable it was that the status of exempted *haute couture* houses not be perpetually challenged.

Without going back over the motives that made a special system necessary for these *couture* houses, houses that are still in existence, Monsieur Schilling would like them to make a useful contribution to the economy. Consequently, he thought that these houses should expand their export activities to Sweden, Spain, Italy, Portugal, etc.

Given the fact that the Berlin *couture* houses have by and large been shut, it seems difficult for Monsieur Schilling to have to admit to these businesses that the Paris *couture* houses remain open.

In view of the need to expand these exports and to avoid criticism from German industries, Monsieur Dr Schilling would envisage suggesting to Berlin via President Michel, who is more specifically responsible for the exports question at the Majestic Hotel, the formation of a 'continental consortium, a true trading concern, buying up articles of *haute couture* made in France in order to re-sell them overseas.

As Monsieur Dr Schilling sees it, this consortium should be a Franco-German body, in such a form that the German industries would not be able to criticize it, as mentioned above.

They would, in fact, be informed that the activity of these Paris *couture* houses was to be part of an overall plan making it possible to obtain raw materials or desirable items.

Monsieur Schilling, who had talked about this with President Michel, consequently reckoned that a 'luxury quota' (for *haute couture*, high fashion and high novelty fabrics) would be fixed annually. It was understood that a percentage of this quota would be exported in the form of finished products.

Bibliography

Unpublished Sources

F7

Police, general: F7 15299. Couture, luxury catalogues.

F12

Commerce and industry:

F12 10192. Rationing department. Correspondence.

F12 10205. Sewing thread (1941–4), *haute couture* (1941–2).

F12 10296. Armistice conventions. Franco-German agreements.

F12 10297. Kehrl Plan, 1940.

F12 10298. Franco-German discussions.

F12 10464. 'Fancy textiles', 1941.

F12 10497. Comité d'organisation de l'habillement et du travail des étoffes.

F12 10499. Rationing.

F12 10503. *Haute couture*: general dossier, correspondence, discussions, decisions.

F12 10548. Comité d'organisation de la soie, 1941–5.

F12 10596. Broom.

F12 10607. Fibranne, 1942–5.

F12 10643. Comité d'organisation de l'industrie du cuir, 1940–4.

F12 10691 and 10692. Comité d'organisation des Pelleteries et Fourrures, 1941–4.

F12 10697. Footwear.

F12 10702 and 10703. Clogs and wooden soles.

F12 10801 to 10807. Textiles and leather (Vichy echelon), 1940–4.

AJ 40

German Archives

AJ 40 608, dossier 2: Reports on the subject of Lucien Lelong's accounts sent to the Militärbefelshaber.

AJ 40 774, dossier 1: fur trade, exports to Germany.

AJ 40 777: Textiles plan.

AJ 40 871, dossier 1: list of people staying at the Ritz.

AJ 40 1006, dossier 4: Jewish matters, various reports, denunciations.

AJ 41. Armistice department:

AJ 41 102. Trade with Germany.

AJ 41 171. Economic section. Various business concerns, in particular, France-Rayonne.

AJ 41 199. Trade, 1940–1.

AJ 38 62. Correspondence with the minister of the Interior.

AJ 38 1337. Toutmain centre.

AJ 38 1563, AJ 38 1576. Files of property claimed.

Archives of the Court of Justice

CJ Z 6 non lieu No 1532. Association des Déjeuners de la Table ronde, Lucien Lelong Affair.

Paris Archives (Villemoisson deposits)

901/ 64/ 1. Payment of the direction of the war department, sub-direction of civil and military mobilization, thirteen dossiers of the Comité régional inter-professionnel d'épuration including the textiles and leathers section, box 323.

Union Française des Arts du Costume

Press file on the *couture* houses: J. Fath, J. Lanvin, Chanel, E. Schiaparelli, M. Rochas, L.Lelong, R. Piguet;

Vogue (1939–40)

Harper's Bazaar (1939–40)

The Lucien François Archives in particular, 'Au balcon de la mode', collection of articles.

Published Sources

Barthes, Roland (1967), *Système de la mode*, Paris: Ed. du Seuil.

Chapsal, Madeleine (1989), *La Chair de la robe,* Paris: Fayard.

Delbourg-Delphis, Marylène (1981*), Le Chic et le Look, Histoire de la mode féminine et des mœurs de 1850 à nos jours*, Paris: Hachette.

Deslandres, Yvonne (1985), *'Mode'* Anne Bony, *Les Années 40*, Paris: Ed. du Regard.

Deslandres, Yvonne and Müller, Florence (1986), *Histoire de la mode au xxe siècle,* Paris: Somogy.

Du Roselle, Bruno (1980), *La Mode,* Paris: Imprimerie nationale.

Green, Nancy (1997), *Ready-to-wear and Ready-to-work. A Century of Industry and Immigrants in Paris and New York,* Durham NC/London: Duke University Press.

Grumbach, Didier (1993), *Histoires de la mode,* Paris: Ed. du Seuil.

Latour, Anny (1961), *Les Magiciens de la mode, de Rose Bertin à Christian Dior,* Paris: Julliard.

Packer, William (1983), *Fashion Drawing in Vogue,* London: Thames & Hudson.

Remaury, Bruno (1996), *Dictionnaire de la mode du xxe siècle,* Paris: Ed. du Regard.

Vincent-Ricard, Françoise (1983), *Raison et Passion. Langages de société: la Mode 1940–1990,* Colombes: Textile/Art/Language.

On the period

Amouroux, Henri (1963), *La Vie des Français sous l'Occupation,* Paris: Fayard.

Amouroux, Henri (1976–1993*), La Grande Histoire des Français sous l'Occupation,* Paris: R. Laffont.

Azéma, Jean-Pierre and Bédarida, François (1992), *Vichy et les Français,* Paris: Ed. du Seuil.

Azéma, Jean-Pierre (1984), *From Munich to the Liberation,* New York: Cambridge University Press.

Azéma, Jean-Pierre and Bédarida, François (1993), *La France des années noires,* vol. 1*, De la défaite à Vichy;* vol. 2, *De l'Occupation à la Libération,* Paris: Ed du Seuil.

Azéma, Jean-Pierre and Wieviorka, Oliver (1997), *Vichy: 1940–1944,* Paris: Perrin.

Baruch, Marc-Olivier (1997), *Servir l'Etat français, l'administration en France de 1940 à 1944,* Paris: Fayard.

Burrin, Philippe (1995), *La France à l'heure allemande, 1940–1944,* Paris: Ed. du Seuil.

Delarue, Lacques (1968), *Trafics et crimes sous l'Occupation,* Paris: Fayard.

Jäckel, Eberhard (1968), *La France dans l'Europe de Hitler,* Paris: Fayard.

Laborie, Pierre (1990), *L'Opinion française sous Vichy,* Paris: Ed. du Seuil

Michel, Henri (1981), *Paris allemand,* Paris: Albin Michel.

Muel-Dreyfus, Francine (1996), *Vichy et l'éternel féminin,* Paris: Ed. du Seuil

Novick, Peter (1968), *The Resistance Versus Vichy: the Purge of Collaborators in Liberated France*, London: Chatto & Windus.

Paxton, Robert (1973), *La France de Vichy, 1940–1944*, Paris: Ed. du Seuil

Perrault, Gilles and Jean-Pierre Azéma (1989), *Paris under the Occupation*, London: André Deutsch.

Rousso, Henry (1992), *Les Années noires: vivre sous l'Occupation*, Paris: Gallimard.

Semelin, Jacques (1989), *Sans armes face à Hitler*, Paris: Payot.

Veillon, Dominique (1995), *Vivre et survivre en France, 1939–1947*, Paris: Payot.

Walter, Gérard (1960), *La Vie à Paris sous l'Occupation (1940–1944)*, Paris: Armand Colin.

On Economic Life

Annuaire général textile. Le livre bleu, véritable guide du textile 1942–1943, Lyons: 1942.

Beltran, Alain, Frank, Robert and Rousso, Henry (eds) (1994), *La Vie des entreprises sous l'Occupation. Une enquête à l'èchelle locale*, Paris: Belin.

Commission consultative des dommages et réparations (1951), *Dommages subis par la France et l'Union française du fait de la guerre et de l'occupation ennemie (1939–1945)*, Paris: Imprimerie nationale. (Vol. VI, MP15, Textiles; MP16, Skins and Leather; vol. VIII, PFI, Press.)

Dioudonnat, Pierre-Marie (1981), *L'Argent nazi à la conquête de la presse française (1940–1944)*, Paris: Ed. Picollec.

Marchand, Claire (1999), *Les Fourreurs juifs de Paris sous l'Occupation*, DEA thesis, University of Poitiers.

'Le marché noir allemand en France' in 'Aspects de l'économie française sous l'Occupation', *Cahiers d'histoire de la guerre* 4 (May 1950), pp. 46–71.

Robert, Léon (1944), *L'Industrie de la rayonne en France*, Paris: Ed. de l'industrie textile.

Rousselier-Fraboulet, Danièle (1998), *Les Entreprises sous l'Occupation*, Paris: CNRS.

Rousso, Henry, 'L'Activité industrielle en France de 1940 à 1944, Economie "nouvelle" et occupation allemande, orientation bibliographique', *Bulletin de l'IHTP 38 (*December 1989), pp. 25–68.

Rousso, Henry, *Les Comités d'organisation. Aspects structurels et économiques*. Master's thesis, University of Paris 1, 1976.

Rousso, Henry, 'L'Organisation industrielle de Vichy', *Revue d'histoire de la Seconde Guerre mondiale* 116 (1979), pp. 27–44.

Rousso, Henry, 'L'aryanisation économique: Vichy, l'occupant et la spoliation des juifs', *YOD (Revue des études modernes et contemporaines hébraïques et juives*) special issue 'Les Juifs de France et d'Algérie pendant la Seconde Guerre mondiale' 15–16 (1982), pp. 51–79.

Veillon, Dominique and Flonneau, Jean-Marie (eds), *Le Temps des restrictions en France: 1939–1945, Cahiers de l'IHTP* 32–33 (May 1996) Paris: CNRS.

Verheyde, Philippe (1997), *L'Aryanisation des grandes entreprises juives sous l'Occupation, contraintes, enjeux, pouvoirs*, Doctoral thesis in History, University of Vincennes.

On the Couture Houses (1940–5) and Fashion

Arbaud, Michel, Aubry, Fernand, François Lucien, et al (1945), *Paris et la beauté féminine*, Paris: Société d'Editions Modernes Parisienne.

Delpierre, Madeleine, Boy, Billy, Garnier, Guillaume, White, Palmer (1984*), Hommage à Elsa Schiaparelli*, Paris: Musée de la Mode et du Costume, Palais Galliera. (Catalogue of an exhibition at the Pavillon des arts, 21 June to 30 August 1984.)

Drost, Julia (1998), *Mode unter dem Vichy Regime. Frauenbild und Frauenmode in Frankreich zur Zeit der deutschen Besatzung (1940–1944)*, Pfaffenweiler: Centaurus-Verlogsgesellschaft.

Fiemeyer, Isabelle (1999), *Coco Chanel, un parfum de mystère*, Paris: Payot.

François, Lucien (1946), *Les Elégances de Paris*, Paris: Commissariat Général au Tourisme.

Garnier, Philippe (1987), *Paris couture, années trente*, Paris: Paris-Musées, Société d'Histoire du Costume.

Guillaume, Valérie (1993), *Jacques Fath*, Paris: Paris Musées, Adam Biro. (Catalogue of an exhibition: 'Jacques Fath, les années 50', 21 June to 7 November 1993.)

Images de mode, 1940–1960, Granville: Musée Christian Dior, 1996. (Catalogue of an Exhibition: 'Le Style des années 40, de la paix à la paix'.)

Macdowell, Colin (1997), *Forties Fashion and the New Look*, London: Bloomsbury.

Mohrt, François (1983), *Marcel Rochas: 30 ans d'élégance et de création*, Paris: Ed. Jacques Damase.

Paulvé, Dominique (1995), *Carven, un demi-siècle d'élégance*, Paris: Gründ.

Robinson, Julian (1980), *Fashion in the 40s*, London/New York: Academy Editions/ St Martin's Press.

Sladen, Christopher (1995), *The Conscription of Fashion: Utility Cloth*, Hants.: Scolar Press.

Steele, Valerie (1998), *Se vêtir au xxe siècle, de 1945 à nos jours*, Paris: Adam Biro.

Trois quarts de siècle de fourrures à Paris, n.p.: Jungmann, 1949.

Un siècle de couture parisienne, Paris: Ed. Léonard, 1976. (Catalogue of an Exhibition at the Palais des Congrès, Porte Maillot, Paris, 19 June to 1 August, 1976.)

Vingt-cinq ans d'élégance à Paris, 1925–1950, Paris: Ed Pierre Tisné, 1951.

On Cultural Life

Added, Serge (1992), *Le Théâtre dans les années Vichy*, 1940–1944, Paris: Ed. Ramsay.

Added, Serge, *La Vie littéraire, intellectuelle et artistique en France de 1940 à 1944*, orientation bibliographique, *Bulletin de l'IHTP* 35 (March 1989), pp. 37–58.

Assouline, Pierre (1985), *L'Epuration des intellectuels*, Paris: Ed. Complexe.

Bertin-Maghit, Jean-Pierre (1989), *Le Cinéma sous l'Occupation, le monde du cinéma français de 1940 à 1946*, Paris: Olivier Orban.

Bertrand-Dorléac, Laurence (1986), *Histoire de l'art, Paris 1940–1944*, Paris: Publications de la Sorbonne.

Chenoune, Farid (1993), *Des modes et des hommes, deux siècles d'élégance masculine*, Paris: Flammarion.

Chimènes, Miriam, ed. (2001), *La Vie musicale pendant la guerre*, Brussels: Ed. Complexe.

Costantini, Clorinda (1980), *La Presse féminine des années d'Occupation, juin 1940–août 1944*, doctoral thesis, Troisième cycle, Université de droit et de sciences politiques de Paris II.

Fouché, Pascal (1987, 2001), *L'Edition française sous l'Occupation (1940–1944)*, Paris: Bibliothèque de littérature française contemporaine de l'Université de Paris-7.

Le Boterf, Hervé (1974, 1975), *La Vie parisienne sous l'Occupation*, Paris: France-Empire.

Loiseau, Jean-Claude (1977), *Les Zazous*, Paris: Ed. du Sagittaire.

Lottman, Herbert R. (1981), *La Rive gauche. Du Front Populaire à la guerre froide*, Paris: Ed. du Seuil.

Ragache, Gilles and Jean-Robert (1988), *La Vie quotidienne des écrivains et des artistes sous l'Occupation 1940–1944*, Paris: Hachette.

Rioux, Emmanuelle (1987), *Les Zazous, un phénomène socioculturel pendant l'Occupation*, Master's thesis, Université de Paris-I Nanterre.

Rioux, Jean-Pierre (1990), *La Vie culturelle sous Vichy*, Brussels: Ed. Complexe.

Essays, Recollections, Evidence

Arnoult, Maurice (1993), *Moi Maurice, bottier à Belleville, histoire d'une vie*, Paris: L'Harmattan.

Audiat, Pierre (1946), *Paris pendant la guerre*, Paris: Hachette.

Beauvoir, Simone de (1962), *The Prime of Life*, trans. from the French by Peter Green, London: André Deutsch and Weidenfeld & Nicolson.

Carné, Marcel (1975), *La vie à belles dents: souvenirs*, Paris: J.-P. Ollivier.

Colette (1944*), Paris de ma fenêtre*, Geneva: Ed. du Milieu du Monde.

Cornut-Gentille, Gilles and Michel-Thiriet, Philippe (1989), *Florence Gould, une américaine à Paris*, Paris: Mercure de France.

Dubois, Edmond (1946), *Paris sans lumière 1939–1945*, Lausanne: Payot.

Feuillère, Edwige (1977), *Les Feux de la mémoire*, Paris: Albin Michel.

Guéhenno, Jean (1947), *Journal des années noires (1940–1944)*, Paris: Gallimard.

Guitry, Sacha (1947), *Quatre ans d'Occupation*, Paris: L'Elan.

Heller, Gerhard (1981), *Un Allemand à Paris, 1940–1944*, Paris: Ed. du Seuil.

Hugo, Jean (1983), *Le Regard de la mémoire*, n.p.: Actes Sud.

Jouhandeau, Marcel (1980), *Journal sous l'Occupation*, Paris: Gallimard

Jünger, Ernst (1990*), Journaux de guerre*, Paris: Julliard.

Lartigue, Jacques-Henri (1986), *L'Œil de la mémoire, 1932–1985*, Paris: Carrère.

Leduc, Violette (1961), *La Bâtarde, an Autobiography*, translated from French by Derek Coltman: London: Peter Owen.

Lifar, Serge (1965), *Ma Vie*, Paris: Julliard.

Luchaire, Corinne (1949), *Ma drôle de vie*, Paris: Sun.

Marais, Jean (1975), *Histoires de ma vie*, Paris: Albin Michel.

Schiaparelli, Elsa (1954), *Shocking Life*, London: J.M. Dent.

Schiaparelli, Elsa (1954), *Shocking, Souvenirs d'Elsa Schiaparelli*, Paris: Denoël.

Signoret, Simone (1976), *La Nostalgie n'est plus ce qu'elle était*, Paris: Ed. du Seuil.

Daily Papers, Magazines and Periodicals

Documents Français (les), Revue des hautes études politiques, sociales, économiques et financières, in particular the issue of January 1944 on French industry and the clothing industries.

Figaro (Le), (1939–42)

Gerbe (La), (1940–4)

Illustration (L'), (1940–4)

Je suis partout, (1940–4)

Jour-Echo de Paris (Le), (1939–42)

Marianne (1939–40)
Matin (Le), 1940–4)
Nouveaux Temps (Les), 1940–4)
Œuvre (L') (1939–44)
Paris-Soir (1940–4)
Semaine (La)
Signal (1940–4)
Toute la vie (1941–4)
Une semaine à Paris (1939–41)

Women's Magazines and Fashion Journals

L'Art et la Mode (1940–4), Bibliothèque des Arts Décoratifs, JP 13.
La Femme Chic (1940–4), JO 50 644, BNF Tolbiac.
Marie-Claire (1939–44), 4° JO 268, ibid.
La Mode Chic (1940–44), JO 64796, ibid.
La Mode du Jour (1940–2) JO 68 231, ibid.
Modes et Travaux (1939–44), UFAC, Paris
L'Officiel de la couture et de la mode de Paris (1940–4), Musée Galliera.
Le Petit Echo de la Mode (1939–44), JO 40047, BNF Tolbiac.
Pour Elle (1940–2), 4o JO 1442, ibid.
Silhouettes (1942–7) Musée Galliera.
Votre Beauté (1939–44), ibid.

Trade Journals

La Coiffure de Paris, JO 65891, BNF Tolbiac.
Coiffures de Paris, JO 64229, ibid.
Fourrures et Pelleteries (1943–4), JO 68402, ibid.
Ganterie, Revue technique de la ganterie française, JO 671321, ibid.
L'Hermine, L'Officiel de la fourrure et de la pelleterie, 4° JO 3460, ibid.
Journal de la chaussure française, JO 65877, ibid.
L'Officiel de la fourrure (1946), Musée Galliera.
Pasquier, *Elégante quand même, comment tailler et exécuter un tailleur, un manteau, une jupe-culotte, transformations pratiques*, Paris: Ed. de Montsouris, 1942, 40 pp., 8° Z 29104 (6).
Pigier, *Cours de coupe*, Paris, 1942, 143 pp., 4° V 14280, BNF Tolbiac.
La Revue de la fourrure, revue mensuelle, organe officiel de la fédération de fourreurs et pelletiers de province, 4° JO 580, ibid.

Revue de vêtement. Organe des industries des vêtements et des commerces fournisseurs de ces industries. Mensuel, no 1, June 1942, FOL JO 3027, ibid.

Textiles. Bulletin du Comité général d'organisation de l'industrie textile, July 1941, 4° V 14 080, ibid.

Chronological Landmarks

1939

1 September: German troops invade Poland. General mobilization.

3 September: Great Britain and France declare war on Germany.

1940

10 May: Beginning of the German western offensive. Belgium and the Netherlands invaded.

18 May: Cabinet reshuffle, Philippe Pétain appointed vice-president of the council.

10 June: The government leaves Paris.

14 June: The Germans occupy Paris.

16 June: Resignation of Paul Reynaud. Pétain replaces him.

17 June: Pétain asks for armistice conditions.

18 June: First appeal by General de Gaulle by radio from London.

22 June: Signature of the armistice agreement at Rethondes.

29 June: Government leaves Bordeaux and settles in Vichy via Clermont-Ferrand.

6 July: The Casino de Paris re-opens.

10 July: At Vichy the National Assembly grants full powers to the Maréchal's government (569 votes against 80).

16 July: Laval the Maréchal's heir apparent.

26 July: The Théâtre des Ambassadeurs re-opens.

5 August: Otto Abetz appointed German ambassader to Paris.

8 August: The Battle of Britain begins.

16 August: Law published involving the temporary creation of the Comités d'Organisation.

23 August: Creation of the Légion Français des Combattants.

24 August: The Opéra re-opens.

10 September: Creation of the Office Central de Répartition des Produits Industriels.

17 September: Rationing of the main food products introduced.

27 September: In the occupied zone, the occupier promulgates an ordinance relating to Jews.

3 October: In Vichy the Council of Ministers institutes a Statut des Juifs.

12 October: The Paris race courses re-open.

18 October: Definition and census of Jewish businesses.

20 October: Food ration books become general.

24 October: Pétain and Hitler meet at Montoire. During October the fashion houses present their collections.

1 November: Jean Luchaire brings out *Les Nouveaux Temps*.

11 November: High school pupils and students demonstrate in Paris.

13 December: Laval dismissed.

15 December: Napoleon's ashes returned to Paris.

1941

5 January: Shoe coupons introduced.

23 January: Decree forbids throwing away, destroying or burning old metal, old papers, pens, rubber, bones, skins, leather.

February: *Le Juif Süss* shown in Paris cinemas.

9–10 February: Pierre-Etienne Flandin resigns. Darlan appointed vice-president of the Council and Minister of Foreign Affairs.

10 February: Reception given by Jean Luchaire on the occasion of the publication of the 100th issue of *Nouveaux Temps*.

21 March: Gala of the Union des Artistes at Bagatelle.

8 May: Publication of an ordinance of the Militärbefelshaber in Frankreich: the ordinance lists professions forbidden to Jews.

30 May: Inauguration of the exhibition 'La France Européenne'.

2 June: Second Statut des Juifs in the Vichy *Journal Officiel.*

22 June: German troops invade the Soviet Union.

24 June: Inauguration by Dr Michel and M. de Brinon of the '*couture* and mode' section at the 'La France Européenne' exhibition in the presence of L.Lelong, J. Fath, J. Lanvin, and G. Lecomte.

July 1941: Franco-German exhibition of the new textiles at the Petit-Palais.

1 July: Temporary clothes rationing book comes into force.

6 July: Journée des Drags.

7 July: Formation of the Légion des Volontaires Français contre le Bolchevisme.

3–14 July: Exposition de la Chaussure 1941.

14 July: Demonstration in the République district; arrests.

23 July: Concours de l'Elégance à Bicyclette in the Pavillon d'Armenonville.

13 August: Demonstration at Porte-Saint-Denis; arrests.

21 August: German officer assassinated on the platform of Barbès metro station.

23 August: Creation of special courts to try communists.

27 August: Assassination attempt by Paul Colette at Versailles against P. Laval and M. Déat.

5 September: Exhibition 'Le Juif et la France' opens at the Palais Berlitz.

11 September: Paris soirée at the Ambassadeurs.

11 September: Collecting broom made compulsory.

4 October: Charte de Travail promulgated.

5 October: Prix de l'Arc de Triomphe.

25 October: The Paris press celebrates the first anniversary of the formation of the corporate body and holds a soirée at Tabarin.

23 November: Winter salon at Tokio.

During December: Re-opening of the race-course at Vincennes.

8 December: America enters the war.

1942

1 March: The 'Le bolchevisme contre l'Europe' exhibition opens in Paris.

3 March: The Allies bomb Boulogne-Billancourt.

6 March: Some twenty Paris *couture* houses present their collections in Lyons.

15 March: Law passed regulating the black market.

27 March: Decree ordering the collection of hair from hairdressing salons.

17 April: Darlan resigns.

18 April: Laval becomes head of government.

May: Publicity gala at Tabarin in the presence of fashionable Paris.

15 May: Arno Breker exhibition opens at the Orangerie.

29 May: Jews living in the occupied zone forced to wear the yellow star.

22 June: Laval launches the first radio appeal on behalf of the Relève and voices his desire for a German victory.

27 June: Paris Grand Prix.

14 July: Patriotic demonstrations in Paris and the provinces.

16–17 July: Round-up at the Vel' d'Hiv in Paris.

27 July: Production of *Songe d'une Nuit d'Été* at the château de Montredon, the home of Comtesse Pastré.

4 September: Publication of the law relating to the utilization and orientation of the workforce. Battle of Stalingrad begins.

26 October: Opening of the presentations of the *haute couture* collections.

8 November: Anglo-American landing in French North Africa.

11 November: The Germans occupy the Southern Zone.

December: Release of *Visiteurs du Soir* at Paris cinemas.

1943

11 January: Thirty metro stations closed.

26 January: The three main Resistance movements in the Southern Zone merge, birth of the MUR (Mouvements Unis de Résistance).

30 January: The Militia formed.

2 February: Von Paulus's army corps surrenders at Stalingrad.

16 February: Law creating the Service du travail obligatoire promulgated.

27 February: La nuit du cinéma takes place at the Gaumont-Palace. Arletty, Charles Trénet, Maurice Chevalier, Gaby Morlay, Marie Déa, Edwige Feuillère supported it.

4 April: Outskirts of Paris bombed.

14 April: Talks between Dr Schilling and Jacques Deligny at the Majestic.

27 May: The Comité National de la Résistance meets for the first time.

3 June: Comité Français de Libération Nationale created, headed by De Gaulle-Giraud.

21 June: Arrests of Caluire.

17 August: Speer-Bichelonne agreement on the creation of Speer-Betriebe.

September: Autumn parade in the *haute couture* houses.

October: Exhibition of substitute products in Paris.

27 November: First night of *Soulier de Satin* in Paris.

1944

6 January: Philippe Henriot becomes Secretary of State for information and propaganda.

17 February: Trial of the so-called red Affiche 'terrorists'.

5 March: Auteuil re-opens.

26 April: Pétain in Paris.

26–27 May: France heavily bombed by the Allies.

6 June: Allied landings in Normandy.

21 June: 76th Paris Grand Prix at Auteuil.

18 August: The collaborationist press newspapers cease publication.

Notes

Chapter 1 The Last Good Days

1. Corinne Luchaire (daughter of the journalist, Jean Luchaire), *Ma drôle de vie*, Paris, Sun, 1949, 104.
2. From *Le Jour-Echo de Paris*, June 1939. (National daily, formed by the amalgamation of two titles shortly before 1939: *Le Jour*, founded by Léon Bailby in 1933, and the old conservative paper *L'Echo de Paris*. In 1940 *Le Jour-Echo de Paris* withdrew to the southern zone – including Marseilles and Clermont-Ferrand – before disappearing in March 1942.)
3. Anny Latour, *Les Magiciens de la mode*, Paris, Julliard, 1962, 258.
4. *Le Jour-Echo de Paris*, 16 September 1939.
5. Among recent books published about this *couturière*, see in particular, Isabelle Fiemeyer, *Coco Chanel, un parfum de mystère,* Paris, Payot, 1999.
6. See the dossier Chanel, Union des Arts du Costume, Museum of Decorative Arts. See also the exhibition catalogue *Paris-Couture – Années 30*, 1987, Ed. Paris Musées et Société de l'histoire du costume, 1987.
7. *La Semaine, l'hebdomadaire de l'actualité mondiale*, 'Modèles de France', no. 38, 3 April 1941.
8. *Mode du Jour*, no. 938, 13 April 1939, 'A presentation of fashion with the great *couturiers*'. (Founded in 1921, this is one of the oldest women's publications, well produced and reasonably priced, printing easily copied designs of gowns, lingerie and knitwear. After a break in June 1940, the paper reappeared in December 1940. Its print run reached almost 100,000 copies and it had more than 20,000 subscribers in 1944.)
9. *Mode du Jour*, no. 880, March 1938.
10. Edna Woolman Chase joined *Vogue* in 1895 when she was eighteen. In 1914 she became editor, a position she retained until she retired in 1952.
11. *Votre Beauté*, interview with Lucien Lelong, September 1939. (Luxury monthly fashion journal, modern in its conception. It was devoted to physical culture, beauty treatments and the presentation of the collections. During the war its print run was between 50,000 and 100,000 copies. It was distributed by individual sales and subscription in the occupied zone, and by subscription only in the free zone. Its editor was Lucien François and occasional contributors included René Rambaud, Fernand Aubry on cosmetics, Antonio on coiffure and Lucien Lelong on fashion.)

12. *Marianne,* August 1939, Henriette Vermond. (Left-wing political and literary weekly, founded in 1936, whose editor was Emmanuel Berl. H. Vermond signed the important women's column. The paper disappeared after June 1940.)
13. *Mode du Jour,* no. 938, 13 April 1939.
14. From *Vogue, Marianne, Marie-Claire, Une Semaine à Paris*, August 1939, which published these reactions to the presentation of the preview of the autumn-winter collection. Everyday styles also loomed large in this trend (see *Nouveauté* or *Le Petit Echo de la Mode*).
15. See the evidence of Boris Kochno: '. . . there was nothing warlike about these improvised soldiers, and their elegant uniforms, often not the regulation uniform, resembled a fancy-dress made to be worn for only a brief period', *Christian Bérard*, Paris, Herscher, 1987, 56.
16. *Le Jour-Echo de Paris*, 7 November 1939.
17. Corinne Luchaire, *Ma drôle de Vie*, 105.
18. Quoted in *Les Années 1940, La vie continue*, 16–25 May 1940, publication *Historia*, no. 98, Librairie Tallandier, 1971.
19. Edmond Dubois, *Paris sans lumière*, Lausanne, Payot, 1946.
20. The phrase is found in *Vogue*, French edition, September 1939. Several women's magazines stressed the need for a practical style dictated by the continual comings and goings. The magazine ceased publication in 1940. It reappeared in 1945.
21. *Fourrures Magazine*, February–March 1940, 29. A number of advertisements extolling the virtues of sheepskin and other jackets appeared in all the trade journals. The following example is taken from *La Revue de la Fourrure*, February 1940: 'Wholesale Furs and Skins, Elie Ramage & Co., 10 rue de Dijon, Chalon-sur-Saône: specialist in sheepskin jackets and waistcoats for soldiers.'
22. Interview with Alice Le Bris-Lehmans, autumn, 1999.
23. *Marianne*, 'Fashion during the war as seen by Maggy Rouff', 20 December 1939.
24. 'We built up a collection in three weeks hoping for some response. This was the "cash and carry" collection with huge pockets everywhere so that a woman, obliged to leave home in a hurry or to go on duty without a bag, could pack all that was necessary to her. She could thus retain the freedom of her hands and yet manage to look feminine.' See Elsa Schiaparelli, *Shocking Life*, London, J. M. Dent, 1954, 115.
25. *Fourrures Magazine*, November 1939.
26. Report by Lucien Lelong, *La couture française de juillet 1940 à août 1944*, Archives nationales CJ Z6 non lieu, no. 15352. (Several contemporary magazines made this comparison.)

27. *Votre Beauté*, editorial by Lucien François, Christmas, 1939. See also: 'At a time when the country needs foreign currency, we must make every effort to increase our export figures. Our overseas clientèle has resumed its usual way of life . . . We have another duty. Twenty thousand working women and 500 male employees make their living from Parisian *couture*. It also has a direct influence on the life of other industries: textiles, silk, furs, lace, etc.' *Fourrures Magazine*, Hélène Simart, interview with Lucien Lelong, p. 7, November 1939.
28. Ibid., April 1940, May 1940.
29. *Fourrures Magazine,* November 1939.
30. 'La mode et la guerre' ('Fashion and the War'), *Marianne*, 6 December 1939.
31. Edward Molyneux, who wasted no time before he closed his boutique and settled in London.
32. 'Infirmière des hommes' ('Nurse to Men'), *Marianne*, 18 October 1939; also, 'C'est pour eux' ('For Them We Do It'), ibid., 27 December 1939.
33. *La Revue de la Fourrure*, No. 12, December 1939.
34. In honour of the British allies (and more specifically the pilots of the Royal Air Force) who were fighting by France's side.
35. This cover was the work of the designer Pagès for the March 1940 issue; see William Packer, *Dessins de mode, Vogue, 1923–1983*, Paris, Ed. Herscher, 1983, 105.
36. Quoted by Henri Amouroux, *Le Peuple du désastre*, Paris, Laffont, 1976, 189.
37. *L'Œuvre*, 16 May 1940. (National daily, which was the organ of radical circles before the war. The paper moved to Clermont-Ferrand in August 1940 but returned to Paris in September 1940, where it appeared from 21 September under the editorship of Marcel Déat, the anti-Vichy, pro-German founder of the RNP movement [Rassemblement National Populaire]. The weekly women's page was signed by pseudonyms: Elyane or Gisèle or the initials PC. It had a circulation of about 195,000.)
38. *Paris-Midi*, offshoot of *Paris-Soir*, which appeared throughout the occupation.
39. *L'Action Française*, royalist-orientated daily, edited by Charles Maurras. On the capitulation, it retreated to Poitiers, Limoges and Lyons, where it supported Maréchal Pétain while remaining hostile to the Germans.
40. *Paris-Soir,* 24 June 1940. (*Paris-Soir,* a daily evening paper, appeared before the war. It was one of the first titles to be published in Paris, from 22 June 1940, under the editorship of a former employee of the paper, Schliesse, then Eugène Gerber. Its circulation of 970,000 in November 1940 stabilized at around 300,000 in July 1942. Closely influenced by the Germans, who subsidized it, the paper had a large number of correspondents. It included a regular women's column, to which Andrée Morane contributed.)

Chapter 2 New Formulas for New Times

1. *Le Matin*, 19 June 1940. (A daily paper aimed at a working-class public. It was run by Maurice Bunau-Varilla. Publication was suspended at the beginning of June 1940 but resumed in Paris on 17 June. Jean Luchaire was its editor in chief until he founded *Les Nouveaux Temps*. After Luchaire left, Jacques Ménard took over the editorship. The paper had many occasional contributors, including Robert de Beauplan, André du Bief and Camille Mauclair. Lucie Hirigoyen contributed to the weekly women's page. The print run fell from 532,000 copies in November 1940 to no more than 200,000 in July 1942.)
2. Blanche Auroy, *Journal d'une institutrice pendant la guerre*, Paris, September 1940 – February 1942, 044, Archives IHTP.
3. Ibid.
4. Jacques-Henri Lartigue, *Instants de ma vie*, Paris, Arène, 1970.
5. *Pour Elle*, 'Paris se refait', 21 August 1940, a long report by Violette Leduc, a cub journalist recommended to the editor by the writer Maurice Sachs. (*Pour Elle*, a weekly fashion journal, founded in August 1940 with German consent and appearing until March 1942. It contained a large number of fashion and beauty items, advice on dress and the reproduction of current models. Launched with a print-run of 404,000 copies, 330,000 were printed in 1941. Regular contributors included Fanny Clair, André Thérive and, above all, Violette Leduc who published regular features on fashion.)
6. *L'Officiel de la Couture et de la Mode*, no. 234, February 1941, 13.
7. *Le Figaro*, 'La page féminine', December 1940. (A national daily before the war, it withdrew to Lyons and was published from there until it was wound up in November 1942. Although its circulation constantly declined, *Le Figaro* had 8,000 subscribers at that date, according to Pierre Brisson. The paper reappeared at the Liberation.)
8. *Le Mot d'Ordre*, 21 August 1940. (A Left-wing daily that appeared in Marseilles in 1941–4, edited by Ludovic-Oscar Frossard.)
9. Jacques-Henri Lartigue, *L'Œil de la mémoire – 1932–1985*, Paris, Carrère, Editions 13, 1986, 179.
10. The first German ordinance on the Jews was promulgated in the occupied zone on 27 September 1940. It defined their identity and commanded that a yellow poster, 'Jewish Business', be placed on Jewish shops. In addition, it forbade Jews in the free zone from returning to the occupied zone. The first statute on the Jews formulated by Vichy was promulgated on 3 October 1940 (this was a purely French initiative): it defined the Jews and excluded them from a certain number of professions. On 18 October 1940 a German ruling ordered a census of Jewish businesses. It was followed by Aryanization with the nomination of *administrateurs provisoires* (temporary administrators). Cf.,

Philippe Verheyde, *L'Aryanisation des grandes entreprises juives sous l'Occupation. Contraintes, enjeux, pouvoirs*, doctoral thesis in history, University of Paris VIII, December 1997, volume 1, chapter 1, 21–44; see also volume 3, appendices, chronological table of laws. Clothing and leather businesses were particularly affected by these regulations.

11. Raymond Corot, *Trente ans de chiffons*, Paris, La Table Ronde, 1964.

12. According to AJ3862, Archives nationales, dossier on the relations of the Commissariat général aux questions juives with ministers, letter from the president of the Chamber of Commerce to the sub-prefect, 30 January 1941. Cf., Philippe Verheyde, *L'Aryanisation*, 46.

13. Lucien Rebatet, *Les Décombres*, Paris, Ed. Denoël, 1942, 481.

14. Ibid., 499.

15. Cf., Myriam Chimènes (ed.), *La Vie musicale pendant la guerre*, Brussels, Complexe, 2001. See the contribution by Josette Alviset, 'La programmation musicale à Vichy: les apparences de la continuité'.

16. Jean Débordes, *Vichy, capitale à l'heure allemande*, Paris, Godefroy de Bouillon, 1988, 77.

17. On 12 July 1940, the National Assembly meeting in Vichy decided almost unanimously that there were good reasons to revise the constitution. Full powers were voted to Philippe Pétain who founded the French state, bringing the French Republic to an end. Only eighty parliamentarians, deputies and senators, opposed it and said 'no' to Pétain. They included Vincent Auriol, Léon Blum, Max Dormoy, Louis Noguères and André Philip.

18. According to Débordes, *Vichy*, 22.

19. Léon-Paul Fargue, 'Paris 1941,' in *Patrie*, first year, 1941, no. 3.

20. Dubois, *Paris sans lumière*, 124–5.

21. Lartigue, *L'Œil de la mémoire*, 199.

22. Alfred Fabre-Luce, *Journal de la France, août 1940 – avril 1942*, Paris, Imprimerie JEP, 1942, 139–40.

23. *Les Nouveaux Temps*, 22 October 1941. (Daily evening paper that collaborated with the Germans, founded and edited by Jean Luchaire in autumn 1940, first issue, 1 November 1940. Its contributors included Guy Crouzet and Guy Zucharelli. Lucien François signed the description of the presentation of the collections in it. Its founders regarded it as the best informed paper of upper-crust Paris. It was considered to be the official organ of Otto Abetz. Circulation: 40,000 in July 1942.)

24. In September 1942, *Silhouettes*, no. 165, praised 'simple and comfortable designs for sports, including one-piece pantsuits' (pp. 18–19).

25. *Marie-Claire*, no. 24, June 1942. (Women's magazine launched in 1937, popular with its clientèle because of its Americanized appearance. Moved to Lyons in September 1940, set up at 65 cours de la Liberté and was published

throughout the war. Its circulation verged on 80,000 in 1940. Contributors included Marcelle Auclair.)

26. Lartigue, *L'Œil de la mémoire,* 203.
27. Ibid., p. 204.
28. *L'Œuvre*, 18 November 1940.
29. Dubois, *Paris sans lumière,* 110.
30. Fabre-Luce, *Journal de la France,* 139–40.
31. *Le Matin*, 23 February 1942.
32. Born Caroline-Edwige Cunati. Cf., *Les Feux de la mémoire*, Paris, Albin Michel, 1977, in which the actress recalls some wartime memories.
33. *Marie-Claire,* 27 December 1941.
34. Jean-Paul Sartre's companion, a young philosophy teacher at the outbreak of war, 'putting an end to ten years of marvellously free life'. During the occupation, Simone de Beauvoir was in Paris where she taught at a high school. She learned to ride a bicycle, wore clogs with wooden soles and ski pants. In those days her external appearance meant nothing to her. 'I had enjoyed keeping up my personal appearance in the days when such activities formed a pleasurable diversion; but I had no wish now to burden my existence with pointless complications of this sort, and so I stopped bothering.' Simone de Beauvoir, *The Prime of Life*, London, 1962, 400.
35. Michèle Bood, *Les années doubles, journal d'une lycéenne sous l'Occupation*, Paris, Laffont, 1974 (5 January 1941).
36. Quoted by Gérard Walter, *La Vie à Paris sous l'Occupation*, Paris, A. Colin, 1960, 110.
37. Auroy, *Journal d'une institutrice.*
38. *Le Figaro*, 15 January 1941.
39. Schiaparelli, *Shocking Life,* 115.
40. *La Semaine*, no. 35, 13 March 1941.
41. Alfred Fabre-Luce, *Vingt-cinq années de liberté. 2: L'épreuve, 1939–1946,* Paris, Julliard, 1963, 64–5.
42. *L'Œuvre*, 4 November 1940.
43. *L'Œuvre,* 18 November 1940.
44. *La Femme Chic*, no. 35, October 1940. (*La Femme Chic* was an A. Louchel publication. This monthly journal was essentially aimed at provincial *couturiers*, suggesting designs for them to reproduce. The fashion column was written by Lucie Neumayer-Hirigoyen. The journal printed 30,000 copies and circulated solely in the occupied zone.)
45. *L'Œuvre*, 18 November 1940.
46. *Le Matin*, 9 November 1940, Lucie Hirigoyen's women's page.
47. Ibid.
48. Fabre-Luce, *Journal de la France,* 144–5.

49. Juliette Clarens, 'L'élégance sous toutes ses coutures,' *L'Illustration*, 5 October 1940. (Illustrated weekly edited by René Baschet. Resumed publication in August 1940. Its principal contributors included Robert de Beauplan, Jacques de Lesdain, Léon-Paul Fargue, and Juliette Clarens.)

Chapter 3 Hard Times

1. From September 1940 bread and pâtés were rationed; in autumn 1941 almost every commodity was subject to quotas. The population was divided into Es (under three years old), Js (children and adolescents), As (21 to 70 year-olds) and Vs (over 70). Cf. Dominique Veillon, *Vivre et Survivre en France, 1939–1947*, Paris, Payot, 1995.
2. *Le Journal de la chaussure française. Revue professionelle du commerce et de l'industrie,* September 1940, JO-65877, BNF-Tolbiac. (Trade journal.)
3. Gauleiter Hans Kehrl, in charge of textile planning for the Reich, wanted 'a division of raw materials between German military requirements and French civilian needs', hence the drawing up of a convention. Throughout 1941 France was deprived of almost all its stocks: it had to hand over 25,000 tons of raw wool, 5,000 tons of worsted, 10,000 tons of cotton. After that only a contract policy prevailed. A similar convention was in force for leather: the Grunberg plan, from the name of the German in charge of leather. Cf. also Michael Margairaz, *L'Etat, les finances et l'économie. Histoire d'une conversion, 1932–1952*, Comité pour l'histoire économique et financière de la France, vol. 1, 1991, 609 and 612–13.
4. This was the law on professional organizations of 16 August 1940.
5. *Journal officiel de la République française*, 30 October 1940, Comité Général d'Organisation de l'Industrie Textile.
6. Or OCRPI. The OCRPI was created on 10 September 1940.
7. Quoted by Michael Margairaz, preface by Philippe Verheyde, *Les Mauvais Comptes de Vichy. L'organisation des entreprises juives*, Paris, Perrin, 1999, 9–10.
8. Georges Ravon, 'Où va l'industrie de la chaussure?', *Le Figaro*, 25 September 1940.
9. Testimony of M. Vialatte, master shoemaker, in *L'Œuvre*, 25 November 1940.
10. *Le Petit Parisien*, 16 January 1941. (Paris daily that withdrew to the free zone but returned to the capital, from where it reappeared on 8 October 1940. It had a large mass readership and a circulation of 680,000 in November 1940.)
11. Cf. *Le Journal de la chaussure,* 22 October 1940.
12. Estimates by professionals vary between 60 million and 80 million. Cf. *Le Journal de la chaussure,* 28 January 1941, 12 September 1942; also *Le Cuir,* 13 December 1941.

13. Jean Bichelonne, a graduate of the Ecole polytechnique, Secretary-general for industry and commerce from 18 July 1940 to 25 April 1942, then Secretary of Industrial Production in the Laval government until November 1942.
14. Archives nationales, AJ 4179, AJ 41 171.
15. Archives nationales, F12 10640, 'a provisional statistic drawing up the balance sheet of the occupation for ten years stipulates that more than 45 per cent of industrial establishments in the Leather sector worked for the Germans': from Philippe Verheyde, *L'Aryanisation,* vol. 1, 128.
16. *Journal officiel,* 3 January 1941.
17. *Les Nouveaux Temps,* 11 February 1941.
18. *L'Œuvre*, 'Chaussures pour première communiantes,' 22 March 1941.
19. *Marie-Claire*, 8 March 1941.
20. Bood, *Les Années doubles,* 203.
21. Colette, *Paris de ma fenêtre*, Paris, Editions de Milieu du Monde, 1944, 217.
22. Better known as Madame Grès.
23. *L'Œuvre, Images de France,* 30 March 1941. *Images de France* was a monthly periodical published by *L'Illustration*. It was not a fashion journal but dealt with art, decoration and tourism, as well as devoting a few pages to fashion. It had a circulation of 33,000.)
24. *La Gerbe*, 24 July 1941. (A collaborationist weekly which first appeared on 10 July 1940. It was edited by Alphonse de Chateaubriant. Jeanne Fernandez was the signature found most frequently on the women's page.)
25. *Le Journal de la chaussure,* August 1941.
26. Archives nationales, AJ 41 171, F 12 10296.
27. Cf. Plan for Leather, Archives nationales, F 3733, F 3720, in Margairaz, *L'Etat, les finances et l'économie,* 613.
28. Archives nationales, AJ 41171, F 12 10296.
29. 'In 1943 the town of Nancy receives an allocation for six months of 3,650 pairs of shoes for town use (low shoes with rubber soles), 507 pairs of walking shoes (laced boots with rubber soles), and 22,425 pairs of fancy shoes (all shoes with wooden soles).' There was general discontent. Cf. Bertrand Heyraud, *5,000 ans de chaussures*, Bournemouth, Editions Parkstone, 1994, 126.
30. Edmée Renaudin, *Sans fleur au fusil*, Paris, Stock, 1979.
31. *Tout et Tout,* 22 March 1941.
32. 'Sales are paid for in cash or are bartered with other goods that are reputed to be scarce. This system makes it possible to buy raw materials outside the allocation and thus improve one's resources. Black market transactions must not leave any trace in the accounts. It is possible to sell up to 50 per cent of production without too great a risk of attracting inspections by the fiscal authorities and the economic police, which are frequent. What they had to fear most were denunciations by a client or a dissatisfied trader because, alas,

denunciation is prevalent everywhere.' Maurice Arnoult, *Moi, Maurice, bottier à Belleville, Histoire d'une vie* (collected by Michel Bloit), Paris, L'Harmattan, 1993, 122.

33. Archives National, F 12 10192.
34. *Les Nouveaux Temps*, 'A la tribune', 7 May 1941.
35. *L'Œuvre,* 15 April 1941.
36. Interview with Jo Cardin-Massé, 1987, and report by the commissioner of police for the Sorbonne district, Archives of the prefecture of police, Telegram 34, carton PJ 33.
37. According to *L'Œuvre,* 27 January 1941.
38. Arnoult, *Moi, Maurice,* 118.
39. *L'Œuvre,* 20 May 1941.
40. *Les Nouveaux Temps*, 26 June 1941.
41. *Silhouettes*, no. 176, August 1943.
42. *Mode du jour*, 1 August 1943.
43. *Au Pilori*, quoted in Dominique Veillon, *La Collaboration*, Paris, Hachette, 1984, coll. Textes et Débats, 235–6. (The paper was called *Hebdomadaire de combat contre la judéo-maçonnerie.* It first appeared on 12 July 1940.)

Chapter 4 Making Do and Looking Smart

1. Dossier, 'Carte de vêtements', Archives nationales, F 12 10499.
2. Ibid.
3. *Le Matin*, 14 February 1941.
4. From *Marie-Claire*, no. 215, 6 September 1941.
5. *Le Figaro*, 7 May 1942.
6. From *Le Figaro*, 5 February 1942.
7. Colette, *Paris de ma Fenêtre*, 104.
8. *Le Petit Echo de la Mode*, Archives nationales, F 41 1247. Its President, Jacques Moy, had been a volunteer in the Free French Forces. The paper appeared at the Liberation with a print run of 350,000.
9. *Pour Elle*, no. 10, 16 October 1940.
10. *L'Œuvre*, 12 August 1941.
11. *Marie-Claire*, 25 January 1941.
12. Paris, Editions de Montsouris, 1942, 47 pp. 8-Z-29104, BNF-Tolbiac.
13. Correspondence, Archives nationales, F 12 10804.
14. Ibid.
15. Service du rationnement, Archives nationales, F 12 10205.
16. *La Revue de la Fourrure*, May-June 1942; these grievances are set out on p. 277.

17. Archives nationales, ibid.
18. Simone Signoret, *La Nostalgie n'est plus ce qu'elle était,* Paris, Seuil, 1976, 75.
19. *Bulletin du Comité d'organisation générale de l'industrie textile*, July 1941, 4° V 14080, BNF-Tolbiac.
20. 'Interdictions', Archives nationales, F 12 10503.
21. Archives nationales, F 12 10503.
22. Maggy Rouff (Anne-Marie Besançon de Wagner), *La Philosophie de l'élégance*, Editions littéraires de France, Paris, 1942, 141–2.
23. Colette, *De ma fenêtre*, in *Œuvres complètes*, Paris, Editions du Centenaire, Club de l'Honnête Homme, 1973, 48.
24. 'The smallest hat that they placed on their heads held the promise of that sublime August storm during which Paris was going to throw off its enemies, its chains and its false prophets at one fell swoop', *Silhouette*, 1945.
25. Interview with Jacques Delamare, manufacturer of cloth flowers, June 1989.
26. Violette Leduc, 'Un chapeau qui n'est pas un chapeau', *Pour Elle*, 4 September 1940.
27. 'Because of electricity cuts the hairdressers worked at odd and irregular hours, and an ordinary set became a hazardous ordeal, with the result that turbans came into fashion; they formed a simultaneous substitute for a hat and a permanent', de Beauvoir, *The Prime of Life*, 400.
28. Ernst Jünger, *Premier journal parisien, 1941–1943*, Paris, Livre de Poche, Hachette, 1980, 52. Ernst Jünger was a German writer who kept a war diary from 1939 to 1945. Assigned to the German general staff in Paris, Jünger patronized the capital's high spots and could be found at Prunier, La Tour d'argent, the Ritz, and so forth. He dined with Cocteau, Jouhandeau, Arletty, and Sacha Guitry.
29. *Le Figaro*, 3 June 1941.
30. Violette Leduc, *Tout et Tout*, reportage, 19 April 1941.
31. Colette, *Paris de ma fenêtre*, 89.
32. Schiaparelli, *Shocking Life*, 164.
33. *Images de France*, February 1941.
34. *Les Nouveaux Temps*, 'L'agressivité des "couteaux"', 12 June 1941.
35. Gérard d'Houville, 'La Parisienne et la mode', in *Paris 1943*, Presses Universitaires de France, n.d., 46.
36. Limitation de l'emploi de tissus rentrant dans la confection de chapeaux de dames, Archives nationales, F 12 10503.
37. Lartigue, *Instants de ma vie*, 202.
38. Lucien Lelong, *La Couture française*, non lieu no. 15352 Archives nationales.
39. Schiaparelli, *Shocking Life*, 131.

Chapter 5 Fibranne, Rayon and Ersatz

1. By artificial fibres we mean all usable products in the textile industry obtained by a chemical process: continuous fibres of rayon, lanital and so forth.
2. *Journal Officiel de la République française*, 7 August 1940. The decree of 9 July 1940 had already made it compulsory to declare stocks of certain textile materials. The measure was extended to artificial fibres, rags and sewing thread.
3. Report of the interview with M. Hartman, in charge of textiles for the German administration of the occupied territories, 14 August 1940: Archives nationales, F 1210297.
4. Note on the plan for Franco-German economic collaboration in the textile industry, Ministry of Production and Labour, Archives nationales, F 1210297.
5. Le Majestic, from the name of the hotel taken over by the German censorship and propaganda departments.
6. Archives nationales, F 1210297.
7. The interview took place in August 1940 before the decision to introduce clothes rationing was taken (see Chapters 2 and 3).
8. Archives nationales, F 1210297.
9. Note on the Franco-German textile plan: Archives nationales, AJ 41 171.
10. Note, 21 November 1940: Archives nationales, F 1210297. Y. Bouthillier, supporter of the armistice and of the national revolution, was one of the theorists whom Maréchal Pétain listened to most. He was Minister of Finance, 12 July 1940 – 6 September 1940, then Secretary of State for Economy and Finance until 18 April 1942.
11. Inquiry into the Lyons textile industry, chief inspector Galmier, Assistant Inspector General of the Economy, to the Secretary of State for Industrial Production, 14 June 1941, Archives nationales, F 12 10548. See also, Jocelyne Vidal-Blanchard, *Les Voies de l'élégance*, Paris, La Martinière, 1997, 76 ff.
12. Fabric Group 'Flesa Albène', 8 August 1941, Archives nationales, F 12 10548.
13. Ibid.
14. France-Rayonne, Archives nationales, AJ 41 171, F 12 10296–10297.
15. Archives nationales, 7 February 1941, AJ 41 171.
16. Ibid.
17. *Le Figaro,* 9 October 1941.
18. *Pour Elle*, interview with M. Guénin, 10 December 1941.
19. Ibid.
20. Investigation by Georges Ravon, *Le Figaro,* March 1941.
21. *L'Œuvre*, 15 March 1941.
22. 'One expression must be banished from descriptions of the new textiles: "ersatz" or its fashionable translation, "substitute products". When you wear

a linen or cotton dress you do not say that you are dressed in a plant or a shrub. But a basic component of this vegetation is cellulose, just like the pines of Norway from which, after many transformations, rayon and fibranne come', in *Silhouettes*, no. 239, July 1941.

23. *L'Illustration*, 'L'effort textile français' ('The French Textile Effort'), 20 September 1941 (supplement). See also *La France Européenne* (monthly review of the Exhibition at the Grand-Palais), no. 1, June 1941, and no. 4, September 1941.

24. André du Bief, 'Leipzig, plaque tournante de l'Europe nouvelle' ('Leipzig, turntable of the new Europe'), *La Semaine,* no. 3, 27 March 1941, 7 ff. A journalist on *L'Ilustration*, André du Bief contributed a considerable number of pieces of investigative journalism for the revue *La Semaine.*

25. *Ganterie* (technical journal of the French glove trade), November – December 1941, Lyons Fair, 27 September – 5 October 1941.

26. Archives nationales, F 12 10804.

27. Ibid.

28. *Images de France*, September 1941. Ganterie, November – December 1941, Lyons Fair, 27 September – 5 October 1941.

29. *Le Matin*, 'Les nouveaux tissus', August 1942.

30. 'The shortage of textile supplies during the Second World War destroys the image of the modernity of the artificial fibres, particularly perceptible during the thirties. From being substitute, artificial fibre became ersatz.' Valérie Guillaume, 'Industries, techniques et politiques industrielles en mutation' ('Industries, techniques and industrial policies in mutation'), in *Mutations/ mode 1960–2000*, catalogue of the spring exhibition, Musée Galliera, Paris-Musée, 2000, 19.

31. *Paris-Soir*, 'Tissus de laine? Non, madame, du bois!' ('Woollen cloth? No, madam, wooden!'), 13 April 1941.

32. *La France Européenne*, 'Economie vestimentaire' ('Clothing Economy'), no. 4, September 1941.

33. *Le Matin*, 4 May 1943.

34. *Le Matin*, 22 February 1943.

35. Archives nationales, F 12 10804.

36. Report by Robert Le Vaux, Rapport sur la fibre de genêt d'Espagne, (Report on Spanish broom), Archives nationales, F 12 10596.

37. *Le Matin*, 18 June 1942.

38. The German SS also 'collected' for cloth manufacture: the hair of the male and female prisoners whom they shaved when they arrived at concentration camps, particularly Auschwitz.

39. *Le Matin*, 14 October 1942.

40. At the Liberation this caused some problems for the editor of the magazine, considered too obliging to the occupier. It is however significant to note that in the articles imposed by the Germans, editors could take up different positions. *L'Officiel de la couture et de la mode de Paris* showed greater caution in the same circumstances and modified phrases it saw as too blatant. Archives nationales, F 41 1464.
41. Marcel Carné, *La Vie à belles dents*, Ed. J. Vuarnet, 1979, 192–202.
42. *Le Journal de la chaussure français*, 4 April 1942.

Chapter 6 Haute Couture on German Time

1. Rita Thalmann (ed.), *Femmes et fascismes*, Paris, Tierce, 1986, 79.
2. Madame Besançon de Wagner, known as Maggy Rouff, was the president of the Association for the protection of the seasonal artistic industries (PAIS). See Didier Grumbach, *Histoire de la mode,* Paris, Seuil, 1993, 28.
3. Lelong, *La Couture française*, non lieu no. 15352, Archives nationales.
4. *Signal*, no. 9, March 1941, 17.
5. Lelong, *La Couture française*, non lieu no. 15352, Archives nationales.
6. Report of the meeting on 24 October 1940, Chambre syndicale de la couture.
   'M. Lucien Lelong is charged (by the Ministry of Labour and Industrial Production) with a study mission in Germany to inform himself of German fashion activities and to explore the basis on which an agreement might be reached permitting the resumption of activity by *couture* and by the French work-force.'
   His colleagues supported him: 'The committee of the Chambre syndicale de la couture approves of Lucien Lelong's journey and has absolute confidence in him to defend the interests of French *couture*.'
7. They had just suffered their first setback with the failure of the Battle of Britain (autumn 1940).
8. Archives of the Chambre syndicale de la couture parisienne, quoted by Grumbach, *Histoire de la mode,* 29.
9. Collective propaganda plan, spring 1941, C.O.V, Group 1, Archives nationales, F. 12 10503.
10. *Les Nouveaux Temps*, 6 March 1941; the same tendency can be found in *Le Matin*, 30 March 1941.
11. Lecture by Lucien Lelong, January 1941, Comité d'organisation du vêtement, 8e V, piece 26,888, BNF-Tolbiac.
12. *Haute couture*, collective propaganda plan, spring 1941, C.O.V, Group 1, Archives nationales, F. 12 10503.
13. *Votre Beauté*, 'Sourires de Paris,' April 1941.

14. *La Femme Chic* and *Les Nouveaux Temps*, 22 May 1941, which express the same idea.
15. *Les Nouveaux Temps*, 'La mode et l'Amerique', 8 May 1941. Report carried out via Radio mondial.
16. *Le Matin*, 1 February 1941, Lucie Hirigoyen's column.
17. 'America had said that France was dead and that no longer would chic come from Paris. But with the fine spring days, *couturiers* and milliners have shown a considerable number of designs that retain full Paris elegance. Remember that, to defend French fashion, thirty-four luxury houses can supply gowns without coupons.' *La Semaine*, no. 40, 17 April 1941.
18. *L'Officiel de la couture et de la mode*, no. 235, March 1941.
19. Lucien François, *Cent conseils d'élégance, précédés d'un éloge de Paris*, Paris, Société d'edition moderne, 1942.
20. Rouff, *La Philosophie de l'élégance*, 224–7.
21. Germaine Beaumont, 'Le poids des choses légères', in *Albums de la Mode Figaro*, winter 1942.
22. Exemption for *haute couture*, decision 1007 – 11 July 1941, creation of a *haute couture* ration card, Archives nationales F 12 10205, F 12 10503. See also Lelong, *La Couture française*, Archives nationales.
23. *Le Matin*, 30 March 1941.
24. *La Semaine*, no. 38, 3 April 1941.
25. Despite intervention by Jean Jardin, chief secretary of Y. Bouthillier, the Department of textiles and leathers refused any new exemption on the grounds of decision no. 1007. Archives nationales, F 12 10205.
26. Secretariat of State for Industrial Production, *haute couture* exemption, Archives nationales, F 12 10205.
27. Decision VI A12, 19 June 1942, Archives nationales, F 12 10503 (see extract in appendixes).
28. Ibid.
29. Note sent to M. Jacques Deligny, Archives nationales, F 12 10503.
30. Of Russian origin, leading French dancer and choreographer at the Paris Opéra, regular attendant at Franco-German receptions in Paris.
31. 'Dejeuners de la Table ronde', Affaire Lucien Lelong, Procès-verbaux, Cour de Justice, Z6. 13552, Archives nationales.
32. Under the title, 'La haute couture passe la ligne' ('*Haute couture* crosses the line'), *Marche, le Magazine Français* devoted its cover to the event (17 March 1942) and kept two whole pages for the show of the collection which Renée Massip described (pp. 10 and 11).
33. *Marie-Claire*, 1 April 1942.
34. *Le Progrès de Lyon*, 7 March 1942 which specified that 'if the wide-open windows had not shown us the Rhône flowing by, we would have thought we were in a salon of a great Paris fashion house.'

35. Interview, Jacques Delamare, June 1989.
36. Note on 'La mode artistique' ('Artistic Fashion'), Archives nationales, F 41 1696.
37. Louis Joseph took refuge in France, then in Switzerland after the defeat of 1940.
38. First journalist to have obtained an interview with Hitler in 1933. He was enthusiastic about the Nazi regime. After the defeat of 1940, he assumed the role of ambassador and acted as the general delegate of the French government in the occupied territories. Married to a Jewish woman proclaimed an 'Honorary Aryan', he was a pliable tool of the occupier.
39. *Manteaux et costumes de promenade*, no. 68, summer 1944, Archives nationales.
40. *La Mode Idéale*, summer 1944, 'La mode dans son rôle de concilier l'utile et la grâce.'
41. *L'Art et la Mode*, the magazine printed between 15,000 and 20,000 copies, Archives nationales F 41 1043.
42. *L'Officiel de la couture et de la mode*, Archives nationales F 41 1464.
43. *Votre Beauté* (225,000 copies, 200,000 subscribers), Archives nationales, F 41 1692, *Le Petit Echo de la Mode*, F 41 1247; *Modes et Travaux*, F 41 1429.
44. 20 July 1942, Group 1 became Branche des industries de création et de vêtement sur mesure (Sector of Industries involved in Creation and in Made-to-measure Clothing). Le Comité du vêtement became 'Comité général d'organisation de l'habillement et du travail des étoffes' (General Committee for the Organisation of Clothing and Work in Materials) headed by Jacques Deligny. Henceforth it was he who ensured relations with the German authorities.

    On 18 March 1943 a decision by Jean Bichelonne, published in the *Journal officiel* of the French state, judiciously filled in the gaps in the decree of 20 July 1942 by defining the terms *couture* and *couturière*, on the one hand, and *haute couture* and *couturier* on the other. It was therefore under the Vichy regime that the terms *couture*, creative *couture* and *haute couture* were regulated.
45. Discussions at the Majestic between Jacques Deligny and Dr Schilling, Archives nationales, F12 10503 (see the extract in Appendix 2).
46. Lelong, *La couture française*, non lieu no. 15352, Archives nationales.
47. Archives nationales, F 12 10643, protection of the workforce in the leather industry.
48. AJ 38-1563, AJ 38-1576, Archives nationales, Paris. Cf. also, Claire Marchand, *Les Fourreurs juifs sous l'Occupation,* DEA, ed. Annette Wieviorka, Gérard Baal and Paul Lévy, University of Poitiers, 1999, 60–1, from where these examples are taken.
49. Of 58,000 businesses registered, 51,200 corresponded to the definition of small businesses. Note to Jacques Deligny, 26 June 1942, *à propos* the concentration of businesses, Archives nationales, F 12 10497.

50. A note dated 25 February 1943 on the concentration of ready-made clothing businesses specifies that in men's clothing 350 businesses out of 1,624 were closed; in women's clothing, 200 out of 1,927; and in men's shirt and underwear and lingerie, 501 out of 4,289: Archives nationales.

51. From Catherine Ormen-Corpet, *Modes. XIXe-XXe siècles*, Paris, Hazan, 2000, 299–300.

52. During the war her *couture* salon was merged with Marcelle Tizean's salon.

53. Lelong, *La couture française*, Archives nationales.

54. Ibid.

55. Madeleine Chapsal, *La Chair de la robe*, Paris, Fayard, 1989, 21 ff. Madeleine Chapsal is Marcelle Chaumont's daughter.

56. Interview with Alice Le Bris-Lehmans, autumn 1999. See also *L'Officiel de la couture et de la mode*, no. 234, February 1941: 'In a Paris regained after tragic times, they [the *couturiers*] anticipated women's wish to be dressed quietly and with dignity; they had also adapted everyday designs to the circumstances of their new lives, without ever forfeiting the element that gives to their elegance, however discreet, an unexpected charm.'

57. Schiaparelli, *Shocking Life*, 131.

58. Cf., Fiemeyer, *Coco Chanel*, 117.

59. For further details, see Verheyde, *L'Aryanisation des grandes entreprises juives*, 354–5.

60. Information passed on by Valérie Guillaume, author of the exhibition catalogue, 'Jacques Fath, les années 50' ('Jacques Fath, the Fifties'), 21 June – 7 November 1993, Musée Galliéra, published in Editions Paris- Musées.

61. Interview with Mme Odette Fabius, May 1989.

62. Archives nationales, AJ 40 1006-4, J. Heim. Subject to increased supervision, Jacques Heim took refuge in the Free Zone; although the house of Biarritz was mentioned in the investigation, it seems that the *couturier* lived mainly in Cannes.

63. 'With a view to eliminating Jewish influence definitively from the French economy, Jewish property as a whole is entrusted to *administrateurs provisoires* (temporary administrators) whose role consists of preserving the value of the said property and of transferring it from a Jewish heritage to an aryan heritage by means of complete and effective aryanisation': *Memento-guide à l'usage des administrateurs provisoires*, quoted by Verheyde, *L'Aryanisation des grandes entreprises juives,* vol. 3, 15 (document appeared in 1942, Commissariat général aux questions juives, Bibliothèque de Droit et de Sciences économiques de Paris).

64. *La Gerbe*, 26 December 1940.

65. *Une semaine à Paris*, no. 937, November 1940, 20–7.

66. Report by M. Cazenave, acting commissioner of Pelleteries et Fourrures, 15 March 1945, Archives nationales, F 12 10691.

67. Maerz Contracts, F 12 10691; See also Archives nationales, AJ 40 774-1, Commerce des fourrures.
68. 'Furs and skins are commodities which have international value largely exploited by Israelite merchants.' This is how the acting commissioner of Pelleteries et Fourrures began his report on the role and activity of the Comité d'organisation during the war.
69. In 1939, there were '708 Jewish fur businesses established in Paris'. In 1940, the businesses placed within the jurisdiction of the Comité d'organisation des Pelleteries et Fourrures numbered '6,250 and rose again to 6,045 in 1944. 93 per cent have a turnover of less than a million francs and more than 96 per cent of them have fewer than 10 employees. Only 17 firms employ 100 employees other than home workers.' Marchand, *Les Fourreurs juifs*, 41, and Verheyde, *L'Aryanisation des grandes entreprises juives*.
70. *La Revue de la fourrure*, December 1940, 180.
71. *Rapport sur certaines particularités de la gestion du président-directeur général du Comité d'organisation des pelleteries et fourrures*, Archives nationales, F 12 10691.
72. The period 1939–45 is not even mentioned in the booklet on the bicentenary of the house of Révillon,. As for the name of Jean-Marie Révillon, it is totally non-existent. Cf., *Rester soi-même en s'inventant un nouveau destin. Révillon, 1923–1973*, text by G. Gentilhomme, Imprimerie Tournon, 1973, n.p.
73. *Journal officiel*, 28 January 1941.
74. *Rapport de Monsieur Albert-Louis Fleury, commissaire-gérant*, 10–25 août 1941, AJ 38 1337, Archives nationales. Cf., also dossier 582 handed to the juge d'instruction on 12 February 1946.
75. The 'Fantaisies Textiles' affair, Archives nationales, F 12 10464.
76. Which is true. They ordered the figures for quantities levied to be lowered: Cf., Compte rendu de l'activité de R. Ribes by M. Cazenave, commissaire provisoire, already quoted, Archives nationales, F 12 10643.
77. 'Thus, a whole gamut of behaviour by the occupied towards the occupiers can be discerned, ranging from the methods of voluntary and forced collaboration, the forms of collaborative conduct, the various forms of dissidence, to the expressions of resistance properly speaking.' (Jacques Sémelin, *Sans Armes face à Hitler*, Paris, Payot, 1989, 60; and Philippe Burrin, *La France à l'heure allemande*, Paris, Seuil, 1995).

Chapter 7 Fashionable Paris Dresses Up

1. 'To some people to care about prestige at such a time could seem futile, but it appeared obvious to me that abandonment of our reputation for good taste and elegance formed no part of the necessary sacrifices, and, on the contrary, that

such a renunciation would have deprived France of one of the most substantial treasures of her heritage,' André de Fouquière, *Cinquante ans de panache*, Paris, Horay, 1951, 360.

2. Lucie Hirigoyen, *La Femme Chic*, December 1940.
3. Lucien François, 'Vive la classe', *Les Nouveaux Temps*, 30 October 1941.
4. *L'Œuvre*, 9 December 1940. Cf. also, 'Lumières à l'Opéra,' *La Semaine*, no. 24, 26 December 1940.
5. 100th issue of *Les Nouveaux Temps*, 11 February 1941.
6. Luchaire, *Ma drôle de vie*.
7. Jeanne Fernandez, *La Gerbe*, 10 July 1941.
8. Gilles and Jean-Robert Ragache, *La vie quotidienne des écrivains et artistes sous l'Occupation*, Paris, Hachette, 1988, 139.
9. Ibid., 133.
10. *Journal de la ganterie française*, September–October 1941.
11. *Marie-Claire*, 6 April 1941, 'To the ladies of Paris – Paris – Have received spring message, understand symbol new fashion – stop – Thanks for lesson courage, dignity and smile. Heartfelt greetings – Signed Women worldwide – 6 April 1941.'
12. 'Vu et retenu à Paris', *Le Figaro*, November 1941.
13. Ragache, *La vie quotidienne*.
14. Gilles Perrault, *Paris sous l'Occupation*, Paris, Belfond, 1987, 27.
15. *Toute la Vie*, 25 September 1941.
16. 'La femme française', *La Gerbe*, 27 November 1941.
17. It clings to the bust, emphasises the waist and enlarges the hips by building up the skirt with gathers or pleats.
18. 'La Mode d'hiver 1943', *Marie-Claire*, September 1942.
19. Philippe Erlanger, *La France sans étoile*, Paris, Plon, 1974, 241.
20. Lily Pastré belonged to the Marseilles upper middle class. Worldly and refined, the countess took an interest in Letters and Arts. In her Château de Montredon, she sheltered several intellectuals in difficulty and Jews on the run, and acted as a true patron.
21. Christian Bérard, stage painter, designer and decorator, highly valued for his original ideas.
22. Kochno, *Christian Bérard*, 61.
23. *Le Figaro*, 28 May 1942.
24. Seeberger and Schall were the names of the photographers whose work appeared most frequently, as well as the Harcourt Studios.
25. *Journal de la ganterie française*, March-April 1943.
26. Regulations suggested by Groupe 1 on behalf of creative *couture*, Archives nationales, F 12 10503.
27. Ibid.,

28. J.-P. Bertin-Maghit, *Le Cinéma sous l'Occupation, le monde du cinéma français, 1940–1946,* Paris, Olivier Orban, 1989, 169.

29. *Toute la vie,* no. 36, 16 April 1942.

30. *Marie-Claire,* 1 February 1942. Suzy Solidor was a regular customer of Jacques Fath, as was Michèle Alfa.

31. List of private apartments at the Ritz: Archives nationales, AJ 40 871. Chanel, who occupied a suite, was among the beneficiaries (12 February 1941).

32. Archives nationales, AJ 40 608, Comptabilité *Paris-Soir.*

33. *Marie-Claire,* 1 February 1942.

34. For example, in *L'Officiel de la couture et de la mode,* a headline 'Seen at the Races' recurred in every issue that appeared in 1941–2. These show that the baronne de Beaufort, Mme Gilbert Orcel and the comtesse d'Oncieux de Chaffardon were favourite models of Seeberger photographs.

35. Serge Lifar, *Ma Vie,* Paris, Julliard, 1965, 254.

36. Interview with Odette Fabius, June 1989. Odette Fabius worked for the Resistance and was deported to Ravensbrück. After having been part of the Alliance network at Marseilles, led by Loustaunau-Lacau and Marie-Madeleine Fourcade, she worked, still in Marseilles, for the OCM-Centurie information network. Cf. also Odette Fabius, *Un lever de soleil sur le Mecklenbourg: Memoires,* Paris, Albin Michel, 1986, 249.

37. Jean Hugo, *Le Regard de la mémoire,* Actes Sud, 1984.

38. *Silhouettes,* no. 185, May 1944, Lucien François, 'Celles qui transnovent'. For the columnist, the ladies who went overboard were those who wore fashion without discernment. And he cited as examples women who wore 'monumental hats', 'aggressive spangles, soles, which make them walk like terror-stricken geese'.

39. The manager of Jacque Fath's salon, Maud, confided: 'We saw many women who drew their substantial incomes from food products, the women one called the BOF.'

40. Chapsal, *La Chair de la robe,* 116.

41. Suzanne Fournier, *Cousu main,* n.p., Editions SSP, 1953, 158.

42. *Votre Beauté,* February 1942.

43. From Anny Latour, *Les Magiciens de la mode, de Rose Bertin à Christian Dior,* Paris, Juillard, 1961, 262 ff.

44. *Le Matin,* 'La vedette et sa robe', 2 January 1943.

45. Ibid., 'Vedettes de la scène', 16 February 1942.

Chapter 8 Vichy, Fashion and Women

1. This term covers both 'a doctrine that is inspired by nineteenth-century reactionary ideologies and a series of institutional, economic, social and

cultural reforms.' Cf. Henry Rousso, 'Qu'est-ce que la révolution nationale?' *L'Histoire*, special issue. *L'année 1940*, no. 129, January 1990.

2. On this question, see the seminal work by Francine Muel-Dreyfus, *Vichy et l'éternel féminin*, Paris, Seuil, 1996.

3. *Votre Beauté*, April 1941.

4. Published by the Office de propagande générale in co-operation with *Votre Beauté*, n.d., BDIC, reserve GR. Fol. 126-3; cf., Muel-Dreyfus, *Vichy et l'éternel féminin*, 131.

5. *Petit Echo de la ligue féminine d'action catholique*, September 1940, quoted by Clorinda Costantini, 'La presse féminine des années d'Occupation, juin 1940–août 1944', third cycle thesis, Université de droit et de sciences politiques de Paris-II, 1980.

6. François, 'Vive la classe'.

7. Muel-Dreyfus, *Vichy et l'éternel féminin*, 132.

8. H. Roudaud, 'Le village des célibataires', in *Mode du Jour*, 26 June 1941.

9. *La Femme Chic*, July 1941.

10. *L'Œuvre,* 'Pour ou contre les pantalonnées', 7 February 1942.

11. Ibid.

12. Bruno du Roselle, *La Mode*, Paris, Imprimerie Nationale, 1980, 203.

13. Lucien François, *Image de la femme et de la révolution nationale*, 1942.

14. Suzanne Panne, 'Jeunes filles . . . restez française', in *Pour Elles*, 2 October 1940.

15. *Votre Beauté*, 'This woman puts on too much make-up, we have restored her to her nature', April 1941.

16. Ibid.

17. Georgette Varenne, *La Femme dans la France nouvelle*, Clermont-Ferrand, Imprimerie Mont-Louis, 1940, 24.

18. The allusion is to the magazine *Marie-Claire,* whose pre-war format was clearly inspired by American publications.

19. 'Mode impérative mode', *La Gerbe*, 24 July 1941.

20. Votre beauté vous parle', *Votre Beauté*, November 1940.

21. Ibid.

22. Varenne, *La Femme dans la France nouvelle*.

23. 'Un brin de rouge? Mais pourquoi pas', *Pour Elle*, April 1941, no. 36.

24. *Votre Beauté*, May 1941.

25. Quoted in *Silhouettes*, no. 183, March 1944.

26. Laurence Bertrand-Dorléac, 'La question artistique et le régime de Vichy', in *Politiques et pratiques culturelles dans la France de Vichy*, Cahier de l'IHTP, no. 8, June 1988, 16.

27. *La Femme Chic*, no. 360, May 1941.

28. According to *Images de France, Le Figaro, La Femme Chic* 1941, 1942.

29. *Mode du Jour*, no. 1019, 29 May 1941.
30. *Paris-Soir*, 28 July 1942.
31. *Le Matin,* 'Pastorales', spring 1941.
32. According to Sylvie Raulet, in Anne Bony, *Les Années 40*, Ed. du Regard, Paris, 1985, 694.
33. Non-Gaullist Resistance paper.
34. Emmanuelle Rioux, *Les Zazous, un phénomène socio-culturel pendant l'Occupation*, dissertation for a master's degree, Université de Paris-X-Nanterre, 1987.
35. On the zazou phenomenon, see Farid Chenoune, *Des modes et des hommes, Deux Siècles d'élégance masculine*, Paris, Flammarion, 1993, 210.
36. Yves Ranc, 'Swing ou pas swing', *L'Œuvre*, 4 March 1942.
37. *L'Illustration*, 28 March 1942.
38. Cf., decisions U1-A11 and U2-A3, Comité général d'organisation de l'industrie textile.
39. Rioux, *Les Zazous*, 25.
40. Ibid., 20.
41. P. Ducrocq, 'Swing qui peut', *La Gerbe*, 11 June 1942.
42. Chenoune, *Des modes et des hommes*, 210.
43. Jean Guéhenno, *Journal des années noires (1940–1944)*, Paris, Gallimard, 1947, 132.
44. Lucie Aubrac, *Ils partirent dans l'ivresse, Lyon: mai 1943, Londres: février 1944*, Paris, Le Seuil, 1984, 85
45. Interview with Denise Vernay.
46. Marylène Delbourg-Delphis, *Le Chic et le look. Histoire de la mode féminine et des moeurs de 1850 à nos jours,* Paris, Hachette, 1981, 178.
47. Linda Watson, *Vogue, la mode du siècle*, Paris, Hors Collection, 2000, 43.

Conclusion

1. Comité régional interprofessionel de l'épuration de la région parisienne (CRIE), Dossiers of the fourth section, textiles, and the fifth, leathers, deposit 901/64/1, 323; Archives de Paris.
2. Intervention by Jacques Deligny on the problem of exports after the war, CO of the textile industry, F 12 10802.
3. Statement by Lucien Lelong to American *Vogue* (December 1944), quoted by Valérie Steele, *Se vêtir au XX siècle*, Paris, Adam Biro, 1998, p. 13.
4. Lucien Lelong, 'Défense de la Mode', *Revue de Paris*, March 1946.

Index

Note: A number in **bold** indicates an illustration on that page.

Index

Index